Worship and Witness in Crisis

Worship and Witness in Crisis

Has the Church Failed the Covid Test?

Edited by
Matthew A. Vogan and Matthew J. Hyde

ISBN 978-1-8380775-5-6

Cover photo by Serge Le Strat on Unsplash

Ettrick Press
98 The Brow, Brighton
BN2 6LN
ettrickpress.co.uk

Contents

Prefatory Note

The editors greatly appreciate the willingness, time and effort of the authors of the individual essays collected in this book. Without their energy and insight, the book would never have seen the light of day.

We want to state clearly that the views presented in individual chapters are those of the individual authors alone. Not all the authors, nor the editors, will necessarily subscribe to all the views expressed, or all the conclusions drawn. All unsigned chapters are by the editors.

The questions posed in the chapter titles are what the contributors were invited to address, basing their response on the Bible and the witness of church history. If you have different conclusions in answering these questions personally, we encourage you to ensure your conclusions are based on the same premises.

The authors come from different church backgrounds, but they all share a concern for the church in this time of crisis. This book is centred on the response in the UK context, and does not touch on the response of the church in other parts of the world which have a different heritage, and different confessional backgrounds to the churches of the United Kingdom.

Contributors

Catherine E. Hyde, MA (Hons), MSc, PhD, is a member of the Free Presbyterian Church of Scotland. After moving from linguistics to statistics she has since co-edited *Christ Victorious: Selected Writings of Hugh Martin* (2019, Banner of Truth Trust) and co-authored *Bible Truth Explored* (2020, Reformation Scotland Trust) and *Our Faith* (2020, Reformation Scotland Trust).

Matthew J. Hyde, BSc (Hons), ARCS, MClin Res, PhD, DIC, is pastor of Galeed Strict Baptist Chapel, Brighton. Matthew is a research scientist in neonatal medicine, based at Imperial College London. He has written or edited over sixty books including *With Mercy and with Judgement: Strict Baptists and the First World War* (2016, Gospel Standard Trust); *The Men of 1662* (2012, Huntingtonian Press); *Enclosed by Grace: Records of the Church Meeting at Port Vale Chapel, Hertford* (2011, Huntingtonian Press).

Rev. Allan W. MacColl, MA, PhD, is minister of Dingwall and Beauly Free Presbyterian Church of Scotland, having previously served the congregation of Ness on the Isle of Lewis. A historian by training, his doctoral dissertation was published as *Land, Faith and the Crofting Community: Christianity and Social Criticism in the Highlands of Scotland, 1843-1893* (2006, Edinburgh University Press).

Jonathan D. Moore, BA, MA, PhD, is part of the Reformed Presbyterian Church of Ireland, and currently serves as an Honorary Research Fellow in the School of History at the University of East Anglia, and as an Adjunct Lecturer and Research Associate at Union Theological College in Belfast. He has recently co-edited *The Puritans on Independence* (2017) and *Reformed Government* (forthcoming) for Oxford University Press.

Rev. Paul Murray, BSc (Hons), BTh, is minister of Kinloch Free Church of Scotland. After a short career in construction, Paul trained for the ministry in the Free Church of Scotland at Edinburgh Theological Seminary. Since August 2017, he has occupied a pastoral ministry on Lewis, his native island.

Rev. Iain Smith, Dip Theo, is a retired minister in the Free Church of Scotland (Continuing) and lives in Stornoway, Isle of Lewis. He has previously pastored Free Church of Scotland (Continuing) congregations at Partick, Glasgow and South Harris. He also pastored a congregation in Tasmania, Australia.

Rev. Douglas W. B. Somerset, BSc, DPhil, has been minister of the Free Presbyterian Church of Scotland congregation in Aberdeen since 2005. He is the Secretary of the Scottish Reformation Society and edits *The Bulwark* and *The Scottish Reformation Society Historical Journal.*

Matthew A. Vogan, BA (Hons), MA, MLitt, served as an elder of the Inverness congregation of the Free Presbyterian Church of Scotland and now in the Edinburgh congregation. He oversees the work of the Reformation Scotland Trust. He has written and edited a number of books, most of which are related to writers from or aspects of Scottish church history, including, *The King in His Beauty: The Piety of Samuel Rutherford* (2011, Reformation Heritage Books); *Scottish Worthies: Alexander Shields* (2019, Scottish Reformation Society); and *Samuel Rutherford: An Introduction to His Theology* (2011, Scottish Reformation Society)

Peter C. Wilkins, BEng, PhD, CEng, is an itinerant preacher, mostly amongst the Gospel Standard group of Strict Baptist

Churches. He was baptised at Uffington Strict Baptist Chapel in 2005 and sent out to preach by the church at Hedge End Strict and Particular Baptist Chapel in 2015. In his secular employment he works for the Ministry of Defence.

Introduction

The spring of 2020 initiated challenges for the church that have been acutely difficult. Navigating conflicts, official guidance and medical issues while trying to minister to a scattered flock has often seemed like an impossible task. Just as the life of wider society was disorganised by the effects of Covid-19, so the church has found itself in a disordered condition. Reviewing our response may seem like the last thing pandemic-weary pastors and congregations would want. There is an understandable desire to put it behind us and try to reassemble the life of the church as we once knew it. The past is the past, our instincts tell us—we cannot change it, so should we just move on?

This book shares that orientation towards the future. But the coronavirus crisis is such a seismic event that we cannot ignore its far-reaching impact. We cannot treat it as a mere interruption in the life of the church. It has been and will continue to prove to be a disruption. Political historian Peter Hennessy commented, 'I would divide British post-war history into before corona and after corona.'[1] It would seem strange to find secular analysis outstripping faith-driven reflection.

The Covid-19 crisis found everyone unprepared, churches included. We responded as we thought best and had little time for working patiently through the principles involved. In seeking to provoke prayerful reflection on the church's response, *Worship and Witness in Crisis* is neither complacent nor condemnatory. It does

---

[1] In an interview with BBC Radio 4: The World at One, on 17th March, 2020. See https://twitter.com/bbcworldatone/status/1239947862001278977?lang=en [Accessed 27/04/2021].

not list our woes, apportion blame, or excoriate any particular scapegoats. Yet reflection is called for. If we fail to reflect carefully, we will not only be unprepared for another crisis but we are likely to find that our impromptu solutions have had long-lasting unintended effects. We may also find ourselves drawn to a reflex response of pragmatism over principle to other issues which may arise in the future.

Instead, this book seeks to examine the response of churches within the United Kingdom in order to learn lessons for the future. The authors come from a variety of church groupings throughout Scotland, England and Ireland, providing some breadth of perspective and experience. Of course, the views stated in the individual chapters are those of the individual authors alone. Not all the authors hold the same position, and they belong to churches who may have made different decisions about the response to Covid-19.

Engaging in this kind of review is certainly biblical. God's call to Israel through the prophet Haggai was, 'Consider your ways' (Haggai 1:5). They had neglected to continue building the temple due to the command of the Persian king (Ezra 4:23-24). As a consequence, God had sent them many evidences of his displeasure in outward things (Haggai 1:9-11). Despite all these warnings they continued to put off their duty by saying it was not the right time to engage in it when they were surrounded by risk (Haggai 1:2). Yet they were happy to live comfortably (Haggai 1:4). They were like their complacent ancestors before the captivity who were at ease in Zion (Amos 6:1) and unconcerned about the afflictions of the people of God (Amos 6:6).

It was to such people that the Lord says, 'Consider your ways.' This very instruction implies that failure to engage in corporate self-examination is perhaps the main reason we err from our duty and continue in disobedience. We need to ponder deeply and respond appropriately to God's dealings with us and our ways towards him. The events of 2020-2021 call loudly for us to do this. Indeed, perhaps they are the wake-up call that the Lord is using to make the church consider her ways. But while it is a tender rebuke, the message, 'consider your ways,' is also bright with hope and promise.

The exhortation to 'consider your ways' is repeated in Haggai 1:7-8 together with an instruction as to how to act in the future. The very fact that it is repeated shows how reluctant we are to bring matters to our consciences. Our natural response is to dig in and refuse to accept that we have got things wrong. After all, it will only create difficulty and loss of face. But the Lord adds rich promises of his gracious acceptance, delight and pleasure in his people and their service if they will listen to his call and obey. These promises are connected with his public worship, something that those whom Haggai addressed had neglected and undervalued.

Scripture and experience tell us that if we do not listen to God's voice to us, other heavier chastisements will be required. In the case of Haggai's message, there was a receptive audience. Their spirits were stirred up to work for the sake of restoring the public worship of God and the glory of his name. Much was accomplished in a short time (Haggai 1:14-15). They were so strengthened as to be able to resist the threat of opposition from civil authority (Ezra 5). All this came from a call to consider their ways. When they heeded that and considered what God required of them, they were found in a better condition.

Worship and Witness in Crisis opens with an overview by Iain Smith of how the church has responded to pandemics in the past. Douglas Somerset then sets the scene by identifying the principles which should guide us in negotiating disagreements within the church, as part of our Christian duty to maintain unity and love among the brethren.

The discussion then turns to ask serious questions about the nature and purpose of worship and of the church itself. Matthew Hyde explores whether the church should ever voluntarily choose to suspend public worship. Peter Wilkins then analyses the importance of gathering physically for worship.

During this crisis we have also faced critical questions about the role of church and state. For some time we have not been required to work out our understanding of such matters, and our analytical tools have become blunted and rusty through years of disuse. Allan MacColl refreshes our memories of how Scripture presents the respective roles of church and state and how the church has striven to implement these biblical principles down through the centuries. Matthew Vogan then homes in on how to understand the principle of 'rendering to Caesar the things that are Caesar's, and to God the things that are God's.'

In recent decades we have been used to reflecting on the preciousness of life in relation to issues such as abortion and assisted dying. Yet in other areas our views have perhaps been less coherently thought through and expressed. Suddenly Covid-19 faced us with immediate practical issues of preserving life and health. Paul Murray explores some dimensions of loving our neighbour that may have been neglected or under-emphasised. Jonathan Moore takes up the question of whether it is ever 'unloving' to go to church to worship God.

It is easy to think like the world and respond like the world when we are under pressure. Matthew Vogan and Catherine Hyde look at how far the church's response to this crisis has been shaped by the assumptions and pressures which prevail in our culture.

In the final chapter, the editors pull together a collection of pointers for how to move forward from this crisis.

Individually and corporately, whatever decisions and arguments we may have made since spring 2020, we have much to consider. 'Let us search and try our ways, and turn again to the Lord' (Lamentations 3:40).

We would like to express appreciation to Rev. David Campbell (Edinburgh) who originally floated the idea for a book on these lines and has provided assistance for the project along the way.

Matthew A. Vogan and Matthew J. Hyde
Editors

April 2021

~ 1 ~
Pandemics and the church

Iain Smith[1]

> I have sent among you the pestilence after the manner of Egypt: your young men have I slain with the sword and have taken away your horses; and I have made the stink of your camps to come up unto your nostrils: yet have ye not returned unto me, saith the LORD. (Amos 4:10)

As the world continues to struggle with the Covid-19 pandemic, we cannot help wondering if this is one of the worst plagues mankind has ever experienced. It is tempting to think along those lines. For the past year, and on a daily basis, we have been inundated with politicians and mainstream media insisting on bombarding us with statistics on infection, serious illness, and deaths from this virus. And then, of course, the abiding threat to the NHS being overwhelmed by a tsunami of coronavirus cases.

We could, therefore, be forgiven for being somewhat distracted from the true nature of what is now plaguing virtually every nation on earth. And without detracting from the seriousness of this illness, the manner by which we are compelled to constantly focus upon it, magnifies the problem beyond its own actual threat to humanity.

King Solomon was of course right: 'there is no new thing under the sun.' The world has seen many diseases and disasters, natural and

---

[1] This chapter is based on a lecture given by the author on Friday, 19th March, 2021, on behalf of the Scottish Reformation Society.

otherwise, which claimed the lives of multitudes of people. But these were not 'new' in the sense that they were unmatched in human history. There are two disasters recorded that will never be surpassed in their devastation.

The first major pandemic to hit the human race was the fall of man into sin. That may not suit as a medical or scientific definition of a virus, nevertheless, sin is a disease that affects all people—which is the true meaning of the word pandemic.

The second 'pandemic' was the widespread evil and iniquity which led to the flood of Noah's time. The scale of that sin-virus is well-summed up in Genesis 6:5: 'God saw that the wickedness of man was great in the earth, and that every imagination of the thoughts of his heart was only evil continually.' To clothe that statement in physical terms, we can use the graphic picture given in Isaiah: 'From the sole of the foot even unto the head there is no soundness in it; but wounds, and bruises, and putrefying sores' (1:6).

No disaster, epidemic, or pandemic can match the Fall in its damaging impact on humanity. Equally, no plaque, pestilence, or disease can match the Flood for its near-annihilation of the entire human race.

In this chapter we will remind ourselves that plagues and pandemics are not modern things. We will briefly mention the references to plagues in the Bible before drawing out some biblical principles which should inform the church's response to plagues. We will then review how these principles have been put into practice by the church during plagues throughout history, and identify some lessons with regards to the church's approach to the Covid-19 pandemic.

1. Plagues in the Old Testament

Following the Flood, God plagued the world with numerous lesser pandemics and epidemics of judgment.[2] The Egypt of the time of Moses was awash with all kinds of deadly diseases as a result of divine judgment. Even God's own people were not spared. In one example, after leaving Egypt, 'those that died in the plague were twenty and four thousand' (Numbers 25:9). In the land of Canaan judgments of famine, drought, and disease occurred on a regular basis. In each instance, God was speaking to his erring people.

God's message is famously articulated in Ezekiel: 'Turn ye, turn ye from your evil ways; for why will ye die, O house of Israel?' (33:11). God's message to his erring people remains the same today. This is the true message from God during the pandemic of Covid-19. But like many of the leaders in Israel, present-day governments and far too many church leaders refuse to listen. Most politicians are far more concerned about the NHS than any spiritual implications associated with the present pandemic.

However, some people of faith did understand what was happening in Old Testament times. Hence the repeated refrain from faithful prophets, for the people to turn in repentance to God. Solomon, for his part, recognised that sin lay at the heart of all the calamities which befell the Hebrews. We have his amazing prayer in 1 Kings 8:47 to confirm this. 'If they shall bethink themselves in the land whither they were carried captives, and repent, and make supplication unto thee in the land of them that carried them captives, saying, We have sinned, and have done perversely, we

---

2 For an interesting treatment of plagues as a judgment from God, see Hendley, W. (1721) *Loimologia Sacra: or, a Discourse shewing that the plague never proceeds from any first natural cause, but is sent immediately from God, and that as a punishment to a people for their sins*. London: T. Bickerton.

have committed wickedness.' What did Solomon expect as a result of this confession? His prayer continues, 'Then hear thou their prayer and their supplication in heaven thy dwelling place, and maintain their cause and forgive thy people that have sinned against thee, and all their transgressions wherein they have transgressed against thee.'

We can also learn from biblical times that public health measures, such as social distancing, are not recent concepts. Social distancing is apparently held up today as a new development borne out of concerns over Covid-19. However, the concept of social distancing can be said to have been introduced by God to deal with the plague of leprosy.

We might note however, that the modern practice of social distancing largely turns God's method on its head, by compelling the healthy to socially distance, whereas God insisted that only the infected should isolate. In Leviticus 13:4 the instruction is given regarding lepers, 'The priest shall shut him up that hath the plague seven days.' That was to be repeated until the leprosy was cleansed.

Noticeably, the Lord Jesus never shunned people with infectious diseases. That was demonstrated when a leper knelt before him asking to be healed (Mark 1:40). In that and other instances, our Lord never hesitated to be in thick of it. Furthermore, when he sent his apostles into the Gentile world with the gospel, he did not attach any caveats to their primary duty of preaching God's message of salvation by free grace, even though he knew that he was sending his servants into a world plagued with every disease imaginable.

2. The Christian mindset in approaching pandemics

Present government policy on dealing with Covid-19 presents the potential death of victims as a constant threat hanging over our heads. The propaganda of fear has left many citizens reluctant to have human contact—even with their own families. For many Christians this fear has obscured biblical teaching on life and death.

Consequently, it is important to be reminded of the mindset by which God's faithful servants in all ages confronted challenges that threatened life. A Christian mindset has the following characteristics.

- It presupposes that this is God's world and that he is in sovereign control of all events at all times.
- It focuses on the resurrected Christ whose endless life is shared by every believer.
- It considers this life as preliminary to life in the eternal paradise of God.
- It considers the Word of God, especially the Ten Commandments, as crucial to moulding the believer's moral and ethical parameters.

Amongst other things, this mindset enables Christians to live life in this world with one eye on eternity, where they will enjoy everlasting fellowship with their Lord. Furthermore, this mindset puts life in this world into the perspective of Paul's estimation of eternal things, when he wrote: 'To be with Christ ... is far better' (Philippians 1:23). History reveals this mindset developing throughout the Gentile world as Christianity exploded over Europe. Acceptance of God's moral code also created the familiar concepts of civility, decency and uprightness. All this was fine-tuned as a result of the Reformation. Ever since, broadly speaking at least, that mindset prevailed until the second half of the twentieth century.

However, the post-war years have witnessed an incremental abandoning of belief in a transcendent God and in biblical morality by so-called progressive thinkers. Over the past few decades this has gathered frightening speed. And into the moral vacuum which this has created, there has grown a new mindset which produced, amongst other things, political leaders who 'know not Joseph.'

The result of this has become painfully obvious in our generation. To the everlasting shame of our leaders, they have legislated to defy God by criminalizing the gospel and usurping the headship of Jesus Christ by insisting that, at their whim, churches must close for as long as they deem pertinent. So strange have they become to Christian church activity, that (in connection with Covid-19 policy) they have referred to God's worship as a 'secular activity.'[3]

Sadly, even among God's people, this distinctive mindset has been eroded somewhat. Many Christians are too willing to submit to the godless political philosophy of our day. They seem to have accepted that the government has the last say on life, who should live and who should die, how life should be lived, and how it must be preserved.

This type of thinking has shown the church to be drifting from the mindset we ought to be fostering as Christian people. Listen to

---

[3] Letter from the Scottish Government Legal Directorate to Mr Brent Haywood, Lindsays WS, Edinburgh, dated 22nd January, 2021. See https://christianconcern.com/wp-content/uploads/2018/10/CC-Resource-Misc-Church-Lockdown-Scotland-Government-Response-210129.pdf [Accessed 23/03/2021].

these Bible texts relative to what our attitude ought to be regarding this present life. 'Men that have hazarded their lives for the name of our Lord Jesus Christ' (Acts 15:26); 'I am ready not to be bound only, but also to die at Jerusalem for the name of the Lord Jesus' (Acts 21:13); 'Hereby perceive we the love of God, because he laid down his life for us: and we ought to lay down our lives for the brethren' (1 John 3:16); 'They loved not their lives unto the death' (Revelation 12:11).

These texts, and many more, urge Christian people to lay hold of what true life really is. It is more than the breath in our nostrils and the beat of our heart. It is more than the life we live on this earth. It is more than enjoying the best things that this life has to offer us. So the lesson here is that Christians should maintain a balance between duties and responsibilities in this life and the reality of the life that shall never end.

The church has been challenged as never before with the arrival of Covid-19. The primary issue for Christians during the pandemic has undoubtedly been the closure of our churches. But let us not forget, a secondary issue which rates highly in the duties and responsibilities given to the church: the pastoral care of the flock. Legislation imposed during the pandemic also prohibited the free access, which ministers ought to have, to the sick, suffering, and dying. This, as we shall see, was a role that men like Martin Luther (1483-1546) considered of the utmost importance during plagues and pandemics. However, in the challenge we face today there seems to be little consensus in the Christian community on how to respond to the virus and the associated government legislation and guidance.

There can be a cultural component to the church's reaction. That is understandable given that our ecclesiology can vary according to denominational nuance, as well as views on church-state relationships. For example, the Christian church in the USA has a different view on these matters to what might be expected from a church in the United Kingdom. Even within individual denominations there can be disunity of approach. However, it is a pity that we cannot come together in a concerted effort in applying clear biblical principles when being confronted by such interference in the affairs of the church by the civil magistrate.

3. The church's response to plagues in history

Before glancing at how previous generations dealt with similar issues in their own day, let us first review some historical plagues.

The most devastating plague of the post-New Testament era was surely the bubonic plague, or Black Death. This scourge wrought havoc throughout European and Mediterranean lands. The first outbreak was during the sixth century, under the reign of Justinian. Statistics were not carefully recorded at that time. However, it is reckoned that upwards of 100 million people died during repeated outbreaks over the next two centuries.

There was another succession of outbreaks from the fourteenth through to the sixteenth century. It seems that the fourteenth century outbreak originally came out of China during the years 1347 to 1350. It is reckoned that this pandemic resulted in the deaths of between 75 and 200 million people in Eurasia and North Africa, peaking in Europe between 1347 and 1351.

Much later in history, an influenza pandemic during the years 1889 to 1890, called 'Russian Flu,' erupted in places as far away as Central Asia, north-western Canada, and Greenland. This pandemic claimed the lives of a million people. A more serious influenza pandemic broke out in 1918, commonly known as

'Spanish Flu.' It raced across the globe, claiming lives numbered in millions in the first 25 weeks alone. It eventually killed upwards of 50 million.

These statistics give some perspective on the current coronavirus pandemic. At the time of writing, reports suggest that over 3 million have died world-wide from Covid-19.[4]

So, what can we glean from history in terms of the response from Christian leaders in some of these instances? We shall limit ourselves to a small number of examples.

In the third century, a pandemic known as the Plague of Cyprian erupted initially in Ethiopia and quickly spread to Rome. It lasted nearly 20 years and at its height killed 5,000 people per day in the city of Rome. Of the second outbreak, Dionysius wrote, 'The healthy pushed the sick away and fled from their dearest ... hoping to avert the spread and contagion of the fatal disease.' By way of contrast, he states that 'most of our brother Christians showed unbounded love and loyalty, never sparing themselves and thinking only of one another ... nursing and curing others.'[5]

When the Black Death broke out in Zurich in 1519, the Reformer Ulrich Zwingli (1484-1531) was away from home. According to a recent article in *Christian History*, 'Though weak already from exhausting work, he hurried back to his city to minister to victims. Before long he himself caught the disease and seemed likely to perish. But his work was not yet done; Zwingli recovered and went

---

4 'Globally, as of 11:47am CEST, 27 April 2021, there have been 147,377,159 confirmed cases of COVID-19, including 3,112,041 deaths, reported to WHO.' As reported on the World Health Organisation's website, https://covid19.who.int/ [Accessed 27/04/2021].

5 See: https://worship.calvin.edu/resources/resource-library/pandemics-and-public-worship-throughout-history/ [Accessed: 23/03/2021].

on to compose his famous plague hymn.'[6] The first verse of that hymn reads:

> Help me, O Lord,
> My strength and rock;
> Lo, at the door
> I hear death's knock.[7]

When the Black Death invaded Wittenberg in 1527 many people fled in fear. However, Martin Luther and his pregnant wife Katherine remained in the city to treat the infected. Luther was surrounded by the disease and in fact, the mayor's wife virtually died in his arms. Despite calls for him to flee, he insisted on remaining. He concluded that it was not inherently wrong for someone to so value their life that they did not remain in the infected city, but only so long as the sick had someone of greater faith than they to care for them.

The experience prompted Luther to write a letter which was later turned into a tract, entitled, *Whether One May Flee from a Deadly Plague*.[8] This was widely circulated. In it, Luther insisted that those in leadership roles in church and state should remain in the community until the crisis would pass. Pastors, he said, must be like the Good Shepherd who lays down his life for the sheep.

The tract also makes plain that Luther saw no single formula for confronting the fear of death. But he wrote that Christ's

---

[6] *Christian History*. (2020) Issue 135 p. 29.

[7] Zwingli, U. 'A Christian Song Written by Huldrich Zwingli when He was Attacked by the Pestilence', in: Jackson, S. M. (Ed.) (1999) *Ulrich Zwingli: Early Writings*. Eugene, Origen, USA: Wipf and Stock. p. 56.

[8] Pelikan, J. J., Oswald, H. C. and Lehmann, H. T. (Eds.) (1999) *Martin Luther's Works. Vol. 43: Devotional Writings II*. Minneapolis, Minnesota, Fortress Press. pp. 119–38.

resurrection should make all Christians fearless in the face of the grave. And on a more practical side, Luther advocated for certain public buildings to be set aside as hospitals for the sick rather than leaving them in their homes. He also urged Christians to fumigate their homes, yards, and streets to stop the spread of the plague. He even advocated social distancing by saying that he would not mix with others unnecessarily.

However, Luther also strongly urged those in the presence of the dying to pour into them the Word of God, teaching them both how to live and also how to die in faith. Anyone dying in unbelief should be urgently warned to repent while there is still time, and a pastor should be called for while they can still understand his words.

In the time of John Calvin (1509-1564), the Black Death erupted in Geneva in 1542. In fact, the plague swept through the city on five separate occasions. During the first outbreak, Calvin led visitations into plague-infected areas and homes. City leaders, realizing that contracting the plague carried a death sentence in most cases, pleaded with Calvin to refrain from these visits because they considered the Reformer's leadership indispensable. However, Calvin, and many other pastors inspired by him, continued their heroic efforts and were able to recount the joy of multiple conversions. One writer has recorded,

> Unknown to many, Calvin privately continued his own pastoral care in Geneva and other cities where the plague raged. Calvin's pastoral heart, already evidenced by the provision of hospitals for both citizens and immigrants, was further

revealed as he collected the necessary resources to establish a separate hospital for plague victims.[9]

When the bubonic plague broke out in London, we have a harrowing and detailed account from a sermon preached by Thomas Vincent (1634-1678) in 1667. The title of the sermon is, *God's Terrible Voice in the City*. Vincent preached his sermon following the Great Fire which swept through London, not long after the plague. However, it was the plague that seemed to burden him most. He records how most of the population who could afford to leave did so. Even many ministers of the gospel deserted their congregations. Those who remained out of choice and duty, Vincent reckoned they deserved true honour. The sermon makes very clear that he himself remained in close quarters with plague victims.[10] If churches closed at all, it was due to multiple deaths and the desertion of pastors rather than to any type of legislation.

Then during the 1850s, again in London, a plague of cholera broke out. As a young village preacher, Charles Spurgeon (1834-1892) admired the Puritan ministers who had stayed behind to care for the sick and dying during the Great Plague of 1665.[11] This informed his response when, in the autumn of 1854, Spurgeon found himself confronted by this major cholera outbreak. It is worth noting five principles of Spurgeon's response. 1) He prioritized local ministry;

---

[9] Parsons, B. (Ed.) (2008) *John Calvin: A Heart for Devotion, Doctrine, and Discipleship*. Lake Mary, Florida, USA: Reformation Trust. p. 65.

[10] Vincent, T. (1997) *God's Terrible Voice in the City*. Morgan, Pennsylvania, USA: Soli Deo Gloria Publications. p. 45-47.

[11] See sermon 290 in: Duesing, J. G. (2021) *The Lost Sermons of C. H. Spurgeon Volume VI: His Earliest Outlines and Sermons Between 1851 and 1854*. Nashville, Tennessee, USA: B&H. [*Due to be published November 2021*]

2) he adjusted his meetings but continued meeting;[12] 3) he cared for the sick; 4) he looked for new evangelistic opportunities; 5) he entrusted his life to God.[13]

Across the Atlantic, in North America during the eighteenth century, President Jonathan Edwards (1703-1758) had to deal with a smallpox plague. This highly contagious virus killed hundreds of thousands each year. It not only caused horrific death but significant scarring and blindness to survivors. So, for Edwards and his fellow Christians, death and extreme suffering were commonplace. Although Edwards never shrank from pastoral duties during this plague, he did recognise the Christian responsibility of taking precautions. This led him to submit himself to a primitive inoculation for smallpox, from which he sadly died.

Francis Grimké (1850-1937) was one of the last students of Charles Hodge (1797-1878) at Princeton. Grimké was a Presbyterian minister in Washington, DC. He died in 1937. He lived through the Spanish flu of 1918 and published a sermon titled, *Some Reflections Growing out of the Recent Epidemic of Influenza That Afflicted Our City*. Grimké informs us that for some of the time during the epidemic, all the churches in Washington were closed for the month of October 1918. This seems to have been by legal requirement, as concert and dance halls were also compelled to close.

---

[12] It is evident that Spurgeon would have had little time for those who fail to follow sensible precautions. In one sermon he said: 'The gospel has no quarrel with ventilation, and the doctrines of grace have no dispute with chloride of lime. We preach repentance and faith, but we do not denounce whitewash; and much as we advocate holiness, we always have a good word for cleanliness and sobriety.' (1866) *The Metropolitan Tabernacle Pulpit*, Vol. 12, Sermon number 705.

[13] See: Chang, G. (2020) *Spurgeon and the Cholera Outbreak of 1854*: https://www.spurgeon.org/resource-library/blog-entries/spurgeon-and-the-cholera-outbreak-of-1854/ [Accessed 24/03/2021].

In any case, Grimké recalls in his sermon, 'This brought home to us as never before what the church really meant to us.' Then, in contrast to what seems to be the prevailing situation with ourselves today, he adds, 'One of the gratifying things to me during this scourge has been the sincere regrets that I have heard expressed all over the city by numbers of people at the closing of the churches.'[14]

4. What are the lessons for us to learn from these facts?

1. We should recognise that this is a deadly contagious virus, but nowhere near as much a killer as other pandemics in history. We dare not minimise the devastating effects of Covid-19, but neither should these be exaggerated. It is virtually impossible for us to know the truth, the whole truth, and nothing but the truth, regarding this virus and its effects. It would be foolish to swallow hook, line, and sinker, the narrative being presented by politicians and the media.
2. We should recognize the important distinction between what the church can *voluntarily* do and what is *imposed* on the church by political legislation. The start point in all discussions on church-state relations is the supreme headship of Jesus Christ over his own kingdom. It is under that headship that Christians find their warrant to worship God freely and without interference. As Alexander Shields (1660-1700), the seventeenth century Covenanter, wrote in his classic work, *A Hind Let Loose*:

[14] Grimké, F. J. (1918) *Some Reflections, Growing out of the Recent Epidemic of Influenza that Afflicted our City*. Washington (?): not stated. p. 9. Churches were reopened in response to protests at the closure.

> It is necessary at all times that Christians should meet together, whether they have ministers or not, and whether the magistrate allows it or not. The authority of God, their necessity, duty, and interest, makes it indispensable in all cases.[15]

We were given no choice in these lockdowns, not even meaningful consultation. In effect, the government swept aside the headship of Christ and criminalized the gospel, without as much as a by your leave. Not to protest this vigorously is to fail the head of the church and to sacrifice the principle of the spiritual independence of the church on the altar of political pragmatism.

3. We should be deeply concerned about the pastoral and spiritual effects of the enforced closure of churches. The lockdown deprived our congregations, and indeed our communities, of all that the gospel and its ministry can do for them. Ministers were prevented from honouring their vow to discharge all the parts of their ministerial work by not being allowed to comfort the sick and minister to the dying.
4. The duty to be 'subject unto the higher powers' (Romans 13:1) should always be balanced by the greater duty established in Acts 5:29, 'We ought to obey God rather than men.' By not being allowed to meet freely for public worship, and to observe the sacraments or to sing God's praise, Christians are coerced into breach of contract with God, because by professing faith in Jesus Christ we are committed to these duties without caveat.

[15] Shields, A. (1797) *A Hind Let Loose: or, An historical representation of the testimonies of the Church of Scotland, for the interest of Christ: With the true state thereof in all its periods*. Glasgow: William Paton. pp. 621-622.

5. The early church, the church of the Reformers, the Nonconformists of 1662 and the Free Church of Scotland of 1843 would not have accepted being told that services had to conform to political policy rather than to biblical teaching. Many of us belong to churches that emerged in history because of political interference. These churchmen of history did not hesitate to protest—we should be just as eager to defend the headship of Jesus Christ.

   Our present circumstances are not about political persecution of the church. There is no suggestion of that—at least not yet. However, these impositions have swept aside what has, until now, been entrenched in our church history. In the case of the Free Church of Scotland this principle was encapsulated in the original title chosen for the 1843 church, which was, *The Church of Scotland, Free*. That is, *free* from any interference from the civil magistrate. William Cunningham (1805-1861) concludes in his *Historical Theology*, that this position was held more clearly and firmly by Scottish Presbyterians than by any other denomination.[16] For their part, the Westminster divines insisted that, 'the civil magistrate may *not* take to himself the keys of the kingdom of heaven' (WCF 23:3).

6. The state of the wider Christian church should be of great concern to us. Mainstream denominations throughout the UK have become an embarrassment. Apostacy by leaders, gross sin at denominational level, heresies in pulpits, shallowness in the pew, have left us as something of a husk of what we once were. Little wonder that we have become an irrelevance to our society.

[16] Cunningham, W (1870) *Historical Theology*. Edinburgh: T & T Clark. Vol. 2.

Also, our nation has evidently abandoned Christian ethics when it comes to behaviour and conduct. This is evident from the corridors of power to the boardroom, from the educational curricula to the enactments of the judiciary, from the discarding of traditional marriage to the rejection of the nuclear family. Crassness, vulgarity, shamelessness, cruelty, and violence, all point to a generation given over by God.

But be that as it may, the bottom line is, 'judgment must begin at the house of God' (1 Peter 4:17). It will not be until we, as Christians, point the finger at ourselves and turn in full repentance to God, that we can sincerely plead with Habakkuk, 'O Lord, revive thy work in the midst of the years, in the midst of the years make known; in wrath remember mercy' (3:2).

7. Let us not forget that this is God's world. Jerome (c.342-420) was a fourth century scholar and church leader of his day. When he heard of the collapse of Rome in 410, he retreated into a cave crying, 'The world is in ruins.' By contrast, when Augustine (354-430) heard about Rome and also the Barbarians closing in on Hippo, his home city in North Africa, he took out his pen and wrote the famous *City of God*.[17] He reminds us that there are two cities—the *city of man* and the *city of God*. Christians may live in the city of man and obey its laws, but our citizenship is in the city of God. Augustine's book found an echo in Scotland when Knox's successor, Andrew Melville (1545-1622), gave his famous *Two Kingdoms* speech to King James.[18] That's an

---

17 See: https://www.5minutesinchurchhistory.com/the-church-in-times-of-crisis/ [Accessed 23/03/2021].

18 See: M'Crie, T. (1819) *The Life of Andrew Melville*. Edinburgh: Blackwood. Vol. 2, p. 66f. and Pitcairn, R. (Ed.) (1842) *The Autobiography and Diary of Mr James Melvill*. Edinburgh: Wodrow Society. pp. 370-371.

approach that would stand the Christian church in good stead today.

8. Finally, probably the most far-reaching lesson to learn here is that something of divine significance seems to be in the air over this past year. Who else but *God* could have paralysed the world, nation by nation, in the twinkling of an eye? Who else but *God* could have bankrupted citadels of business which seemed unassailable only twelve months ago? Who else but *God* could have grounded entire fleets of aircraft throughout the world? Who else but *God* could have made city centres resemble ghost towns? More significant still, who else but *God* could have done this to the Christian community, where we cannot freely sit together in his house, where we cannot commemorate the death of our Saviour, where we cannot baptise our children, where we cannot meet in Christian companionship, where we cannot greet each other with the right hand of fellowship, where we can hardly recognise each other due to living behind face masks? It is almost as if a corporate excommunication has been imposed on the church. There is an ominous, foreboding feel to it all. We can argue all day long on the question, is the coronavirus a judgment? Whatever answer you give to that question, it is evident to any objective thinker that there is no way all of this could ever have occurred as a matter of happenstance.

9. What God is doing in the church and the world may not be entirely clear to our finite understanding. May our cry be with the Psalmist, 'Be merciful unto me, O God, be merciful unto me: for my soul trusteth in thee: yea, in the shadow of thy wings will I make my refuge, until these calamities be overpast' (Psalm 57:1).

~ 2 ~
How may the church preserve unity in the midst of disagreement?

Douglas W. B. Somerset

The Covid-19 crisis has brought disagreements into the church over several matters such as the streaming of sermons, the singing of praise in public worship, the maintaining of public worship in the face of prohibition by the civil magistrate, the wearing of masks in church, and the morality of the various Covid-19 vaccines. It is part of the providence of God that the church should be tested in this way, to see how Christians respond. Through this, they learn more about their own hearts, and their need of the wisdom of Christ to guide them, and more also about the hearts of others. Do we respond in a wise, gracious, and prayerful way to the divine testing, or do we behave much as the world and simply follow our own inclinations or impulses?

It is not the purpose of this chapter to discuss any of the matters of disagreement mentioned. Instead, our concern is—assuming disagreement in the church—to consider how we may fulfil the Christian duty of maintaining love and unity in the church. Different Christians will come to different opinions in these areas of disagreement, and there will also be different conclusions as to how important or fundamental these issues are. Nevertheless, as more than one person has pointed out, it would be ironic if in our zeal for the outward requirement of the sixth commandment to preserve the life and health of our neighbour, we transgress the spiritual aspect of the commandment by nursing bitter thoughts in our hearts towards those who disagree with us.

In this chapter we want to consider six points: 1) the need to approach disagreements humbly and with a readiness to learn; 2) the need to beware the danger of division; 3) the need to maintain a sense of proportion; 4) the need to realise our own limitations; 5) the need to remember our duty towards our brother; and 6) the need to continue steadfastly in ordinary Christian work.

1. We need to approach disagreements humbly and with a readiness to learn

The Lord does not generally give all the wisdom to one person in the church, but divides it among many. 'Where no counsel is, the people fall: but in the multitude of counsellors there is safety' (Proverbs 11:14). The apostles were able, under divine inspiration, to speak with absolute authority, but even they had to *discuss* the non-imposition of the ceremonial law on the Gentiles in Acts 15. Any one of them could have been moved by the Spirit to declare the truth there and then, but instead, as an example to the church in subsequent generations, the matter was aired at great length 'with much disputing' (Acts 15:7). Eventually, through the mutual wisdom given by the Spirit, the assembly arrived at the truth, apparently unanimously (v. 22).

The lesson from this is that Christians need to approach their disagreements in a humble spirit and with a readiness to learn. They believe that the Lord has given them one important aspect of the truth; and let them, in the discussion, try to express that aspect of truth as clearly, biblically, and graciously as they can. By all means, let them retain the element of truth that they do have: 'Buy the truth and sell it not' (Proverbs 23:23). But at the same time, the Lord has very likely given to others further aspects of the truth, and perhaps more important than that which he has given to them. Let them hear what others have to say; and before they start searching for counter-arguments to defend their own position, let them first try to understand the perspective of their brethren. It is unlikely that their brother is wholly wrong and has nothing whatever to contribute to the debate. They may think that his contribution is poor; but let them sift through it for nuggets of gold and add these to the general pool of wisdom. Job's three friends were largely in the wrong, and the Lord's wrath was kindled against them (Job 42:7), and yet the Holy Spirit has seen fit to preserve their words in Scripture, so there is obviously much of profit and value that we can learn from their words, rightly understood. There is a general principle here about learning even from those who are largely mistaken.

Having understood what his brother has said, the disputing Christian must then do two things. Firstly, he must be ready to modify his own views in the light of the wisdom that his brother has now contributed. His views may have been broadly right before but not completely right, but with this additional light now received, he can refine his position and make it more biblical and more accurately articulated. Secondly, once he understands his brother's perspective, he can try, if he thinks that his brother is in error on certain matters, to explain to him, in meekness and patience, where and why he is wrong (2 Timothy 2:24-25). In this way, the hope is that both of them will converge towards the truth.

What sometimes happens, alas, is very different. People make up their minds beforehand, and arrive at the discussion as if they had nothing to learn, and with a determination that their own position is going to prevail. Their manner of arguing is 'eristic'—that is, seeking victory rather than truth. While their brother is speaking, their principal thought is how to demolish his arguments most effectively, and they refuse to move an iota from their original position. The result, not infrequently, is that the decision of the assembly, while perhaps broadly correct, is crude and ill-formulated, and makes many problems for the future.

Let each remember therefore, in humbleness, that he does not have the monopoly of wisdom. Let it not be said to him, as Job said mockingly to his friends, 'No doubt but ye are the people, and wisdom shall die with you' (Job. 12:2). Let us value the wisdom that God has given to others. 'Iron sharpeneth iron; so a man sharpeneth the countenance of his friend' (Proverbs 27:17). 'Every purpose is established by counsel, and with good advice make war' (Proverbs 20:18).

2. We need to beware the danger of division

The second thing to remember is that there may be much more likelihood or danger of division and separation than we realise. When Paul and Barnabas agreed to 'visit their brethren in every city' (Acts 15:36), they little thought how soon they would be separated from each other by disagreement. But they differed over whether to take John Mark, and 'the contention was so sharp between them that they departed asunder one from the other' (v. 39). This is a pointed warning to Christians lest the same thing should happen to themselves. 'The beginning of strife is as when one letteth out water: therefore leave off contention, before it be meddled with' (Proverbs 17:14).

In the case of Paul and Barnabas, the separation was merely practical or 'administrative' rather than ecclesiastical or fundamental. They were reconciled in due course, and there was no associated split in the church. Doubtless the wisdom and grace of Paul—and probably of Barnabas too—had much to do with this. In the absence of this, however, any rent in the seamless garment of Christ may get worse, leading to a complete outward separation (whatever spiritual unity may persist). Several incidents in Scottish church history illustrate this. In each case, the disagreement involved men who are highly esteemed to this day, and led rapidly to a harmful separation with long-term consequences. Let us look now at three examples of this.

(i) The Protestors and the Resolutioners

In 1649, the Scottish Parliament passed the Act of Classes, barring 'malignants' (those hostile to the National Covenant and the Solemn League and Covenant) from the army and important public offices. In December 1650, however, following Cromwell's invasion, much of this legislation was repealed in the 'Public Resolutions' which allowed more people to fight in the army. The General Assembly of the Church of Scotland approved the Public Resolutions by a majority (the Resolutioners), but a highly significant minority (the Protestors) opposed them. In 1651, the Protestors were barred from the General Assembly, and soon afterwards they set up their own presbyteries and synods. The Resolutioners included such eminent figures as David Dickson (1583-1662) and George Hutcheson (1626-1674), and the Protestors such famous names as Samuel Rutherford (1600-1661) and William (1621-1665) and James Guthrie (1616-1661). James Durham (1622-1658) and Robert Blair (1593-1666) endeavoured to remain neutral.

The split continued throughout the 1650s until the restoration of Charles II and the government persecution of both parties from 1661 onwards. In addition to the extreme bitterness of the 1650s, the split hindered united action and, in the words of Thomas M'Crie (1772-1835), 'made them an easy prey to their common enemies' when the crisis of 1661 came.[1] It also fed into the second split of 1680 (which we will look at in the next section as our next example) and brought into the Scottish church a readiness to separate which had not been there before. As Principal John Macleod (1872-1948) said, 'The Reformed Church never got over the bad results that can easily be traced back to this schism which rent its unity in the days of the Commonwealth.'[2] The consensus of conservative Scottish church history has been that the Protestors were right in their assessment of the Public Resolutions, but were excessively vehement in their opposition, and that the resulting division was worse than the reasons behind it. The most useful thing to come out of the controversy was James Durham's *Dying Man's Testament to the Church of Scotland, or A Treatise on Scandal*, published posthumously in 1658, in which he makes the following general comment on divisions:

> Although sometimes the fault of division may be more on one side than another, yet seldom is any side free [from fault], at least in the manner of prosecution; and therefore often it turned in the close to the hurt of both, and the one side becomes more schismatical and erroneous ... The other side again have often become more cold and secure in the practice of holiness, carnal and formal in pursuing ceremonies and external things, with less affection and life in the main, because the edge of their zeal

[1] Associate Synod of Original Seceders (1827) *A Testimony to the Truths of Christ*. Edinburgh: Guthrie and Tait. p. 29.

[2] Macleod, J. (1943) *Scottish Theology in relation to Church History since the Reformation*. Edinburgh: The Publications Committee of the Free Church of Scotland. p. 84.

was bended toward these differences; and generally people have been stumbled and offended by them.[3]

(ii) The moderate Covenanters and the Cameronians

A second division arose in 1680 over Indulgences and the payment of the Cess.

The Indulgences (1669, 1672, 1679, 1687) were various declarations issued by the kings (Charles II and James VII/II), allowing Presbyterian ministers who had been prohibited from preaching in 1662 to resume their ministry under certain constraints. A number of ministers took these Indulgences, believing that it was better to preach under constraints than not to preach at all, but the majority of the ministers and people rejected the Indulgences on the ground that the king had no authority from Christ to ordain conditions under which preaching might take place.

The Indulgences immediately brought division (and were intended to do so by some of the enemies of the church), but more divisive still was the question of how to respond to ministers who had taken the Indulgences. Some people went to hear them because they wanted to hear the gospel; others refrained from hearing them because they thought the indulged ministers unfaithful. This led to the question of whether those who heard indulged ministers in their parishes should be admitted to the covenanting prayer societies, and whether indulged ministers should be allowed to preach at the covenanting field meetings; and these questions in turn led to yet further divisions and further questions. The complications of the situation were expressed by the field-preacher Thomas Douglas (d. 1695):

---

[3] Durham, J. [edited: Coldwell, C.] (1990) *The Dying Man's Testament to the Church of Scotland or, A Treatise Concerning Scandal.* Dallas, Texas, USA: Naphtali Press. p. 244.

> I am not for a sinful union with the indulged, nor for a sinful union with those that are for a sinful union with the indulged, and because of this my ministry has been rejected in many places ... Neither am I for a sinful separation from them that are not for a sinful union with the indulged, and because of this my ministry has been rejected these two years past and more by some.[4]

Equally divisive was the Cess. This was a tax levied to fund the military persecution of the Covenanters. Should one pay the Cess; and if not, how should one behave towards one's neighbour who did pay the Cess (even though, perhaps, he was heartily opposed to the persecution of Covenanters, and perhaps sheltered persecuted Covenanters in their plight)? Furthermore, there were no covenanting church courts at the time to resolve these questions, even supposing they had been able to do so.

In the late 1670s, there were powerful revivals connected with the covenanting field-preaching, but these came to an end with the 1679 Indulgence and the defeat of the Covenanters at the battle of Bothwell Bridge. The Covenanters were divided before the battle with a similar problem to that which had faced the Protestors and Resolutioners in 1650: should they allow into their army men with whom they did not wholly agree in religious things? In the ensuing separation of the Cameronians or 'Society People' from the other Covenanters, Richard Cameron (d. 1680) was supported by John Brown of Wamphray (d. 1679) and Robert MacWard (d. 1681), both of whom had been Protestors in the earlier split, and was opposed by Robert Fleming (1630-1694), Thomas Hog (1628-1692), John Welsh (d. 1681), and others. Alexander Peden (d. 1686) endeavoured to remain neutral. In 1685, about 160 Covenanters

[4] Grant, M. (1988) *No King but Christ*. Darlington: Evangelical Press. p. 254.

were imprisoned in the 'Whigs' vault' in Dunnottar Castle, and one of the points taken up by Alexander Shields (1660-1700) in his letter to the Cameronians there was how they should behave towards the other prisoners, and whether they should hold separate worship in the large chamber in which they were all confined.[5] By 1687 the division had become so sharp that other Covenanters were, on occasions, ready to betray the Cameronians to the authorities.

The division was partly resolved after the 1689 Revolution Settlement, when the bulk of the Cameronians returned to the Established Church with Alexander Shields, but about a third did not, and the Reformed Presbyterian separation has continued to the present day, in Scotland, Ireland, and America. The lasting effect was a mutual bitterness, a weakening of the conservative wing of the Church of Scotland, and the unhealthy example of a standing division.

(iii) The Burghers and the Antiburghers

The third division was 'the Breach' which arose in the Secession Church in 1747. The Secession Church had separated from the Church of Scotland in the 1730s and had about twenty ministers by the early 1740s. In 1744 a 'burgess oath' was imposed in Edinburgh, Glasgow, and Perth for those wishing to engage in commerce or hold political office. The purpose of the oath was to exclude Jacobites (with the 1745 rebellion threatening), but the oath was poorly worded and could be interpreted as endorsing the very things in the Church of Scotland from which the Seceders had separated. After two years of heated conflict, the Secession split into Burghers and Antiburghers in 1747, with the Antiburghers

[5] Shields, A. (1726) *A letter concerning the due boundaries of Christian fellowship; specially, with whom 'tis lawful to join in divine worship, and from whom 'tis duty to withdraw*. Edinburgh. pp. 31-32.

deposing and excommunicating the Burghers in 1748. The Burghers included Ralph (1685-1752) and Ebenezer Erskine (1680-1754) and, later, John Brown of Haddington (1722-1787), while the Antiburghers included Adam Gib (1714-1788) and Alexander Moncrieff (1695-1761).

Apart from the lasting bitterness and the family divisions, the Breach, so soon after their separation from the Church of Scotland, made the Seceders appear quarrelsome and unreasonable in the eyes of the world. It also opened the door, particularly among the Antiburghers, to a considerable number of further splits.

The Breach was effectively healed in 1827 at the reunion of the conservative remnants of the Burghers and Antiburghers to form the Original Secession Church. Looking back on the Breach of 1747, the *Original Secession Testimony* of 1827 comments:

> It is difficult to believe that an ecclesiastical body which had hitherto preserved such unanimity and concord in their deliberations and decisions upon a variety of questions, some of which were of a very delicate and complicated nature, could have divided on the subject of a burgess oath, had not the leaven of prejudice and suspicion insinuated itself, soured their minds, and fomented any difference of sentiment which at first existed among them.[6]

3. We need to maintain a sense of proportion

In the light of the examples just given, we see the need to maintain a sense of proportion in any disagreements that arise in the church. Satan is continually trying to drive people to extremes, and

[6] Associate Synod of Original Seceders (1827) *A Testimony to the Truths of Christ*. Edinburgh: Guthrie and Tait. p. 58.

disagreements in the church are no exception to this. We need to 'judge righteous judgment' (John 7:24) concerning the relative importance of these subjects of disagreement. We are not to brush aside as trifles matters which may have important consequences (as for example, the issue of kneeling at communion has more than once been dismissed in this way in British church history). Paul would not 'give place by subjection, no, not for hour' to those compelling Titus to be baptised (Galatians 2:5). In itself, circumcision was nothing (Galatians 5:6), but to yield in that instance would have been to forsake the gospel because to the minds of the Judaizers circumcision was essential (Acts 15:1). Such an error must be withstood. There are fundamental matters on which compromise is impossible.

On the other hand, however, we are not to exaggerate the importance of any issue, nor to give it an undue place in comparison to other duties that we have, for example towards the unity of the church or the propagation of the gospel. The composition of the Scottish or covenanting army in 1651 and again in 1679 was, doubtless, a matter of urgent practical importance, but was it more important than the unity of the church; and did a difference of opinion on this point justify the ensuing separation, and the refusal to recognise each other's ministry?

Part of the danger is that of being stampeded by Satan. He is allowed, in divine providence, to throw in an apple of discord or a bone of contention, and often the people of God are not watchful enough. They should not be 'ignorant of his devices' (2 Corinthians 2:11). They should not take up the bait of discord as brute beasts without spiritual reflection on their circumstances. They should be pausing and asking, 'What is the Lord's purpose in this test? What is Satan aiming at? What does my spiritual and biblical training as a "good soldier of Jesus Christ" (2 Timothy 2:3) direct me to do? In engaging in this matter that has come before me in providence, I am not to be unmindful of other standing duties that I have as well. I have a duty of prayer, a duty of love, and a duty of watchfulness. If I fail in these duties, then even if I come down on the right side in the particular matter brought before me, I have failed overall as a servant of Christ.' The believer is to admonish himself in this way.

Another danger is that of exaggerating the extent of the disagreement. One way in which this may happen is when we try to deduce what seem to us logical inferences from a brother's point of view, and then charge him with holding these supposed conclusions, which, in fact, he may utterly repudiate. Thus we exaggerate the real difference between us. Anthony Burgess (d. 1664), a Westminster divine, stated in his sermons on John 17:

> [Do] not charge such consequences upon one another's doctrine, that are not natural, and which they do abhor. This in doctrinal disputes has been oil to the flame ... Some gathered from Paul's preaching of free grace that therefore men might sin that grace might abound; but Paul cries 'God forbid' at this (Romans 6:15) and says the damnation of such logicians is just (Romans 3:8).[7]

We should endeavour to ensure that our account of differences between brethren is strictly accurate and should spare no pains in understanding the view of those we differ from.

---

[7] Burgess, A. (2020) *Christ's Prayer before his Passion: Expository Sermons on John 17*. Grand Rapids, Michigan, USA: Reformation Heritage Books. Vol. 1, p. 534; also Vol. 2, pp. 344-346. Burgess's sermons on John 17:11 and 21 are very apt to the church today, when many so easily move church, and there is little seeking for fundamental unity, or true understanding of the sin of schism.

The Christian has to weigh the intrinsic importance of the matter of disagreement brought before him with the likely effects to the church if that disagreement escalates. Today, many become contentious, allow breaches between brethren, or secede from churches, for reasons that are hardly worthy ground for such actions. Again, Burgess comments that we must be sure that we do not take such drastic action 'for some less corruption, but that which does eat up the very vitals of religion.'[8]

The likelihood of disagreements escalating is not small. In 1748, a disagreement arose between Jonathan Edwards (1703-1758) and his congregation in New England regarding the profession of faith that people were making in coming to the Lord's Table. The disagreement rapidly came to a height, and in 1750 Edwards wrote to a ministerial friend: 'This controversy, in the progress of it, has proved not only a controversy between me and my people, but between me and a great part of New England; there being many far and near who are warmly engaged in it.'[9] Whatever the merits of the dispute (and we think that Edwards was right in the stand that he took), the main point here is that it shows how quickly Satan can fan a small flame into a blaze. Let us not be assisting him in the work by inconsiderately piling on fuel ourselves.

4. We need a sense of our limitations

The infinite Wisdom of God is able to resolve every problem, but we may not be able to, and we need to be aware of our limitations

---

[8] Burgess, A. (2020) *Christ's Prayer before his Passion: Expository Sermons on John 17*. Grand Rapids, Michigan, USA: Reformation Heritage Books. Vol. 2, pp. 347.

[9] Edwards, J. (1990) *The Works of Jonathan Edwards*. Edinburgh: Banner of Truth Trust. Vol. 1, p. 340.

in this regard. Just as God does not give all the wisdom to one person in the church, so he does not give it all to one generation. Martin Luther (1483-1546)—and through him the early German Protestant church—received great light on the doctrine of justification compared with previous Christian understanding, but he and they fell into grievous error regarding the Lord's Supper; and Luther's stubbornness—and even pride—in that matter caused a division that has lasted to this day.

It would have been better for the church if the early German Protestants had simply rejected the doctrine of the mass (both the sacrifice of the mass and transubstantiation) and left the positive doctrine as an open question for the time being. But in their desire to annihilate their Roman Catholic controversialists, they wanted to have something definite to assert against their doctrine of the mass, and they prematurely committed themselves and their followers to a position which had minimal biblical support. It would not be difficult to give examples of the same thing happening since in other branches of the church with other doctrines.

If a problem is too hard for us, let us not force a half-baked solution on the church, perhaps entailing a legacy of trouble on those that come after us. It is better to have no decision than a wrong one. In a case of uncertainty, as Paul says to the Romans, 'One man esteemeth one day above another: another esteemeth every day alike. Let every man be fully persuaded in his own mind' (Romans 14:5). Christians can reasonably expect and pray for wisdom to solve the problems that are immediately before them, and to know what *their* present duty is; but they may be taking too much on themselves if they endeavour to prescribe for others. Let us not pretend to greater light than we have.

5. We need to remember our duty to our brother

We have to remember that, even in situations of disagreement and controversy, our duty to the spiritual well-being of our Christian brother is undiminished. In Romans chapter 14, Paul addresses an issue regarding the eating of meat that had arisen in the church in Rome.[10] Some of the Christians were eating meat freely while others would not touch meat at all, being under the mistaken apprehension that it was sinful to do so. Their misapprehension, while erroneous, was sincere, and they genuinely believed in their consciences that it was wrong for them to eat meat: 'He that eateth, eateth to the Lord, for he giveth God thanks; and he that eateth not, to the Lord he eateth not, and giveth God thanks' (v. 6).

Paul plainly resolves the issue in dispute in the chapter: 'I know, and am persuaded by the Lord Jesus, that there is nothing unclean of itself: but to him that esteemeth any thing to be unclean, to him it is unclean' (v. 14). Thus those who were eating meat, whom he characterises as 'the strong' (15:1), were in the right; and those refraining from meat, whom he calls 'the weak', were mistaken. That which they 'esteemed to be unclean' was not in fact unclean, though it was to them as long as they retained their misapprehension.

But that was not the entirety of the matter. Paul also addresses how the 'weak' and the 'strong' should regard each other and behave towards each other; and presumably this counsel was largely intended for the future, when similar situations might arise, and when, in the absence of an inspired apostle, it might be a long time before the church could arrive at a definitive answer to the

---

[10] Professor John Murray (1898-1975) has a useful discussion of this chapter, entitled 'The weak and the strong', in Vol. 4 of his *Collected Writings* (1982) Edinburgh: Banner of Truth Trust. pp. 142-157.

contentious issue. How should those in disagreement behave towards each other in the meantime?

The basic rule in these circumstances is that the strong are not to despise the weak, and the weak are not to condemn the strong: 'Let not him that eateth despise him that eateth not; and let not him which eateth not judge him that eateth: for God hath received him' (v. 3). Of course, in the absence of a definitive answer to whatever the issue is, we cannot say who the strong and the weak are; but presumably each man regards himself as strong, and those that disagree with him as weak, and thus Paul lays a greater burden on the strong than he does on the weak. The strong and the weak are not to despise nor condemn one another, but furthermore they are not to cause one another to stumble: 'Let us not therefore judge one another any more: but judge this rather, that no man put a stumbling block or an occasion to fall in his brother's way' (v. 13).

This duty of not causing one another to stumble may require some of the strong to deny themselves in what they believe, rightly, to be lawful: 'It is good neither to eat flesh, nor to drink wine, nor any thing whereby thy brother stumbleth, or is offended, or is made weak' (v. 21). Furthermore, they may have to deny themselves, not only so as not to provoke a sinful response in their brother, but also so as not to tempt him into conformity with their own practice against his conscience. 'And he that doubteth is damned if he eat, because he eateth not of faith: for whatsoever is not of faith is sin' (v. 23).

In this chapter, Paul sets a very high standard of brotherly care indeed. We are to have as high a regard for our brother's spiritual well-being as for our own: 'Thou shalt love thy neighbour as thyself.' We are to avoid, if possible, being the occasion of sin to our brother; and this includes not only provocative and railing language and trampling on his feelings, which obviously may stir up sin in his soul, but even drawing him into conduct which is lawful but against his conscience.

In disagreements in the church, the great duty of love is not to be forgotten. Indeed the aim of peace and edification remains: 'Let us therefore follow after the things which make for peace, and things wherewith one may edify another' (v. 19).

6. We must continue steadfastly in ordinary Christian work

Christ has left his servants behind in this world to engage in the ordinary duties of the Christian life, and particularly the duty of advancing his kingdom. They are never to desist from this duty: 'Therefore, my beloved brethren, be ye steadfast, unmoveable, always abounding in the work of the Lord, forasmuch as ye know that your labour is not in vain in the Lord' (1 Corinthians 15:58). One of the features of Christ's public ministry, as recorded in the Gospels, is how rapidly he passes on to each succeeding duty. Nothing diverted him from this great work of advancing the kingdom.

There is a danger that unusual providences may have exactly this effect—that they cause Christians to become unmindful of ordinary duty, and to spend their time instead prying unprofitably into the divine purposes, which perhaps are too deep for them. This is how it was with Job's three friends when they came to comfort him. Instead of doing so, which was their ordinary Christian duty, they sought to fathom God's dealing with him, and their attempts were in vain. They were 'miserable comforters' as a result (Job 16:2). James Durham comments:

> The cause of their mistake in all this debate between him and them [was] that they mistook plain practical things and did pry into God's deeps. Observe: (1) It is one of the great grounds of our mistakes, and the fountain from whence they rise, when we mistake plain practical things, and go to search out God's mind in things not so needful to be known, and not so easily won to. (2) And the remedy for this on the other side is to be more studious to fear God and to eschew evil.[11]

Durham goes on to apply this to the divisions of his own day (those between the Protestors and the Resolutioners mentioned above):

> Observe, there are even some things in the way of God's providence and dispensations that folks are not called to study, or to be anxious about though they cannot find it out ... And on the other hand, when God keeps up some things, it is surest to be practising the plain things that we know, and not to be curious nor anxious in seeking to find out secret and hid things; though there is a difference among us about some things, yet there are many things about which there is no difference, as about prayer, making use of the scripture, holy walking, etc. When God takes a mysterious and indiscernible way of doing things in his sovereignty, it is surest and safest for us to be taken up about the practice of holy duties, rather than to pry into his depths.
>
> God has taken a sovereign way of proceeding with us, and though we will be loath to cast at [*Scots*: show repugnance for] anything that is allowed us for duty, in respect of, or in reference to, the finding out of God's mind, yet there may be an exceeding on that side in searching out what he has kept secret.

---

[11] Durham, J. [edited: Coldwell, C.] (2003) *Lectures on Job*. Dallas, Texas, USA: Naphtali Press. pp. 164-5.

> We will not condemn the work, but the fruits show there has been too great inclining to that hand. And it were better for us if we were more in the practice of things plain and obvious to all, than so exercised.[12]

We must not allow uncertain interpretations of providence to hinder us from plain duties; and if we are abounding in these duties, we will be the better able to understand providence, and to make allowance for the conduct of our brethren. The most active Christian tends to be the least censorious.

Conclusion

The Lord has allowed multiple points of disagreement to come into the Christian church during the coronavirus crisis. Let us reflect upon them and discuss them calmly and prayerfully, conscious of our emptiness, conscious of our duty, conscious of the deceitfulness of sin and the subtlety of Satan, and conscious of the fulness that there is in Christ, 'in whom are hid all the treasures of wisdom and knowledge' (Colossians 2:3). 'If any of you lack wisdom, let him ask of God, that giveth to all men liberally, and upbraideth not; and it shall be given him' (James 1:5). The wisdom that is from above will be 'first pure, then peaceable, gentle, and easy to be intreated, full of mercy and good fruits, without partiality, and without hypocrisy' (James 3:17). Let us endeavour, with this wisdom, 'to keep the unity of the Spirit in the bond of peace' (Ephesians 4:3).

---

[12] Durham, J. [edited. Coldwell, C.] (2003) *Lectures on Job*. Dallas, Texas, USA: Naphtali Press. pp. 165-6.

~ 3 ~
Should the church ever suspend public worship?

Matthew J. Hyde

> Let us hold fast the profession of our faith without wavering; (for he is faithful that promised;) and let us consider one another to provoke unto love and to good works: not forsaking the assembling of ourselves together, as the manner of some is; but exhorting one another: and so much the more, as ye see the day approaching. (Hebrews 10:23-25)

The question, 'Should the church ever suspend public worship?' was one that most of us hoped we would never have to ask—or provide an answer for. It was probably just because this was so, that when the Covid-19 pandemic reached the shores of the United Kingdom in 2020 that most churches and church leaders were so unprepared when the government announced a national lockdown which included the closure of places of worship. Most of us, with the best intentions, made rushed or pragmatic decisions. Only now, as the months have passed, have ministers and elders been able to consider carefully, in the light of Scripture and the history of the church, what the answer to this question should be. Perhaps we all should begin by confessing we did not get everything right in March 2020.

In order to learn from this experience, and to teach and prepare future generations in the church on this issue, we will in this chapter seek to answer this narrow question: should the church ever suspend public worship? To come to a right conclusion on this matter we must establish why the church holds worship services in the first place—what is the mandate for public worship? We will explore this as a biblical principle, and then through the history of the church. We will consider how the church has reacted to pressures to cease public worship in history, before answering the question as to whether there are any circumstances in which it is right to suspend public worship. We will briefly ask who has the authority to suspend public worship, and then discuss whether there are aspects of public worship which can be omitted or modified in exceptional circumstances. In conclusion, we will seek to apply our findings to the situation faced by the church during the Covid-19 pandemic.

1. What is public worship?

The term 'public worship' has a range of meanings. It means, for one thing, worship which is *open to all*. Perhaps an example would be a preacher at Hyde Park Corner, preaching to all that pass by. This may also include the sense of *publicised*, or appointed, with a time and a place appointed by authority.

There are however additional layers of meaning in the definition of 'public worship' as used by the confessions of the church. 'Public' is also used with the meaning, '*of the community*,' that is, the community of the church of Christ. The church of Christ gathers together for the shared, communal, collective, worship of the whole. This is sometimes called 'corporate worship,' in a reference to the 'body' (*corpus* in Latin) of Christ. It can take place behind locked doors, and it can be as few as 'two or three gathered together,' (Matthew 18:20) but it is a gathering of the church for the worship of God—with the spiritual presence of the head of the church with them.

And gatherings for 'public worship' are for the purpose of *the public glory of God*. This is the most obvious, visible option that God's people have for expressing how much they adore him and want to honour him. They give him public glory when they gather and worship him according to the forms or pattern set down in his Word.

Worship may be held in many other contexts—the family, private devotions on our own, preaching on the street, at a Christian conference, in parliament before the commencement of each day's business, for example—but none of these settings constitutes public worship. They are not the formally constituted worship of the church of Christ. They are a gathering of the family, or of a society, but they are not the gathering *of the church*.

2. What is our mandate for public worship?

Sadly, today, public worship is regarded by many in a loose way. According to Al Martin, 'Many view the public worship of God as helpful, and perhaps even a necessary arrangement, but they have no appreciation of it as an institution of God.'[1] The truth of the matter is that public worship is an institution of God and not of man. It is a divine ordinance—something mandated by God, not something man has dreamt up in order to please God. We can trace the institution of worship right back to creation and the Garden of Eden.

Man's purpose in creation

Ultimately, God created us to glorify him and to enjoy him for ever (Westminster Shorter Catechism, Q1). The Lord has made all

[1] Martin, A. N. (2020) *The Man of God (Volume 3): His Shepherding, Evangelizing and Counseling Labors*. Montville, USA: Trinity Pulpit Press. p. 268.

things for himself (Proverbs 16:4) and to his honour and glory (Romans 11:36). Everything we do is to be for his honour and glory (1 Corinthians 10:31). Believers glorify God individually by our submission to him and our praise and love for him. Primarily, however, the church glorifies God when we come together for public worship. It is as we draw near to God in worship that we are brought to know God, and this knowledge draws out greater praise and worship from us. God has put us under permanent obligation to worship him according to the pattern set out in his Word. 'Give unto the Lord the glory due unto his name; worship the Lord in the beauty of holiness' (Psalm 29:2).

> Ascribe unto the Lord, O ye kindreds of the people,
> ascribe unto the Lord worship and power.
> Ascribe unto the Lord the honour due unto his Name;
> bring presents, and come into his courts.
> O worship the Lord in the beauty of holiness;
> let the whole earth stand in awe of him.
>
> (Psalm 96:7-9, Myles Coverdale's translation, *The Book of Common Prayer*)

The link between the sabbath and public worship

In order to assist us to pay the debt of worship we owe to him, God set apart the sabbath day as a day for man (Mark 2:27), specifically for his own worship. Martin Luther (1483-1546) writing on Genesis 2:3 states,

> By the sanctification of the sabbath it is plainly shown that man was especially created unto the knowledge and worship of God. For the sabbath was not instituted on account of sheep, or oxen, but for the sake of men; that the knowledge of God might be exercised and increased by them, on that sacred day.

Luther goes on to point out that God 'willed that, on the seventh day, both the Word should be preached; and also those other parts of his worship performed, which he himself instituted.'[2] The link between the sabbath day and the institution of public worship is such that the failure to keep public worship must be deemed a breaking of the sabbath.

Some have argued that when Cain and Abel brought their offerings, they did so on the sabbath day, basing this on the expression 'in the process of time' or 'at the end of the days' in Genesis 4:3. If so, this would have been a recognition very soon after creation that the sabbath day was a day to worship God formally (using the forms or patterns of worship which God required). Again, the expression 'to call upon the name of the Lord' in Genesis 4:26 may be an indication of the start of public worship—that as soon as there came to be more than one family on the earth, families gathered together for public worship as well as worshipping individually or in families.[3]

God confirmed our duty both to keep the sabbath and to worship him on the sabbath when he gave the law at Sinai (Exodus 20:8). The conjunction of the public worship of God with the sabbath day continued throughout the Old Testament (e.g., 1 Chronicles 23:31). It was the practice of the Lord Jesus to attend sabbath day public worship in the synagogue (Mark 1:21; Luke 4:16—'as his custom was').

After the resurrection of Jesus from the dead on the first day of the week, the Old Testament seventh-day sabbath gave place to the

---

[2] Luther, M. [translated: Cole, H.] (1858) *The Creation: A Commentary on the first five chapters of the Book of Genesis*. Edinburgh: T. & T. Clark. p. 112.

[3] On both of these theses see for example, Bonar, H. (1875) *Earth's Morning: or Thoughts on Genesis*. London: Nisbet. pp. 226 and 269.

first-day sabbath-keeping (σαββατισμὸς, *sabbatismos;* Hebrews 4:9) of the New Testament Lord's Day. Gathered worship on the first day of the week was the apostolic pattern (Acts 20:7; 1 Corinthians 16:2). John tells us in Revelation that he was in the Spirit on the Lord's Day (Revelation 1:10). The keeping of the Lord's Day and its public worship is to continue until Christ returns (Hebrews 4:9 and 10:25).[4]

The church is commissioned to worship

In addition to the mandate to worship inherent in creation, and the mandate given to the Old Testament church at Sinai, the New Testament church has received its own mandate to worship publicly in the Great Commission which Jesus gave to his apostles. 'And Jesus came and spake unto them, saying, All power is given unto me in heaven and in earth. Go ye therefore, and teach all nations, baptizing them in the name of the Father, and of the Son, and of the Holy Ghost: teaching them to observe all things whatsoever I have commanded you: and, lo, I am with you always, even unto the end of the world. Amen' (Matthew 28:18-20). Jesus has set the church the task of preaching—for the dual purpose of conversion and discipleship—and administering the sacraments. Both these functions are only rightly performed within the confines of public worship.

Based on the Great Commission, the Belgic Confession (1561) sets out three marks of the true New Testament church. Two of these marks are, 'if the pure doctrine of the gospel is preached therein' and 'if she maintains the pure administration of the sacraments as instituted by Christ' (Article 29). It could be argued that if a church suspends the observance of the sacraments and fails to maintain the public preaching of the gospel, it almost unchurches itself.

---

[4] See the comments of John Owen on Hebrews 4:1-11 in his *Commentary on the Epistle to the Hebrews*.

Rather, in obedience to the Great Commission, Wilhelmus à Brakel (1635-1711) states that for the true church, the 'sole desire is that she may be visible: for this reason she continually strives to manifest herself, not with a sword in hand but by a faithful confession of Christ and his truth. ... It is for this purpose [the Lord's people] *gather together* to hear the Word of God and to use the sacraments'[5]—to the honour and glory of their Lord and Saviour who has commissioned them to worship publicly.

The church is saved to worship

We need to remember too that ultimately the church is saved *to worship*. Peter teaches that the Lord's people are being built together as a building for the worship of God (1 Peter 2:5) and Paul agrees (1 Timothy 3:15). The Lord's Day worship of the church is both a picture and a foretaste of the worship which the church will give in heaven. A poet once described heaven as the place where:

> Congregations ne'er break up,
> And sabbaths have no end.[6]

It is an evidence that we are saved that we worship. Paul wrote of the Thessalonians, 'they themselves shew of us what manner of entering in we had unto you, and how ye turned to God from idols to serve the living and true God' (1 Thessalonians 1:9). When we are saved in Jesus Christ, we become, by adoption, the sons of God. We are part of the family of God. As John writes, 'We know that we have passed from death unto life, because we love the brethren. He that loveth not his brother abideth in death' (1 John 3:14). This

---

5 à Brakel, W (1999) *The Christian's Reasonable Service*. Grand Rapids, USA: Reformation Heritage Books. Vol. 2, p.41-42.

6 Originally from Daniel Burgess (1645-1713) *Hymn on the Sabbath Day*. See Julian, J. (1915) *Dictionary of Hymnology*. London: John Murray. Revised Edition. p. 582.

love is manifested by a desire to be with the Lord's people and to worship God together. Although the believer's worship must be first of all a personal and individual response to the love of his heavenly Father, it is not an isolated response. The 'I' and the 'my' is always in the context of 'we' and 'our.' This is why we pray, 'Our Father,' praying with and for others and not just for ourselves. Corporate worship is the natural expression of our adoption into the family of Christ.

Worship is to be corporate

The Bible makes clear that corporate worship is to be the main worship of the church of God.[7] While we may worship individually or within families and other social groups, the centre of Lord's Day worship is the worship of the church. It is only to corporate worship that the ordinances of the preaching of the Word and the sacraments are delivered.

God deemed from the outset that it was not good for man to dwell alone, and so he created woman. We are by nature social creatures—we need one another (Genesis 2:18). Perhaps the isolation of lockdown has taught us this need again as a society. Some see this need as a partial expression of the fact that we are created in God's image—the relationship between the three persons in the Trinity is in some ways mirrored in relationships between us.[8] Certainly the need for gathering is as deeply ingrained in our DNA as is our duty to worship God. James Bannerman recognised this when he wrote, 'The very law and light

---

[7] The whys and wherefores of corporate worship are dealt with further in Chapter 4 of this volume ('How important is it for believers to gather together physically to worship God?'). Here our main object is simply to demonstrate that the worship of the Lord's Day is to be corporate worship.

[8] For example: Beeke, J. and Smalley, P. (2020) *Reformed Systematic Theology: Man and Christ.* Wheaton, Illinois, USA: Crossway. Vol. 2, p.167.

of nature tell us that the public worship of God is a standing and permanent ordinance for the whole human race.'[9] This can be seen by the fact that corporate worship is central to every man-made religion. It can also be seen in contemporary culture by the establishment of atheist 'churches' to satisfy the natural instinct for gathered worship (Romans 2:14-15).[10]

In the Old Testament, post-Sinaitic worship was inherently corporate. With the exception of the Passover, it was tabernacle-focused and temple-focused (Exodus 15:17-18). The 'holy convocation' of the sabbath speaks of sacred gathering or assembly (מִקְרָא־, *miq·rā-;* Leviticus 23:3). Later, synagogue worship was instituted and this again was corporate worship—those unable to get to the temple gathered locally for the reading and expounding of the Word of God. The Greek term synagogue (συναγωγή, *synagōgē*) is given its meaning in James 2:2 where it is translated in the King James Version (1611) as 'assembly'. The Old Testament principle of gathered worship is summed up in the injunction of Psalm 100:4: 'Enter into his gates with thanksgiving, and into his courts with praise.' Furthermore, while this was specifically written in the context of Jewish worship, the psalm is clear that this is to be the custom of 'all lands' (v. 1) or 'all people' (Scottish Metrical Version), and the psalmist joins this command inseparably to the fact that we are God's creatures. 'Know ye that the Lord he is God: it is he that hath made us, and not we ourselves' (v. 3).

In the New Testament the disciples gathered together in the upper room (Acts 1:12-14; 2:1-4); they came together for worship and the

[9] Bannerman, J. (2015) *The Church of Christ: A Treatise on the Nature, Powers, Ordinances, Discipline, and Government of the Christian Church.* Edinburgh: Banner of Truth Trust. p. 341.

[10] See: www.sundayassembly.com [Accessed 11/03/2021].

breaking of bread—or went up to the temple (Luke 24:50-53). They also gathered together in homes for prayer (e.g., when Peter was in prison, or for worship), but as this was a gathering of more than just the people living in the home, it was by definition something more than family worship—it was the corporate worship of the church gathered in that place. Luke describes the worship of the New Testament church as specifically centred on fellowship in both the preaching of the apostles' doctrine and the breaking of bread (Acts 2:42). These are not things conducted in private or by the individual. When Paul comes to deal with the singing of praise in worship, he emphasises the plurality of the singers, yet their one mouth or voice (ἐν ἑνὶ στόματι δοξάζητε, *en heni stomati doxazēte*; Romans 15:6)—they were gathered together in one place to sing. In Colossians he develops the idea that worship has implications for those who gather. The singing of praise to God (the vertical aspect of worship) has a secondary purpose of admonishing one another (the horizontal aspect) (Colossians 3:16)—yet this is only possible in gathered worship.

None of these aspects of corporate worship can be properly fulfilled in a virtual or online service. Even though such services may be edifying, in measure, they fall short of the fulness of the promise: 'For where two or three are *gathered together* in my name, there am I in the midst of them' (Matthew 18:20).[11]

Church history demonstrates obedience to this mandate

Just confining ourselves to the United Kingdom, the very existence of church buildings which trace their origin back to the earliest

---

[11] This is dealt with at length in Chapter 4 of this volume ('How important is it for believers to gather together physically to worship God?'). There is of course a distinction between livestreaming of worship from the physically gathered church, and livestreaming of worship devoid of any physical gathering.

days of Christianity in these shores indicates the fact that the church has always gathered for corporate worship.

The parish system adopted in the United Kingdom (although also in Europe) allowed for corporate worship in every locality by ensuring the provision of a church building and a minister to officiate. The English parish system dates back to the eighth Archbishop of Canterbury, Theodore of Tarsus (602–690), and churches were evidently built in keeping with the populating of the land.[12]

In the 1830s, with the advance of urbanisation after the Industrial Revolution, the parish system failed to provide access to public worship in Scotland. In response, Thomas Chalmers (1780-1847) led the push for church extension, with the erection of 222 new churches between 1834 and 1841.[13] This demonstrates the emphasis the Evangelical party of the Church of Scotland put on public worship, and the importance they attached to giving all the opportunity to worship corporately.

This is further demonstrated in the case of Thomas Guthrie (1803-1873). The poor in his Edinburgh parish could not afford to attend worship, because entrance to the packed church was by ticket, or payment of pew rent. Guthrie was so burdened by this that he established additional services of public worship on Lord's Day afternoons which were open freely, and to which the poor were given priority admission.[14] The thought of leaving the populace

---

[12] Pounds, N. J. G. (2000) *A History of the English Parish: The Culture of Religion from Augustine to Victoria*. Cambridge: Cambridge University Press. pp. 17-32.
[13] Wolffe, J. Church Extension. In: de S Cameron, N. M. (1993) *Dictionary of Scottish Church History & Theology*. Edinburgh: T & T Clark. p. 182.
[14] Hyde, M. J. (2017) 'Thomas Guthrie and the Magdalene Chapel.' *The Bulwark*. April-June. pp. 24-30.

without access to the public worship of God on Lord's Day was unthinkable to our forefathers.

As Nonconformists in England were put out of the established church, the first thing they did was to build new churches to host gathered worship—and while they were building they met in the open air. While this phenomenon was seen most clearly in the rise of the Methodist movement, it also occurred following the ejection of many ministers from the church under the Act of Uniformity, 1662.

In Scotland, after the Disruption of 1843, where land could not be obtained for a church building at Strontian (on the west coast of Scotland), the congregation built a floating church and met on the loch.[15] It was reported of Rev. Donald MacDonald (1825-1901) that when he came as pastor to Sheildaig, Scotland, in 1872, nearly thirty years after the Disruption, there was still neither church nor manse as sites had been refused by the local landowners. But he gathered his congregation outdoors on the hillside and,

> laboured among circumstances of peculiar difficulty, preaching on the hillside in all kinds of weather, exposed to summer heat and winter cold, within the sound of Atlantic breakers. Sometimes he had to brush snowflakes off his Bible before he could see his text.[16]

Private worship or family worship has never been deemed an acceptable replacement for the physical gathering of the church of Christ by any denomination of the church in our land.

---

[15] Brown, T. (1893) *Annals of the Disruption*. Edinburgh: MacNiven and Wallace. pp. 427 and 655.

[16] Stewart, A. and Kennedy Cameron, J. (1989) *The Free Church of Scotland: The Crisis of 1900*. Edinburgh: The Knox Press. pp. 80-81.

The mandate to the church remains inviolable

The mandate God has given us for worship is still the same today. Our times and circumstances may have changed, and the technology available to us may come and go, but God has not changed. God's purpose for us in creation has not changed—we are to worship him, and worship him gathered as mankind. Our needs have not changed as a fallen humanity—we need the preaching of the gospel. Our needs as redeemed believers have not abated—we need the public means of grace as much as ever. 'Forsake not the assembling of yourselves together' remains the command of Scripture for the New Testament church. We worship in anticipation of the Lord's return and the fullness of public worship to come. It is when we are fulfilling this mandate that the church collectively waits for the Lord to come (1 Corinthians 11:26—especially in the keeping of the Lord's Supper), and cries, 'Even so, come, Lord Jesus' (Revelation 22:20).

3. The church has maintained public worship in extremity

The burden of this mandate on the church, and her obedience to this mandate in the past, is most clearly seen when we survey the history of the church and see that despite the various situations the church has found herself in, public worship has been maintained—even at risk to life and limb. We can only give some illustrations of this, to show the breadth of the church's experience across time, place, and situation.

In time of persecution

The Lord's words were, 'In the world ye shall have tribulation' (John 16:33). There has probably not been a time when the church in some place throughout the world has not been meeting in the middle of persecution. During the Reformation, and later during the Covenanting times in Scotland, the church continued to meet despite the threat of death for doing so. During the 1680s it became punishable by death to preach at or to attend a conventicle.[17] Examples of those who suffered during this period include Marion Harvey (aged 20 years) and Isobel Allison (a young unmarried woman) who were hanged on the 26th January, 1681, for the crime of 'conventicling'—gathering for public worship.[18] Even people like 16 year old George Wood (martyred 1688) could be shot on the spot for carrying a Bible because it was assumed he must be going to a conventicle.[19] It would have been much easier to have stopped public worship until the threat had subsided, but faithfulness to the mandate for worship was counted more precious than life.[20]

After the Great Ejection of 1662, Nonconformists in England faced persecution aimed essentially at preventing them gathering—the number who could worship was limited to five individuals (Conventicle Act, 1664), and virtually impossible geographical limits, within which ministers were permitted to preach, were set. But public worship continued. Many of the records of those meetings make searching reading—does public worship mean as much to us as it did to them? The records of Broadmead Baptist Church in Bristol recount the ingenious ways that the various Nonconformist churches sought out in order to continue the

[17] Such punishment makes the fines imposed by our government during the Covid-19 pandemic look paltry.

[18] Hewison, J. K. (1913) *The Covenanters: A History of the Church in Scotland from the Reformation to the revolution*. Glasgow: Smith. Vol. 2, pp. 344-346.

[19] *Ibid*. p. 512.

[20] For a full justification of this course of action see: Shields, A. (1797) *A Hind Let Loose: or, An historical representation of the testimonies of the Church of Scotland, for the interest of Christ: With the true state thereof in all its periods*. Glasgow: William Paton. pp. 617-651.

preaching amongst them. For example, Brother Gifford's assembly stood the preacher over a trapdoor and surrounded him by tall men, so that if soldiers came the minister could be let down through the floor to safety. This assembly were brought to the point where they report on behalf of all the Nonconformist churches in Bristol,

> Our ministers being taken from us, one dead and the rest imprisoned, we feared their death likewise in such a bad prison, and we being pursued closely every meeting, hardly one escaped, but we were followed from the bishop's men.[21]

Yet they continued to faithfully meet for public worship every Lord's Day.

Then we could consider worship under Communist rule in the Soviet bloc. One only has to read the accounts recorded by the missionary Andrew van der Bijl (b. 1928; better known as Brother Andrew) to know something of what the persecuted church in those countries went through in order to worship.[22] Haralan Popov (1907-1988) records his ministry in Bulgaria during the same period. He had already been tortured and imprisoned for 13 years, yet on his release he returned to the ministry. He reports how people gathered over several hours before a meeting in order to escape detection, so that when he arrived (last) there was often a gathering of 25-30 people to join the worship. These meetings were generally held late at night. He comments that normally it is virtually impossible for people gathered in such numbers not to make some noise—even when not speaking—and yet except for

---

[21] Hayden, R. (1974) *The Records of a Church of Christ in Bristol, 1640-1697*. Bristol: Bristol Record Society. pp. 150-152.

[22] Sherrill, J. and Sherrill, E., with 'Brother Andrew' (1968) *God's Smuggler*. London: Hodder and Stoughton.

the worship these meetings were absolutely silent so as to avoid detection.

> 'My dear brothers and sisters in Christ,' I would begin. 'We meet here to worship our Lord and hear his Word. He is here with us this night.' On and on I would continue. It was dangerous to meet, so when we did meet, the meeting lasted up to three or four hours.[23]

The people then left as they came, slowly in twos or threes, many going straight to their work in the dawning light, having spent the whole night in going to and from and attending gathered worship. Popov says, 'Such small underground churches were springing up all over the country as the persecution drove the believers to this depth of sincerity and dedication, willing to risk their homes, their jobs and even their freedom to assemble and worship together.'

In time of war

In his biography of Dr D. Martyn Lloyd-Jones (1899-1981), Iain Murray records the struggle to continue worship at Westminster Chapel during the heavy aerial bombing of London in the Second World War. Murray makes it clear that in his opinion the struggle faced by the minister to keep worship going was largely due to spiritual deficiency in the diaconate. 'A large pre-war attendance had disguised the extent to which lower standards prevailed.'[24] The steadying influence of Dr Lloyd-Jones on the church was clearly based on his conviction that the public worship of God was essential and on his faith in a faithful God. This is seen in much of

---

[23] Popov, H. (1970) *Tortured for his Faith*. London: Lakeland. pp. 110-111.

[24] Murray, I. H. (1990) *David Martyn Lloyd-Jones: The Fight of Faith 1939-1981*. Edinburgh: Banner of Truth Trust. p. 14.

his preaching in this period. For example, he said in a sermon on Matthew 10:28,

> There are things that really matter in this life, and they are the things that will alone matter in eternity. And with regard to these things we can defy any and every enemy. These are things that bombs cannot smash, that tanks cannot crush. These are things beyond the range of the most powerful gun ... No man can touch your soul and no man can kill your soul.[25]

When a bomb fell just outside the chapel during one morning service, the minister paused only momentarily before continuing with his prayer. It was reported that 'the whole congregation ... was steadied by one man's prayer.'[26] The service continued without further incident. Lloyd-Jones evidently felt the need for preaching at such a time, as many who were sheltering in air raid shelters were unprepared to meet their God. Despite many churches being totally destroyed, Westminster Chapel was preserved, though damaged, and there are abundant testimonies of the Lord's work among those who gathered at this time. Although initially the congregation seemed to decline, the end result was congregational growth.

We could also consider the case of the Dutch churches under Nazi occupation in the Second World War. Rev. Willem C. Lamain (1904-1984) was pastor in Rotterdam South. He writes of a time of bombing on 3rd-4th October, 1941.

---

[25] Murray, I. H. (1990) *David Martyn Lloyd-Jones: The Fight of Faith 1939-1981*. Edinburgh: Banner of Truth Trust. p. 27.

[26] Murray, I. H. (1990) *David Martyn Lloyd-Jones: The Fight of Faith 1939-1981*. Edinburgh: Banner of Truth Trust. p. 115.

> The next morning, we were told that because of the unexploded bomb in the square in front of the church, no church services could be held. The square was roped off and the spot where the bomb lay was guarded.

Undoubtedly this is an example of the civil authority legitimately preventing access to a place of worship. But Lamain continues,

> That Sunday I preached four times. First I preached in the auditorium of a school which could barely hold 500 people, even though there were more than a thousand waiting to be seated. At 10.30 a service was held in a Reformed church and at 2.30 I preached in the old Reformed Church in Rotterdam-South. At 7.00 in the evening I preached in another church.

Lamain made the comment about general conditions,

> It happened sometimes during these services that the air raid alarms sounded and then no one was allowed outside until the danger had passed. Often these were unforgettable evenings. Death and eternity were not far from us then.[27]

Lamain goes on to recount how he preached with spies in his congregation and details his struggle to remain faithful to the truth even though he faced possible imprisonment and internment in concentration camps.

Even on the battlefields of the First and Second World Wars, the British Army maintained public worship on the Lord's Day. Stephen Clark, a Strict Baptist serving on the Somme in 1917,

---

[27] Lamain, J. W., Beijeman, H. and Natzijl, H. (2003) *The Life and Work of Rev. W. C. Lamain*. Stevens Point, Wisconsin, USA: Worzalla. p. 190.

records how the chaplain came on a Lord's Day afternoon to hold a service amongst the artillery of the Front Line.

> We got together in a gun pit, and after singing a hymn, the chaplain read a portion of Scripture, and, to my delight, I heard an extempore prayer. After praying for our safety of body and soul, and an honourable end to the serious conflict and victory to our armies, he gave a short address, encouraging us to seek that life which is in the Lord Jesus Christ, who is Eternal Life. I have said that sermon was the most profitable of the whole time. I felt a little refreshed for the hard times that were ahead of us all.[28]

The letters of J. Gresham Machen (1881-1937), the American Presbyterian, written when he was serving as a padre in France during the First World War, similarly record meetings for worship held in the sound of enemy fire.[29]

In time of plague

When it comes to the church gathering for public worship in time of plague, the examples are many.[30] The outbreak of bubonic plague in London during 1665 caused many ministers of the establishment to flee to the safety of the countryside. For several weeks it would appear there was little preaching in London, until the Nonconformists ventured to gather the people for worship. Remarkably, Thomas Vincent (1634-1678) claims, 'About the beginning of these ministers preaching, especially after their first

---

[28] Hyde, M. J. (2016) *With Mercy and with Judgement: Strict Baptists and the First World War*. Harpenden: Gospel Standard Trust Publications. p. 185.

[29] Waugh, B. (2012) *Letters from the Front: J. Gresham Machen's Correspondence from World War I*. Phillipsburg, New Jersey, USA: Presbyterian and Reformed Publishing.

[30] A useful review is Earngey, E. (2020) 'Plagues and Protestants'. *Churchman*. Summer. pp. 107-123.

fast together, the Lord begins to remit, and turn his hand, and cause some abatement of the disease.'[31]

The plague spread from London by trade to the village of Eyam, Derbyshire. The Rector of Eyam, Rev. William Mompesson (1638-1708), closed the doors of the church to try and limit the spread of the plague. Yet he did not cease public worship, but gathered his congregation outdoors to preach to them—spaced several feet apart—in a 'delft,' or dell, which can still be seen today. The village still perpetuates his memory for the example he set in time of crisis.[32]

The outbreak of cholera in the United Kingdom, especially in 1832, gives many similar examples. Some ministers, such as Robert Findlater (c.1753-1832) of Inverness, died through being exposed to cholera in the course of maintaining their pastoral ministry. Far from decreasing the number of meetings during this time, they held additional nightly prayer meetings.[33] Others, such as Rev. William Krause (1796-1852) later of Dublin, then ministering in Cavan, felt the importance of continuing preaching as he bemoaned that, 'Many are taking precautions for the body, but very, very few for the soul. How insensible is the heart, until the Spirit of the Lord acts upon it!'[34]

---

[31] Vincent, T. (1997) *God's Terrible Voice in the City*. Morgan, Pennsylvania, USA: Soli Deo Gloria Publications. p. 53. Vincent backs up this claim with weekly figures of the number of plague deaths within the city.

[32] Beaumont, R. M. (1989) *The Reverend William Mompesson 1638-1708: Hero of Eyam*. Nottingham: Technical Print.

[33] Findlater, W. (1840) *Memoir of the Rev. Robert Findlater*. Glasgow: Collins. p. 308.

[34] Stanford, C. S. (1854) *Memoir of the late Rev. W. H. Krause, A.M., Minister of Bethesda Chapel, Dublin, with selections from his correspondence*. Dublin: Herbert. p. 177.

We have been able to locate no trace of any evidence that churches or chapels were closed during the deadly Spanish Flu pandemic of 1918-20, amongst either the Free Church or the Free Presbyterian Church in Scotland or the Strict Baptists in England. Conversely many of the scant references to the pandemic (in obituaries, for example) are of the nature that the deceased was in their pew on Lord's Day and died a few days into the same week.[35] In Holland, suggestions from the government that worship should be suspended were fiercely opposed, and worship continued—although some denominations took measures to put in place preventative actions, for example reducing the number of worshippers attending a service, or using individual instead of common cups at the Lord's Supper.[36] Some church closures occurred in America, but these were heavily protested against and lasted for little more than a few weeks.[37]

The church's sense of purpose in times of crisis

Indeed, the pattern in history has been that rather than suspending worship in extreme circumstances, the church has obtained a new sense of purpose. Extreme circumstances usually sharpen the relief

---

35 For example, see the obituary of Ebenezer Watts, in: *The Gospel Standard* (1919) p. 139.

36 See: https://www.rug.nl/research/centre-for-religious-studies/religion-conflict-globalization/blog/coping-with-covid-19-in-dutch-christianity-comparison-with-the-1918-spanish-flu-pandemic-24-04-2020?lang=en [Accessed 13/03/2021].

37 See for example Ott, M. *et al.* (2007) 'Lessons learned from the 1918-1919 influenza pandemic in Minneapolis and St. Paul, Minnesota.' *Public health reports.* 122(6) pp. 803-10. Similar questions on the inconsistency of closing places of worship while allowing them to be used for other purposes were asked about these church closures as we heard during the Covid-19 closures: 'Why were church services closed while Red Cross workers gathered in crowded conditions in those very same churches?' Also see https://www.9marks.org/article/what-did-dc-churches-do-when-the-spanish-flu-struck-again/ [Accessed 17/03/2021]

between life and death for both preacher and hearer. Traditionally, the wider preaching of the gospel—with its message of certainty and hope—has been seen as the answer to the extreme circumstance. It is still common in the Church of England for church doors, which are normally locked, to be open in times of disaster—local or national—and for additional times of public worship to be arranged in response.

George Wishart (1513-1546), the Scottish Reformer, is reported by John Knox to have gone to Dundee to preach when he heard that the plague of pestilence had arisen there. He said to those he left behind, 'They are now in trouble and they need comfort. Perchance this hand of God will make them now to magnify and reverence that Word, which before, for the fear of men, they set at light price.' His ministry was greatly blessed, and 'so raised up the hearts of all that heard him that they regarded not death, but judged those more happy that should depart, than such as should remain behind; considering that they knew not if they should have such a comforter with them at all times.'[38]

Thomas Vincent wrote of the services held by the Nonconformist ministers in London during the plague of 1665:

> Now they were preaching, and every sermon was to them, as if they were preaching their last. Old Time seems now to stand at the head of the pulpit, with its great scythe; saying with a

[38] Laing, D (Ed.) (1846) *The Works of John Knox*. Edinburgh: Wodrow Society. Vol. 1, pp. 129-130. Wishart took sensible precautions to prevent the spread of plague in his congregation, as Knox recounts: 'On his coming to Dundee, the joy of the faithful was exceeding great. He delayed no time, but even upon the morrow gave signification that he would preach. The most part were either sick or were in company with those that were sick, and for this reason he chose the head of the East Port of the town for his preaching place. Those who were whole sat or stood within the Port, the sick and suspected without.'

> hoarse voice, 'Work while it is called today, at night I will mow thee down.' ... If you ever saw a drowning man catch at a rope, you may guess how eagerly many people did catch at the Word, when they were ready to be overwhelmed by this overflowing scourge which was passing through the city; when death was knocking at so many doors; and God was crying aloud by his judgments; and ministers were now sent to knock, cry aloud, and lift up their voice like a trumpet: then the people began to open the ear and the heart, which were fast shut and barred before.[39]

Rev. Willem Lamain noticed when preaching during the Nazi occupation of the Netherlands that, rather than emptying the church, the fear of the invaders filled it, and he commented, 'In those days we did not have to preach to empty pews and chairs—the churches were filled beyond capacity.'[40] His observation is not an isolated case, rather this is a common theme of reports of such situations in history.

4. Are there any circumstances when it is right to suspend public worship?

The available evidence suggests that the church has never regarded it as a possibility that the God-given mandate to worship can be suspended, even in extreme circumstances. In general, matters of life and death, national security, or the demands of government have never been regarded as sufficient reasons to cease gathered worship.

---

[39] Vincent, T. (1997) *God's Terrible Voice in the City*. Morgan, Pennsylvania, USA: Soli Deo Gloria Publications. pp. 50-51.

[40] Lamain, J. W., Beijeman, H. and Natzijl, H. (2003) *The Life and Work of Rev. W. C. Lamain*. Stevens Point, Wisconsin, USA: Worzalla. p. 190.

We have struggled to locate instances where worship has been suspended—or certainly suspended for more than one Lord's Day. The overall weight of evidence suggests that unlike the church's response to coronavirus-related restrictions in 2020, in the past there has never been such a willingness on the part of the church to allow worship to be universally suspended. Such a reaction is evidently something new in the annals of the church of Christ.

Of the anecdotal evidence we have, only 'acts of God,' or impossible situations, appear to have ever been grounds for suspending worship. Some examples include impassably high snow drifts, or extreme weather physically preventing gathering, although our forefathers pushed through most things to attend public worship, being content to sit outdoors while it snowed as they worshipped, such was their hunger for the Word and their desire to worship their gracious God.[41] Other examples include natural disasters (for example earthquake or flooding), or the church building being put physically out of action due to bomb or fire damage, or death or illness affecting all available officiants at worship. It is noticeable that with all of these examples, any cessation of public worship is very temporary—normally no more than one Lord's Day—and in cases when the usual building was unavailable for worship, alternative accommodation was urgently sought.

It would also seem that being prevented from holding public worship was seen by our forebears as a judgment from God. It must surely cause us to pause, if God's judgments on us are truly so severe that he has taken away from us the means of grace and

---

[41] For a remarkable example of this, see a photograph of an open-air service at Ferintosh, Scotland, in 1873, where all that can be seen is a forest of umbrellas because of the inclement weather, in Ansdell, D. (1998) *The People of the Great Faith: The Highland Church 1690-1900*. Stornoway: Acair. p. 113.

removed his honour and glory from among us. But how should we respond to this kind of judgment? Surely by redoubling our dedication to publicly worshipping the Lord with more sincerity and whole-heartedness. It would clearly be a wrong response to the judgment to weaken our commitment to public worship. Our Nonconformist forebears certainly regarded the events of 1662, for example, as God's judgments on them, but they did not interpret the judgment as calling them to give up their principles, submit to the state and cease preaching. Rather, must we not come and seek to use the means of grace in such troublous times, with a cry of, 'If I perish, I perish!' (Esther 4:16) believing that God will still be entreated of by his people, for 'he delighteth in mercy' (Micah 7:18).

Given the weight of the mandate for public worship—prescribed in creation, commanded in the law, reaffirmed by the Lord Jesus, and forming the inward desire of the Lord's people (Psalm 27:8)—it is clear that only the most exceptional circumstances can be grounds for the cessation of public worship, and then only for the briefest period of time. This is surely what was assumed by the Westminster Assembly when they regard as forbidden 'all neglect, contempt, hindering, and opposing the worship and ordinances which God hath appointed' (Westminster Larger Catechism, Q109).[42]

---

[42] Here we are dealing with the question of the church suspending public worship. Whether individuals can or should absent themselves from public worship on some of the grounds mentioned is entirely another question. It would clearly be wrong for anybody to attend public worship with symptoms of Covid-19 or any other infectious illness.

5. Who can suspend public worship?

We are certain that the state has no right to stop public worship.[43] If any party on earth has the right to suspend public worship, it is the church authorities themselves. Perhaps they may be said to have that right when it comes to the suspension of aspects of worship. However, the church needs to remember their position—they are the body of Christ, not the head (Colossians 1:18, 24). Just as physically it is the head which rules the body and not the reverse, so it is with the church—authority belongs to the Lord Jesus Christ as king in Zion.

Jesus is clear on this point. The Great Commission is prefaced with the statement, 'All power is given *unto me* in heaven and in earth. *Go ye therefore* ...' (Matthew 28:18-19). Jesus has given the church a commission, and promised them his presence in that commission, but the authority (the 'all power') resides with himself. He has given no licence for the church to turn aside from the commission, to vary it, or to neglect it. The maximum authority of the church is not absolute, or inherent to the church. Instead it is ministerial—it is the authority to carry out the commission Christ has given.

Paul says of the relationship between Christ and his ministers, 'We are ambassadors for Christ' (2 Corinthians 5:20). An ambassador never acts alone, or on their own initiative, because they do not have the authority to do so. They act on the instruction of the sovereign whose interests they represent. So, the church and her ministers can only act on and within the mandate they have received from their sovereign Lord. In this case, the mandate is

[43] This question is dealt with at length in Chapter 5 of this volume ('How should the church and state interact during a crisis?').

written into our very being in creation and confirmed throughout the canon of Scripture.

6. What about suspending components of worship?

Although the mandate to worship is clear, it does not, *per se*, dictate the form that public worship should take. Our very being calls us to worship our Creator, but does not dictate the manner in which we should do so. The Lord's Day itself calls us to give time to worshipping our Redeemer, but again it does not specify the manner in which we should spend that time.

However, the Word of God does lay down essential *elements* of worship (sometimes also called the *parts* of worship). It does state that New Testament public worship on a Lord's Day must include: (1) *prayer* (Acts 2:42; Acts 16:13; Philippians 4:6; 1 Timothy 2:1-2); (2) *Scripture reading* (Acts 17:11; 15:21); (3) *preaching and hearing of the Word* (Matthew 28:19-20; Luke 24:47; Acts 20:7; 2 Timothy 4:2); (4) *singing of praise* (Ephesians 5:19; Colossians 3:16); and some would also include (5) the *taking of a collection* (1 Corinthians 16:2). Obviously, it also mandates the observation of (6) the ordinances of the church—*baptism and the Lord's Supper* (Matthew 28:19; Acts 2:42; 1 Corinthians 11:23-29)—on the appropriate occasions (1 Corinthians 11:25-26).

As well as the elements of worship there are also the practical factors associated with worship, often termed the *circumstances* of worship. These include, for example, the frequency of services, their duration, the time of day, the place of meeting, what language to use, and so on. These factors are rightly determined by the local church according to practical considerations, on the basis of common sense and Christian prudence.

The *circumstances* of worship may be altered by the church, in a decent and orderly manner, according to local conditions. An example of this could be the changes made to service times at Westminster Chapel during the Second World War, where the evening service was brought forward to 3.30pm, because of the difficulty of blacking out the windows of such a large building, and because it was not felt right to expect worshippers to come long distances on dark nights without any permissible use of light to guide them.[44] Similarly, in times of persecution, services may be held at night, and in private houses instead of the church building. As in previous times of plague, so during the Covid-19 pandemic, a local church could decide to hold only one service on the Lord's Day, to reduce the length of the service, to hold the service outdoors, to physically distance the attendees (and so on), all so as to reduce infection risk. The church has a duty to take into account local factors and alter the circumstances of worship in a considerate manner.

Making changes to the *elements* of worship, however, is more controversial. The elements all have the mandate of God's Word, and who are we to change them, even in a time of crisis? During the Covid-19 pandemic, the supposed increased risk of spreading the virus through singing has made praise in worship particularly controversial. Is it right for the church to cease singing in these circumstances?

To think through the rights and wrongs of suspending elements of worship, firstly we would say that God, who knows the end from the beginning, was not unknowing of the crisis situations which would arise in the history of the church when he set out the

---

[44] Murray, I. H. (1990) *David Martyn Lloyd-Jones: The Fight of Faith 1939-1981*. Edinburgh: Banner of Truth Trust. p. 105.

elements of public worship. We must not ascribe mystical powers of protection to participating in any particular act of worship. Outbreaks of the virus have certainly been attributed to the act of collective singing, and there is good scientific rationale behind regarding it as being risky to share food and a cup, as is required in the observance of the Lord's Supper. But surely we must approach the various acts of worship with faith in the merciful and gracious God who has mandated them, despite knowing the risk. Nothing is without risk, and if we are willing on a natural level to put ourselves in the hands of those who have professionally carried out a risk assessment, surely we have far more grounds to trust in God when it comes to worshipping him according to his prescribed pattern.

Secondly, some of the elements as prescribed in Scripture still leave considerable room for individual interpretation. While singing is an essential part of worship, for example, Scripture does not dictate the proportion of the service which should be taken up with singing, the number of verses sung, nor the number of times praise may be sung during the act of worship. So, when singing has been controversial as regards the spreading of the Covid-19 virus, there may well be flexibility to reduce the act of sung praise to a single occasion of a couple of verses. Another practical option which would maintain singing within the worship service might be to sing only at the end of the service—reducing exposure to aerosols, and allowing any attendees who struggle with the level of risk involved to leave early. Similarly, the length of prayer and preaching could be reduced according to circumstances—perhaps in many cases the circumstances requiring the shortening of them are the natural means used by the Spirit to increase the blessing.[45] To stick doggedly to form and custom in times of crisis could suggest that we make more of the form than the Spirit, and that we are in danger of drawing near with our lips, while our heart is far off. While we are to exercise faith, we are not to be fatalistic when God has given us licence to exercise sanctified common sense in a matter.

The Lord's Supper is another element of public worship which has proved controversial during the pandemic. We feel that the seriousness of suspending the Lord's Supper has not been recognised by the church in general. The *Belgic Confession*, among others, cites the observance of the sacraments as a mark of the true church. Indefinite suspension of the sacraments—as has been the case in some churches during this crisis—obscures this mark of the true church. The solemnity of this is immense. Again, changes to the *circumstances* of the observance of the sacraments could be considered in order to make it possible to hold the ordinance again. For example, it is not essential to the sacrament to hold the multiple services of a communion season, and those administering the sacrament could make a point of hand-washing and using antiseptic gel before distributing the elements. There is not space here to discuss whether a common cup can be replaced by individual beakers to reduce transmission risk. Congregations and church leaders need to give careful consideration both to distinguishing what are and what are not the scripturally mandated aspects of the ordinance, and also to whether changes

[45] The blessing arriving from the preaching, or answers from prayer, is never proportional to their length. Rev. M. Heikoop's memoir records a service shortened by the circumstances of the Nazi invasion of Holland which was greatly blessed, despite its natural constrictions. Fama, J. (1996) *The Life and Labors of The Rev. M. Heikoop*. Netherlands Reformed Book and Publishing Committee. pp. 126-128,

to these aspects are to be preferred to not holding the sacrament at all. Martin Luther, who did not hold to the regulative principle, said that it was better to omit the sacrament altogether than to make any unscriptural innovation in the ordinance.[46]

Thirdly (and only thirdly), we should distinguish between the fundamental mandate for worship itself, and the secondary mandate for specific elements of worship. This is the distinction between 'natural law' and 'positive law.' It is 'natural,' because of how God has created us, that we must hold public worship, but it is 'positive,' in the sense of a specific requirement that God makes known to us, that we must worship him by (for example) reading the Scriptures but not by (for example) offering animal sacrifices (in the New Testament church). Based on this distinction, it might be concluded that it can never be right to cease public worship *per se* because of refusal to make changes to the elements. If singing is so controversial in a congregation that the choice facing the church is between holding worship and not singing, or not holding worship at all, then it may be reasoned that it is better to hold worship without singing as long as it is 1) agreed by the church in an orderly manner, 2) only for a pre-agreed, and minimum, length of time, 3) acknowledged explicitly by the church what they are missing out on in taking such a step.

Following his ejection from the ministry of the Church of England, in 1662, because he refused to conform to the use of the *Book of*

---

[46] In the context of using something other than wine in the observance of the Lord's Supper, Luther said: 'One should not use anything other than wine. If a person cannot drink wine, omit it [the sacrament] altogether in order that no innovation be made or introduced.' As quoted in MacLeod, D. (2020) *Therefore the Truth I Speak: Scottish Theology 1500-1700*. Fearn: Mentor. p. 40.— In the context of a discussion of the debate between Knox and Cranmer on elements and circumstances in the observance of the Lord's Supper.

Common Prayer in public worship, Richard Baxter (1615-1691) became involved in controversy over his attendance at a service led by a 'conformist' minister using the *Book of Common Prayer*. In his reply he makes it quite clear that for him it was more important to attend 'imperfect' public worship, than to fail to keep public worship at all.

> The Covenant bound us to our best to reform: but did not bind us to sin, that is, to forsake all Christian churches among us, and all publick worship, when we cannot reform as we desire. As I am bound to amend all the disorders and faults of my own prayers, but not to give over praying till I can amend them.[47]

Such was the high view of public worship amongst the English Nonconformists.

Perhaps this last point is the hardest. We need to be careful we do not lay aside any element of worship lightly. We become so accustomed to something that only its loss makes us value it or understand what it meant. In times of persecution there have certainly been services held in secret without singing, because of the fear of detection, arrest, and possibly certain death. While there was undoubtedly benefit from gathering for worship without praise, it is interesting to note that worshippers in this situation acknowledged that there was definitely something missing from worship—they were conscious of a painful absence. Haralan Popov records of services held in secret during Communist persecution of the church in Bulgaria: 'Sometimes we took the risk of singing a hymn (we sang very softly to keep from being overheard). Tears would flow as we met and sang the beautiful

[47] Keeble, N. H. *et al.* (Eds.) (2020) *Reliquiae Baxterianae: Or, Mr Richard Baxter's narrative of the most memorable passages of his life and times.* Oxford: Oxford University Press. Vol. 2, p. 282.

songs of the church, just like the believers of early days.'[48] This emotional experience was surely more than mere emotionalism—no doubt the Lord owned and blessed their faith in keeping worship as best they could according to his prescription. It took faith—great faith in the face of imprisonment and death—and venturing faith on their part was blessed by God.

Conclusion

In conclusion, we come back to the question of whether the church should have suspended worship in response to the Covid-19 pandemic. In answer we would consider the following points.

1. The church needs to have a right understanding of the nature, universality, and permanence of the divine institution of public worship. Gathered worship is not under the authority of man but is ordained by God. Consequently, to suspend gathered worship could be described as a tacit denial of God's creation of us, the institution of the sabbath, and the very existence of God himself. This should solemnise our minds concerning this matter and cause us to not act with haste when it comes to closing the doors of our churches on the Lord's Day.
2. Paul's words should sound a warning to us all if we fail to glorify God in his appointed ways. 'For the invisible things of him from the creation of the world are clearly seen, being understood by the things that are made, even his eternal power and Godhead; so that they are without excuse: because that, when they knew God, *they glorified him not as God*, neither were thankful; but became vain in their imaginations, and their foolish heart was darkened' (Romans 1:20-21).

[48] Popov, H. (1970) *Tortured for his Faith.* London: Lakeland. p. 110.

3. Based on the fact that worship is ordained by God, we may conclude that only God can take it away. This he may do by things that we call 'acts of God.' But how solemn it is to think of God removing his own glory or preventing his people from giving him his due. Surely God has such a high regard for his honour that he would never sacrifice his own public worship unless it is because such worship is ultimately dishonouring to him. Can *we, the church,* therefore justify ceasing public worship at any time simply on the grounds of providential circumstances? Surely if God takes away public worship from us, it is his direct act, not just what we may term 'general providence.' It is God saying he would rather take away his glory than permit his people to gather to glorify him! It is God taking away the preaching of the gospel to sinners, which is so bound up with his love (John 3:16). If God takes away public worship, we can be certain it is because of sin in us and the church. Closure of public worship should therefore make us tremble and drive us to self-examination and to seek repentance before God.
4. The church has no duty to obey the government when it comes to the matters of public worship. The church is directly under the mandate of God, and God does not give man in any sphere the option to obviate what he has commanded. If the church agrees with the government's assessment of the riskiness of public worship, that is one thing, but authority over the matters of worship rests with the church in a ministerial way, and with God in the ultimate way. 'Render to Caesar the things that are Caesar's, and to God the things that are God's' (Mark 12:17). How far we are removed from the spirit of our fathers who signed their names to the National Covenant of 1638, stating,

> Neither do we fear the foul aspersions of rebellion, combination or what else our adversaries from their craft and malice would put upon us, seeing what we do is so well warranted, and ariseth from an unfeigned desire to maintain the true worship of God, the majesty of our King, and the peace of the kingdom, for the common happiness of ourselves and posterity.[49]

5. God may make it difficult for us to attend public worship in order to test our faithfulness to his mandate, and our appetite for, or the value we place on, his worship. In time of his judgments as recorded by the prophet Amos, we are told that God sifts Zion (Amos 9:9). We need to face the question as to whether the church's willingness to close her doors during Covid-19 is a symptom of the spiritual decline in the church and a lack of appetite for the worship of God.
6. God is not ungracious. His bar for public worship is low—it is where 'two or three' are gathered together in his name (Matthew 18:20). The church does not need to condemn those who for legitimate health reasons cannot attend worship in the circumstances of this pandemic. But surely it is better for the ministers and elders to open the church even to find that no one else assembles with them, than for them to forsake their posts and shut down the witness of the church in time of trouble.[50]

---

[49] Rushworth, J. (1680) *Historical Collections, The Second Part etc.* Vol. 2, p. 740-741.

[50] The life of the Rev M. Heikoop records the following regarding his ministry in Utrecht during May, 1940. 'Because of the political diversity among the people of the city, there was heavy gunfire. Through the midst of such peril the pastor went from his home to the church on that Sunday evening. But the congregation did not come. The danger in the streets made people fear to come. The police also prevented the citizens from leaving their homes. The minister went home again without having accomplished his purpose.'—

> God has provided the church with sufficient freedom in the ordering of worship that we can mitigate the risks—we can meet outside instead of inside, sing just a few verses at the end of the service, shorten the service, and take the government's sound and sensible advice for the safe ordering of public worship at this time.

Taking all this together, should churches have closed their doors during Covid-19? If after all we have considered about worship, the church doors are shut for public worship, surely it must be one of the most trying times ever experienced by the Lord's people, and a time of sorrow and repentance. Any closure should have been kept to the shortest time frame possible, and it should not have occurred simply because the government made it illegal to gather but based on the immediate risks in the locality and within the congregation.

Perhaps most of us may have been party to a very different course of action than the one suggested here. If we feel now, in calm consideration of these matters before an all-seeing God, that we have erred in our handling of the situation, may we learn from it and lament over it. Let us come with Jeremiah and put our mouth in the dust, if so be there might be hope. May we seek to stir each other up and teach our children better, so that, as far as is within our power, the church would be better prepared for the future.

However, we cannot help feeling that it could be said concerning the minister that evening, that he had faithfully discharged his responsibility. (Fama, J. (1996) *The Life and Labors of The Rev. M. Heikoop*. Netherlands Reformed Book and Publishing Committee. p. 128.)

~ 4 ~
How important is it for believers to gather together physically to worship God?

Peter C. Wilkins

> For where two or three are gathered together in my name, there am I in the midst of them. (Matthew 18:20)

Historically, most sections of the professing Christian church have taught that it is the Christian's privilege and duty to play an active role as a member of a local church. The vast majority have asserted that the Christian's normal practice ought to include gathering for corporate worship on the Lord's Day; and—almost as universally—asserted that the Christian who fails to do so is guilty of breaking the fourth commandment. This has been discussed in Chapter 3 of this volume ('Should the church ever suspend public worship?').

But what is 'gathering'? Does the word 'gather' necessarily mean *physical* gathering? There have always been those who have argued that it does not. Many of us have probably encountered professing Christians who, having become dissatisfied with their place of worship, have isolated themselves. Sometimes these people have argued that whilst they do not gather physically, they do gather spiritually. There are also professing Christians who do not acknowledge any duty or need to gather with other Christians at all.

People like these have no doubt always existed. But today, the question of what 'gathering' *is* has become more urgent. Through technology, we can *almost* 'go to church' without 'going to church'. We can 'virtually gather' with fellow Christians without any of us having to leave our homes. It is easy to see the advantages of 'gathering' virtually. It saves having to heat a draughty building, and, if you have children, having to organise them to leave the house; and of course, topically, it eliminates the risk of the transmission of infectious disease. But is what we gain enough to balance out what we lose?

In this chapter we try to examine this question; to ask, what is 'gathering'? How important is the physical element? Few would argue that a 'virtual service' is the *same* as a 'real service'. When we attend a 'virtual service', we know that we do not have exactly the same experience as we would if we were 'really there'. Few would claim that it is 'as good'. But is it *good enough*? Should we class 'virtual gatherings' as 'gatherings' in the biblical sense? Does, for example, Christ's promise concerning the 'two or three' apply when the 'gathering' is virtual?

Disagreement within the professing church on this point is easy to find. The Archbishop of Canterbury said recently that when we

> use the wonders of technology to be in touch with each other ... we recover the sense that Jesus says, 'Where two or three are gathered in my name I am there with them.' And they don't even actually have to be physically gathered, virtually gathered does very well indeed. Jesus is quite up-to-date on this stuff.[1]

---

1 https://anglican.ink/2020/04/09/on-the-need-to-keep-church-buildings-closed-justin-welby/ [Accessed 13/04/2021]

Others have argued the opposite—that 'virtual gatherings' cannot be seen as equivalent to physical gatherings, and that to try to *make* them equivalent is misguided and even dangerous.

How should we think about this issue?

1. The first principle is that we *should* think about it—all of us. If corporate 'gathered' worship is important (and few Christians would argue that it is not) then we must be wary of letting others decide our position for us—even other Christians, let alone non-Christians.

2. Secondly, we should think about it *logically*. This is an issue that can confront us very suddenly; the danger is that we rush into a position which seems sensible and pragmatic without considering all of the implications.

3. Thirdly, we should think about it *sympathetically*; bearing in mind especially those who, for whatever reason, may never be *able* to gather physically for worship, and remembering that it is sometimes better to deviate from our principles in a right spirit than to hold rigidly to them in a wrong spirit.

4. Fourthly, we must think about it *spiritually*. No doubt there are benefits of 'virtual services'. But are they mainly spiritual benefits, or not? And are the things we lose mainly spiritual, or not?

5. Fifthly, and most importantly, we must think about it *biblically*. It is of course true that today's 'virtual gatherings' were not possible when the Bible was written. But if the distinction between 'virtual' and 'real' gathering *is* important, that *will* somehow be reflected in what the Bible says, because scripture is sufficient.

Point 3 above mentions those who *cannot* gather. We all know such people. Perhaps they are ill; perhaps frail; perhaps they simply have no means of getting to a church (as in a local assembly of Christians, not a building). These people need the sympathy and the practical support of the church. There have been cases where a member of a church has become housebound, and that church has held services in that member's home, but in many cases this is impossible. 'Relayed' services can, in cases like this, be a lifeline. Advances in technology that enable those isolated Christians to experience something *closer* to being physically present are to be welcomed, and used. And the Lord is able to bless those means such that these isolated ones do not lose out; and able to fit and enable them to play an active role in the church. But relaying services to one or more isolated Christians who, for whatever reason, *cannot* attend, is very different to holding 'virtual' services where most or all of the 'congregation' are listening remotely even though they *could* attend physically.

There is an enormous difference between those who *would* gather if they *could*, and those who *could* gather if they *would*. Both need treating sensitively and sympathetically. But the argument, 'If "listening in" is good enough for those who *cannot* attend, why not for *everyone*?' does not hold water. Some Christians may not be *able* to work—that does not mean that Christians generally do not *need* to work. So the fact that some Christians *cannot* gather does not mean gathering is not important for Christians generally.

It is worth also remembering that there are Christians who cannot gather because there are no churches in their locality—or because there are only 'churches' which are so far removed from what a church *should* be that they are no longer churches. This in itself is a difficult line to draw. It would be wrong to refuse to gather with a local church simply because we disagreed with that church's position on minor matters, but which matters are minor? The person who can honestly say, 'There are no other Christians that I *can* gather with,' is in a very different situation to the person who can only say, 'There are no other Christians that I *want to* gather with,' or even, 'that I *feel comfortable* gathering with.' There may sometimes be a difference between the kind of church we would *like* to be a part of and the kind of church we are *called* to be a part of. Some might go so far as to say that if a Christian is living in a place where he cannot gather, he is living in the wrong place, but this is too simplistic. Whatever our view, we must again treat people in these difficult circumstances sympathetically.

So this chapter is not so much about situations where Christians *cannot* gather, but about situations where Christians *choose* not to gather. There may be occasions when a particular local church decides not to gather for a time, as discussed elsewhere in this book, and resort to 'virtual services'. But in order to decide when that is justified, we need to understand *why* we gather—and what we *lose* when we choose not to. As a first step, consider what the Bible says about the gathering of God's people.

1. The biblical view of gathering and scattering

In the Old Testament

Firstly, the Old Testament implies that the *physical* gathering of the people of God is associated with his blessing.

In Deuteronomy 4:10, Moses recalls that the Lord had said to him at Mount Sinai, 'Gather me the people together, and I will make them hear my words.' Being omnipresent and omnipotent, the Lord could have made the people hear his words *without* them being physically gathered, but his *will* was to speak to a physically gathered people. Moses refers to that day three times later in the same book as 'the day of the assembly,'[2] and this link between assembling and hearing was not just a one-off, but was repeated every seven years (Deuteronomy 31:12).

Some may say, 'Well, of course—they *had* to assemble physically, because they did not have the technologies that we now have.' But God was as omnipresent then as he is today; and he could have conveyed his word to his people as they sat in their respective homes. But he did not.

We also see that there was only one tabernacle, and later only one temple, described as 'the place which the LORD shall choose' (Deuteronomy 12)—not just *a* place, but *the* place. Physically gathering was therefore an essential part of being a Jew: and there were three great yearly feasts where the nation assembled—*physically.* Isaac Watts (1674-1748) was right that Christians 'have no such lengths to go,' but he did go on to say that 'where'er [God's] saints *assemble* now, *there* is a house for God.'[3]

This emphasis on gathering endured even after the destruction of the temple. One term that the Jews use to refer to a synagogue is בית כנסת (*beit knesset,* 'house of assembly')—still the name of the Israeli parliament. The word 'synagogue' itself is derived from a Greek verb meaning 'to gather together'—in James 2:2 it is translated as 'assembly.'

Again, some might say, 'The Jews *had* to assemble physically because their worship had so much of the physical element—sacrifices, rituals, etc.—but ours is *spiritual.*' It is true that right worship *is* spiritual; but it always has been. It was spiritual in the Old Testament synagogue, as much as it is in the New Testament

---

[2] Ash, C. (2009) *The Priority of Preaching*. Fearn: Christian Focus Publications. p. 79.

[3] Watts' paraphrase of Psalm 132.

church. However, 'spiritual' does not mean 'disembodied'; and Christian worship also has many physical elements, like singing, speaking, eating, and drinking. The Jews could have offered those exact same sacrifices, and carried out those same rituals, in their homes; but they were expressly forbidden to do so, and threatened with excommunication if they did (Leviticus 15:4).

On the other hand, in Genesis 11:9, physical *scattering* is seen to be the result of human pride; in Genesis 49:7, the result of human anger and wrath; in Deuteronomy 4:27, the result of idolatry; in Deuteronomy 28:64, the result of disobedience; in Psalm 60:1, the mark of God's displeasure. To be 'cut off from his people' (as in Genesis 17:14) was a terrible punishment for a Jew.

So at the very least, when we and our churches are scattered to their homes today, we ought not to be complacent about it; we ought not to say it does not really matter. We ought rather to ask, *why?* During the recent pandemic, the Lord could have arranged things such that the church remained untouched (as he did for the Israelites when he judged Egypt, Exodus 10:23)—but he did not. As John Preston (1587-1628), the influential Puritan, wrote,

> When there is an evident sign, that God hath a controversy with a kingdom and the churches, and a sign of his wrath is proclaimed from heaven, then every man must do something. Now fear the Lord, be zealous, repent and do your first works; begin now to mend your pace to heaven.[4]

The words of the Lord through Micah are surely appropriate here: 'The Lord's voice crieth unto the city, and the man of wisdom shall see thy name: hear ye the rod, and who hath appointed it' (Micah

---

[4] Preston, J. (2016) *The Golden Sceptre Held Forth to the Humble*. Birmingham, Alabama, USA: Solid Ground Christian Books. p. 10.

6:9). The clear scriptural principle is that the Lord does not scatter those with whom he is pleased. Therefore, when we are scattered, we ought to at least consider the possibility that we have offended him.

In the New Testament

Secondly, this emphasis on physical gathering is carried over into the New Testament.

Jesus promised his presence to those 'gathered together' in his name (Matthew 18:20). The word translated 'gathered together' is the Greek word συνάγω (*sunagō*: a combination of the words σύν, meaning 'with' or 'together', and ἄγω, meaning 'lead' or 'bring'). It is used 61 other times in the New Testament; and in almost every one of those other 61 places, the plain and obvious reference is to a physical gathering. It is the word used to describe the kind of gathering that happens when wheat is harvested into a barn (Matthew 13:10); when fish are caught in a net (Matthew 13:47); when birds collect at a carcase (Matthew 24:28); when strangers are taken in to a home (Matthew 25:35); when fragments of bread are collected into baskets (John 6:13); and when branches are collected to be put onto a fire (John 15:6). (See also Matthew 2:4; 13:2; 22:10; Mark 7:1; Luke 22:66; John 6:13; Acts 4:6, 20:8.)

We have already seen that there are those, like the Archbishop of Canterbury, who say that when *Jesus* used the word, he did not necessarily mean 'physically'. But it is plain to see that he used a word that has the idea of physical gathering. He could have said '*gathered together in spirit* in my name,' or '*of the same mind* in my name,' or even '*in communication with one another* in my name.' But he did not. How might one gather fish into a net, or bread into a basket, but 'not physically'? They are either gathered, or not gathered. There is a clear danger here of denying the clarity of scripture, if not its inerrancy. The man who asks someone to gather wheat into his barn is unlikely to be very pleased if they return claiming to have done it, 'but not physically.'

Perhaps some might point to 1 Corinthians 5:3-4, Colossians 2:5, or 1 Thessalonians 2:17 as evidence that it is possible to 'gather in spirit': Paul writes of being present 'in spirit' or 'in heart.' But there is no suggestion that Paul is talking about being 'present' with them for corporate worship; in many of these instances his meaning seems to be that his 'heart is towards' those he is writing to; that he is 'thinking of them.' To use these expressions to argue that all Christians have an innate ability, as a matter of routine, to 'gather together spiritually' is far-fetched. If that were true, it would be difficult to understand why Paul and John both have a desire to be *with* the Christians they write to: 'Having many things to write unto you, I would not write with paper and ink: but I trust to come unto you, and speak face to face, *that our joy may be full*' (2 John 1:12). Even when Paul speaks of being with the Thessalonians 'in heart,' he still obviously feels painfully separated from them, and speaks of how he endeavours 'the more abundantly to see [their] face with great desire' (1 Thessalonians 2:17). Similarly, Paul realised there he could not 'impart ... some spiritual gift' to the church at Rome—though he was an inspired apostle—when he was not physically with them (Romans 1:11).

Again, others might point to the essential spiritual union that there is between all Christians, at all times; and wonder if this might be what Jesus was referring to. But the words of Christ clearly indicate that the 'gathering together' that he speaks of is not something permanent, but something that happens from time to time. The nineteenth century Anglican hymnwriter Hugh Stowell (1799-1865) was right to speak of a 'common mercy seat' around which 'friend holds fellowship with friend' even though they may be 'sundered far'[5]; and it is a wonderful thing (and a mark of the new birth) to feel real love to and union with Christ's people, even those we have not met, and a terrible thing to allow this unity to appear disrupted—but it is untenable to argue that this is what Christ was talking about when he spoke of the two or three being gathered together. Stowell might have been horrified if he had known that people would one day make his words an excuse for the neglect of gathered corporate public worship.

The early church gathered together as a matter of routine (Acts 2:1, 44; 4:23; 20:7; 1 Corinthians 11:18; 14:26). When writing to the Corinthian church, Paul takes it for granted that they will gather (1 Corinthians 5:4).

And then, significantly, the Epistle to the Hebrews exhorts us not to forsake 'the assembling of ourselves together' (Hebrews 10:25). Here, the word used is ἐπισυναγωγή (*episynagōgē*)—the same basic word as Christ used in Matthew 18:20, but with the prefix ἐπί (which, when it appears on its own, is usually translated *on*, *upon*, or *in*). A very similar word is used to describe what a hen does to its chicks (Matthew 23:37) and what a crowd does when pressing around a door (Mark 1:33)—again, it is *physical*. John Owen (1616-1683) comments on this exhortation:

> ... a voluntary neglect and relinquishment of those assemblies destroys any church-state, if it be persisted in ... believers in all ages have constantly ventured their lives in the observance of them through a thousand difficulties and dangers, esteeming them always aliens from their communion by whom they were neglected.[6]

---

[5] From the hymn, 'From every stormy wind that blows.'

[6] John Owen, *Commentary on the Epistle to the Hebrews*, comments on Hebrews 10:25.

Again, some have argued that the 'assembling' that the apostle described can be non-physical. But this again is an assertion based on no evidence. The writer knew that some were forsaking this assembly. How did he know that? The most obvious answer is because they simply were not there. It seems unlikely that he would have had much time for anyone who said, 'Oh, I do not assemble *physically*—I do it *spiritually*.' And if this is acceptable, why not spiritualise away *all* the precepts? 'Oh, I have not been *physically* baptised; I prefer to think of it as a *spiritual* thing;' or, 'Oh, I know he said, "Do this in remembrance of me," but I like to think that I can do it *spiritually*—surely the physical element is not so important.' When we make these arguments, we are claiming to be wiser than God, and tending towards gnosticism—that everything *physical* is *evil*.

Finally in this section, we could expand on some of the terms that the Bible uses to describe the church. The word translated 'church' in the New Testament (ἐκκλησία, *ekklēsia*) is made of up the word ἐκ (*ek*, meaning 'out of', 'from', 'by', or 'away from') and a derivative of καλέω (*kaleō*, meaning 'call')—the 'called out.' William Tyndale generally (and arguably more accurately) translated it as 'congregation.' We find the church described as a flock of sheep following the same shepherd (John 10:27); as 'one body' (Romans 12:5) under the same head; as one 'household' (Ephesians 2:19); as one 'temple' (Ephesians 2:21); as 'one family' (Ephesians 3:15); as one 'wife' of one husband (Ephesians 5:32); as one 'house' (Hebrews 3:6). There is an undeniable physical aspect to all of these terms.

So the Old and New Testaments are united in pressing upon us the importance—it is no exaggeration to say, the *vital* importance—of 'gathering'. And both present this gathering as something *physical*. This alone ought to be sufficient to make us think of 'virtual services' only as a very last resort, and certainly not in any way a substitute for physical gathering. There are many disadvantages to not gathering physically—we cannot sing together, we cannot hear together, we cannot enjoy the same kind of fellowship. But really, the worst thing about not being gathered is that we are not gathered.

During the recent pandemic, when at times various governments have outlawed gathered worship, a group of various church leaders appealed to the Court of Session in Edinburgh against the Scottish government's ban on gathering. In the introduction to his judgment, the judge recorded that

> the essence of the petitioners' case is that an integral part of Christianity is the physical gathering together of Christians for prayer, proclamation of the gospel, the celebration of communion and the administration of the sacrament of baptism. The essential physical element of these aspects of their faith is absent from virtual, internet events.

In the judgment itself, the judge said:

> While certain church practices—the reading of prayer, preaching and teaching—may be observed, or even, in the case of live streaming, participated in to a certain extent, on a computer screen or a television whilst alone, in the solitude of one's own home, that does not amount to collective worship.[7]

---

[7] *Opinion of Lord Braid In the cause Reverend Dr William J U Philip and others*, 24th March 2021, https://www.scotcourts.gov.uk/docs/default-source/cos-general-docs/pdf-docs-for-opinions/2021csoh032.pdf?sfvrsn=0, [Accessed 27/04/2021].

Even a secular judge is clear that when Christians cease gathering, they cease collective worship.

Is 'gathering' something mechanical—something in which the physical element is the *only* important aspect? No, certainly not. To 'gather together' in the name of Christ is *more* than being together physically. But it is not *less* than being gathered together physically. Physical gathering *by itself* is of course inadequate. A husband and wife may be physically together without loving one another, and we would say that was a poor marriage. But if a husband or wife had no desire to be physically together, if they felt it was 'just as good' to 'meet virtually', even if just temporarily, when they could be together physically, we would equally call that a poor marriage.

2. The disadvantages of 'virtual gathering'

Let us go on to consider some of the disadvantages of 'virtual gathering'[8]. We all know there *are* disadvantages. How many times have you ended a phone or video call by saying, 'It would be good to meet up *properly* next time'? How would you feel if, having arranged to visit someone's house for dinner, they instead suggested that they have some food delivered to you and that you speak to each other on the phone or via a videocall whilst eating it? These things have their place, and there will be circumstances when we are thankful for them—but I suspect we would all be upset if a close friend said they were just as happy to meet

[8] Of course, the term really contains a contradiction. When we talk to someone on the phone, or via video call, we cannot say that we are *with* them. Similarly, when we are 'attending' a 'virtual service', whilst we may give thanks for the provision and the fellowship, we cannot give thanks for being 'gathered' or 'assembled', because we are not.

'virtually' as in person. What do we lose when we do not gather in person for worship?

When we choose to 'gather virtually', we choose to exclude ourselves from the promise of God's presence

Of course, God is everywhere. But he was just as omnipresent in Old Testament days—yet the people had to gather physically in the temple; and David longs for it in Psalm 84:2. *He* knew God was everywhere; yet he *longed* to be in God's 'courts.' Why? Because that was where God had *promised* to be. David was obviously familiar with those promises (e.g. Exodus 29:43), as was Solomon (1 Kings 8:38).

When the Christian stays at home and listens to a service online, Christ *may* be with him. But when he gathers with the people of God in the name of Christ, Christ *must* be with him—because he is promised. That is why our forefathers would walk for hours, through rain and wind, to attend a service. They saw something that perhaps we have lost sight of.

If a friend promised to meet me on Platform 3 of Waterloo Station, it would be foolish of me to hang around outside the station, hoping that I will happen to see him passing by. If I want to meet him, I will go to the place where he has promised to be. If I fail to go to Platform 3, and we do not meet, I cannot blame *him*. Similarly, if we desire to meet Christ, we will not be content to be where he *may* be. If we can (and again, there may be times when we cannot), we will be where he has *promised* to be.

The Puritan David Clarkson (1622-1686) speaks of this in a sermon.

> But you will say, Is not the Lord present with his servants when they worship him in private? It is true; but so much of his presence is not vouchsafed, nor ordinarily enjoyed, in private as in public. If the experience of any find it otherwise, they have

cause to fear the Lord is angry, they have given him some distaste, some offence; if they find him not most, where ordinarily he is most to be found, and this is in public ordinances, for the Lord is most there where he is most engaged to be, but he has engaged himself to be most there where most of his people are. The Lord has engaged to be with every particular saint, but when the particulars are joined in public worship, there are all the engagements united together. The Lord engages himself to let forth, as it were, a stream of his comfortable, quickening presence to every particular person that fears him, but when many of these particulars join together to worship God, then these several streams are united and meet in one. So that the presence of God, which, enjoyed in private, is but a stream, in public becomes a river, a river that makes glad the city of God. The Lord has a dish for every particular soul that truly serves him; but when many particulars meet together, there is a variety, a confluence, a multitude of dishes. The presence of the Lord in public worship makes it a spiritual feast, and so it is expressed, Isaiah 25:6. There is, you see, more of God's presence in public worship, ergo public worship is to be preferred before private.[9]

When we choose to 'gather virtually', we choose to make it much harder for us to 'give'

Do you attend worship solely in order to *get* something? That is certainly *one* reason to attend, but it is not the *only* reason; it is not even the *main* reason. John Gill (1697-1771) says that corporate worship is to be attended to *firstly* 'on the account of God, who has appointed it, who approves of it, and whose glory is concerned in

---

[9] Clarkson, D., 'Public worship to be preferred before private—Sermon on Psalm 87:2', In: (1865) *The Practical Works of David Clarkson, BD*. Edinburgh: James Nichol. Vol. 3, pp. 190-191.

it.'[10] The Christian who gathers solely or mainly in order to get something is missing the main point—the church assembles first and foremost to *give*.

In his diary, James Morrison (1910-1982), minister in the Free Church of Scotland, speaks of announcing a communion service to be held the following week by saying, 'Think of this time as one of *giving* more than *getting*.'[11] This attitude is clearly appropriate for a communion service ('This do *in remembrance of me*'—remembering is a form of *giving*)—and equally appropriate for every service of public worship. I once heard someone suggest that singing was 'the only part of the service where the congregation has anything to do.' That is a pitifully low view of what public worship is. The true worshipper attends as a *participant*, not an observer; as part of a *congregation*, not an audience. And that is true of every part of the service. During the reading of the Word, we all read and hear it *together*. In the prayers, the preacher is *leading* the congregation in prayer—not praying whilst the congregation eavesdrops. And during the preaching of the Word, the congregation certainly has something to do—*hear*. I asked a preacher many years ago how he prepared to preach. He told me, but then asked me a question: 'How do *you* prepare to hear?'! Good preaching without good hearing bears no fruit.

Part of this 'giving' is in the simple act of gathering *publicly*. The sight of a group of Christians gathering together is in itself a witness to those who see it. Passing a closed church during the recent lockdown, a taxi driver was heard to say, 'That shows how much their religion means to them.' David Clarkson was undoubtedly right: 'The Lord is more glorified by public worship

---

[10] Gill, J., *Commentary on the Whole Bible*, comments on Hebrews 10:25.

[11] Collins, G. N. M. (1984) *Gleanings from the Diary and Ministry of James Morrison*. Edinburgh: Lindsay and Co. p. 105.

than private. God is then glorified by us when we acknowledge that he is glorious. And he is most glorified when this acknowledgement is most public.'[12] The Scottish minister William Lindsay (1802-1866) wrote that 'above all, [assembling] is for the purpose of presenting our united acknowledgments to God, of paying to him the homage which is his due, and of professing his name before the world.'[13] When we 'meet virtually,' God may still be glorified; but he is less glorified. This alone ought to make us extremely hesitant to resort to 'virtual services.'

We gather also to give *to one another*. This means not only the preacher giving to the congregation—though he certainly ought to be doing that, and not just words but his *whole self*[14]—but *all* of the other members of the assembled church are 'giving' to one another; 'the whole body fitly joined together and compacted by that which every joint supplieth, according to the effectual working in the measure of every part, [making] increase of the body unto the edifying of itself in love' (Ephesians 4:16).

You may be just as able to hear what the preacher is saying as you sit at home listening over the internet; you may be more comfortable and find it easier—but what about that empty seat in the building? What about that word of greeting that will now be left unsaid? Especially in these days of generally small congregations, one person being absent can make a great difference. You may think nobody notices when you are not there, but they almost certainly do. You may even think you do not *need*

---

12 Clarkson, D. (1865) *The Practical Works of David Clarkson, BD*. Edinburgh: James Nichol. Vol. 3, p. 189.

13 Lindsay, W. (1867) *Lectures on the Epistle to the Hebrews*. Edinburgh: Smith, English, and Company. Vol. 2, p. 122.

14 Ash, C., 'Why I Object to Screen Preaching', https://www.thegospelcoalition.org/article/why-i-object-to-screen-preaching/ [Accessed 17/03/2021].

to be there because you have 'nothing to do.' But everyone who gathers has 'something to do.' You would feel pain even if it was only the tip of your little finger that was cut off. When a part of the body is missing, the whole body feels it. So it is with the gathered church.

When we choose to 'gather virtually', we choose to deny ourselves preaching

This is strong language; some will say, too strong. But consider what preaching is. If it is no different to giving a lecture, or reading the news, then it is quite possible to preach remotely. If it just involves the one-way flow of information from the mouth of the preacher into the ears of the hearers, then preaching remotely is just the same—indeed, writing the sermon down and posting it to the 'hearers' to read would be just the same—it would be the same words, in the same order. The only thing missing would be the preacher's tone of voice.

But preaching *is different*. It is not just one man talking and other people hearing. It is not one man being active and a number of others being passive. Something mysterious, something spiritual is happening. There is a real, if intangible, *connection* between speaker and hearers. Dr D. Martyn Lloyd-Jones (1899-1981) puts it well:

> There is always an element of exchange in true preaching ... the man who reads his essay gets nothing from his audience, he has it all there before him in what he has written; there is nothing new or creative taking place, no exchange. But the preacher—though he has prepared, and prepared carefully—because of this element of spiritual freedom is still able to receive something from the congregation, and does so ... Thank God, it often occurs that when the preacher, poor fellow, is at his worst for various reasons—perhaps has not had time to prepare as he

> should have done, or various physical factors and other things may be operating to militate against the success of the occasion—the responsiveness and eagerness of his congregation lifts him up and enlivens him.[15]

That is one reason why, as one put it, 'preaching and assembly are inseparable. Preaching, properly understood, cannot be done by telecommunication, but only in assembly.'[16] From the preacher's point of view, there is all the difference in the world between preaching to a gathering of expectant faces and speaking to a blank screen. David Ellis hits the nail on the head:

> We surely must agree that the kind of 'meetings' we rely on in the present circumstances fall far short, in lots of ways, of the ideal ... the Word is opened, read, and commented upon via Zoom, but the image is cold, almost clinical. The Word is to be preached in the context of assembly![17]

Anyone who has ever had to retreat from a service to a vestry or a hall with a noisily uncooperative child, or for any other reason, will know that even if they can still hear the preacher—even if they can still *see* the preacher—it is just not the same. They are no longer '*in* the service.' They are no longer worshipping *with* the rest of the congregation—they are at best listening to them worship. The preaching is still going on, and they are still hearing the same words—but they are not *involved* in it any longer. They have become an *observer*; no longer a participant. No doubt it is better

---

15 Lloyd-Jones, D. M. (1998) *Preaching and Preachers.* London: Hodder and Stoughton. p. 84.

16 Ash, C. (2009) *The Priority of Preaching.* Fearn: Christian Focus Publications. p. 80.

17 David Ellis, 'Something to Think About from a Struggling Saint.' *Banner of Truth Magazine* 690, p. 11.—Evidently written when the author was restricted to 'virtual services' during the Covid-19 epidemic.

than *nothing*, just as hearing your family around the meal table over the phone is better than *never* hearing them—but it is *immeasurably* inferior to being there with them.

Some may be ready to say, 'What about Mr X, who was remarkably blessed by a sermon preached over the internet?' Well, it is entirely possible that he *did* have a remarkable blessing. The *ordinary* means God uses are not the *only* means God can use. A preacher once related how the Lord used an advertisement for beer, seen on a billboard from a train ('TAKE COURAGE,' it said) to encourage him. But, wisely, he did not attempt to encourage his congregation using the same means!

God can bless *any* means—read sermons, recorded sermons, broadcast sermons, even silence!—but Hugh Latimer (d. 1555) wisely said,

> God can save my life without meat and drink; need I none therefore? God can save me from burning, if I were in the fire; shall I run into it therefore? No, no; I must keep the way that God hath ordained, and use the ordinary means that God hath assigned, and not seek new ways. This office of preaching is the only ordinary way that God hath appointed to save us all by. Let us maintain this, for I know none other; neither think I God will appoint or devise any other.[18]

It is in public worship that the Lord does his greatest works. 'It pleased God by the foolishness of preaching to save them that believe' (1 Corinthians 1:21). That preaching takes place where the church *assembles*. As Martin Luther (1483-1546) wrote, 'The highest

---

[18] Latimer, H., Sermon on Matthew 22:21, http://anglicanhistory.org/reformation/latimer/sermons/stamford.html [Accessed 17/03/2021].

form of worship is the preaching of God's Word.'[19] If we desire people to be saved, we must prioritise gathering, if only to maintain preaching.

Am I saying that 'virtual preaching' is valueless? No—it can be of tremendous value, as many of us will have found by experience, and it can be greatly blessed. It is without a doubt a form of *ministry* (it is unhelpful that the words 'preacher' and 'minister' have in many circles become synonymous—*all* Christians are called to minister, but not all are called to preach). Where a pastor or preacher is *unable* to travel to be with his people, to have him speak to them virtually may be the best form of ministry available, both for them and him—the *closest possible thing* to preaching, perhaps. But it is not *preaching*.

There are also 'in between' options. The congregation may gather, and the preacher may speak remotely from his home. This is arguably closer to the ideal (especially if the preacher is visible and not just audible) than for the congregation to listen from their respective homes. But it is still far from the ideal. In fact, one could argue that it would be better to have a sermon *read* by someone who *is* physically gathered with the congregation than a 'live' sermon 'piped in' from someone who *is not*.

When we choose to 'gather virtually', we choose to make it impossible to carry out the other functions of the church

Baptisms self-evidently require physical assembly, at the very least of the person being baptised and the person doing the baptising. It is the function of the church, not of the private individual; as the 1689 Baptist Confession of Faith puts it in Chapter 28, it is to be

[19] Luther, M. [translated: Cole, H.] (1837) *A Manual of the Book of Psalms*. London: R. B. Seeley and W. Burnside. p. 350.

'administered by those only who are qualified and thereunto called, according to the commission of Christ.'

So with the observance of the Lord's Supper; it is surely important that Jesus instructed his disciples to share the bread and wine as he was sitting down *with* them. Surely the *gathering* was part of what he meant when he said, 'This do in remembrance of me,' just as much as the eating of the bread and the drinking of the wine is. Again, there may be times when a church deems it prudent to move away from the ideal for a time—but when we do, we ought to do so with the most extreme caution. Asserting that it is possible to observe the ordinance without gathering is no different to asserting that it is possible to observe it without bread, or without wine. The outward things of the ordinance may be less important than the inward; but they are still the outwards things *that Christ instituted*. And this is confirmed by Paul's emphatic teaching in 1 Corinthians 11:20: it is when Christians 'come together … into one place' that the ordinance is to be held. 'Observing the Lord's Supper' without gathering, or without bread, or without wine, arguably means that we are not really observing the Lord's Supper.

We could also think of church discipline. Jesus' words are very clear. The offended brother is to '*go* and tell' the offender his fault; if the offender will not hear, the offended brother is to '*take* with' him 'one or two more'. Jesus could just have said 'tell', without saying 'go', and he did not. Being physically present with the offender is clearly important. Surely the same is true of any other steps that might be taken with respect to the offender, right up to excommunication—it is important that the church be gathered together to consider and decide these steps. The same is surely true of other meetings of the church, for example to hear someone's testimony or consider a member's call to preach. We might also mention the tradition in some parts of the church for preachers to be ordained by the laying on of hands—something that clearly requires physical gathering.

Some may decide to gather physically for *these* purposes—baptisings, church disciplinary meetings, the Lord's Supper, and perhaps also other 'extraordinary' services such as weddings and funerals—but not for 'normal services.' Such a decision surely reveals a wrong attitude towards the regular services of the church. 'Normal' preaching services are not 'less important' than church meetings, the Lord's Supper, or wedding or funeral services—they are at least *as* important, if not more so.

When we choose to 'gather virtually', we choose to have more control than is good for us

We naturally like control. There are some preachers we like more than others. There are some books of the Bible we like more than others. There are some kinds of preaching that we prefer to other kinds. We think we know what we need. But in reality, we only know what we *want*. Choosing what to hear appeals to us in the same way that choosing what to eat would have appealed to us when we were children—and the outcomes can be just as unhealthy.

When we gather physically, there is an element of submission. We sit, and we listen. We recognise—or ought to—the preacher as the messenger that God has appointed for us to hear on that occasion. When he comes with a message which searches us, which turns our comfortable religion upside-down, which brings God before us as a consuming fire, which makes us shrink, which makes us uncomfortable—we do not get up and leave, even if it is only common politeness that keeps us in our seats. How much more if we recognise the truth that the words he is speaking, as he unfolds them out of the Word of God (and only so far as he does that) *are* the words of God!

But when we are at home, it is too easy to take a 'pick-n-mix' approach to who and what we hear. Some have spoken of this as something positive: 'We can now attend wherever we want and hear whoever we want.' But few seem to consider the strong possibility—if not certainty—that what they *want* is not what they *need*. When we are at home, if we are bored of our pastor's ministry, we can hear someone else. If we do not like what we are hearing, we can turn it down, or leave the room, or read a book, or make a cup of tea. And nobody will know. But it would be a dangerous thing—potentially even fatal—to allow patients to choose their own medicine, particularly if they chose entirely on the basis of which pills looked nicest or tasted best!

When we choose to 'gather virtually', we choose to deny ourselves the clearest views of God

As David Clarkson put it, why did David desire above all else to 'dwell in the house of the Lord' in Psalm 27:4? 'To behold the beauty of the Lord.' When David remembered seeing God's 'power and glory' in Psalm 63:2, where did he remember seeing them? 'In the sanctuary.' When the church in the Song of Solomon is looking for the place where Christ feeds his flock, where is she directed? To 'the footsteps of the flock' and to 'the shepherds' tents' (Song 1:8). Why are pastors and teachers given to the church today? 'For the edifying of the body of Christ' (Ephesians 4:12)—not so much the edifying of the members *individually*, but of the body *as a whole*.[20]

---

[20] Clarkson, D. (1865) *The Practical Works of David Clarkson, BD*. Edinburgh: James Nichol. Vol. 3, pp. 191-192.

When we choose to 'gather virtually', we choose to deny ourselves the vital influence of other Christians

This can be a *warming* influence. Again, Clarkson says,

> Live coals, if ye separate them, and lay them asunder, will quickly die; but while they are continued together, they serve to continue heat in one another. We may quicken one another, while we join together in worshipping God; but deadness, coldness, or lukewarmness may seize upon the people of God, if they forsake the assembling of themselves together.[21]

How many times have you struggled to motivate yourself to go out to a week evening service—yet come away thankful that you did?

It can be a *preserving* influence. The wise man says, 'Woe to him that is alone when he falleth; for he hath not another to help him up.' A person who thinks he does not need his fellow Christians is in direct opposition to the Apostle Paul: 'The eye cannot say unto the hand, I have no need of thee: nor again the head to the feet, I have no need of you.' (1 Corinthians 12:21) No doubt we have all seen people who have isolated themselves from the rest of the church, and subsequently drifted further and further away until they are altogether out of sight.

It can be an *encouraging* influence.

> When I gather with my brothers and sisters to hear the word preached, it is still possible to hit the 'off button'. I can look out of the window; I can read Wesley's instructions for congregational singing in *Christian Hymns;* I can read the 39 Articles at the end of the *Book of Common Prayer;* I can doodle; I

[21] Clarkson, D. (1865) *The Practical Works of David Clarkson, BD*. Edinburgh: James Nichol. Vol. 3, p. 193.

> can daydream. But it is not quite so easy. For I have sitting around me brothers and sisters who might notice, and I would hate to be seen to be inattentive. And I have sitting around me brothers and sisters who may talk to me afterwards about the sermon; and it will be embarrassing if I have no idea what it was about.
>
> Further, when we listen together, you know what word I have heard, and I know what word you have heard. I've heard it. You know I've heard it. I know that you know I've heard it! And you expect and hope that I will respond appropriately to that word, just as I expect and hope that you will do the same. We are accountable to one another for our response, and this stirs us up and encourages us to respond as we know we ought.[22]

Some may say, 'In our place of worship we are each focused on ourselves and the Lord.' This sounds plausible; perhaps even admirable. But we should be cautious about being comfortable in a situation where a number of individuals are worshipping *individually*, rather than aspiring to a situation where a body of Christians are worshipping *corporately*. When we gather for worship, we are meant to be *gathering* for worship. Sometimes people pray during public worship that we might 'lose sight of one another.' There is perhaps an element of truth in that request—we must all hear for ourselves, and God does deal with his children individually, and each of us needs to *worship*, not watch *others* worshipping—but losing sight of each other completely is in effect to treat the other members of the body as irrelevant, when our

[22] Ash, C. (2009) *The Priority of Preaching*. Fearn: Christian Focus Publications. p. 99.

greatest privilege and benefit is to be one of many members in the body.

If we love God, we will love God's children—and if we love God's children, we will be concerned for them, and look out for them, and enjoy being with them. It is in this sense, surely, that Paul exhorts, 'Look not every man on his own things, but every man also on the things of others' (Philippians 2:4). So many gospel precepts are, like this one, very much more difficult (if not impossible) to observe when we are scattered from the 'others.' The early Christians seem to have gathered *daily* for worship and fellowship (Acts 2:46). Something is wrong if we think of that as something we would have to *endure,* rather than something that we would *enjoy*!

When we choose to 'gather virtually', we choose not to follow those who have gone before us.

Some of those who have gone before, who gathered despite all attendant difficulties, have already been mentioned in Chapter 3 of this volume ('Should the church ever suspend public worship?') How David longed for public worship! Solomon, Hezekiah and Josiah all had a great desire to begin and maintain public worship—building, repairing or reopening the temple. The apostles and the early church prioritised meeting together, even risking their own lives for the privilege—as many since have done down through the ages. Yes, we have technology that they did not have. But can we pretend to believe that if they *had* had our technology, they would have chosen it above gathering?

Finally, when we choose to 'gather virtually', we choose to deny ourselves the nearest thing on earth to heaven

Quoting David Clarkson again:

> In heaven, so far as the Scripture describes it to us, there is nothing done in private, nothing in secret, all the worship of that glorious company is public. The innumerable company of angels, and the church of the first-born, make up one general assembly in the heavenly Jerusalem (Hebrews 12:22, 28). They make one glorious congregation, and so jointly together sing the praises of him that sits on the throne, and the praises of the Lamb, and continue employed in this public worship to eternity.[23]

Our gatherings here are not only part of the process by which the Lord *prepares* us for that great gathering above; they are also *foretastes* of that gathering.

When speaking of the 'general assembly (πανηγυρει, *panḗgurei* 'mass meeting' or 'universal gathering') and church of the firstborn' in Hebrews 12:22, the writer does not say the Hebrew Christians 'are coming' to it or 'will come' to it—instead, they 'are come' (or 'have come') to it. There is of course a spiritual element to this (because some of those who make up the assembly are already in heaven); but the words used do imply a physical element also (because we who are not yet in heaven must assemble on earth to be part of this meeting).

Again, for what purpose does the Lord give pastors, teachers, etc.? What is the objective of these gifts? It is so that the church would '*all come* in the *unity* of the faith, and of the knowledge of the Son

---

[23] Clarkson, D. (1865) *The Practical Works of David Clarkson, BD*. Edinburgh: James Nichol. Vol. 3, p. 194.

of God, unto a perfect man, unto the measure of the stature of the fulness of Christ;' and 'grow up into him in all things, which is the head, even Christ' (Ephesians 4:13, 15). They are 'quickened ... *together*,' and 'raised up *together*,' and made to 'sit *together* in heavenly places' (Ephesians 2:5-6). It is all *together*.

How much have the Father, the Son, and the Holy Spirit each done in order to ensure the physical gathering of the church in heaven! His people will gather there in *glorified* bodies, yes; but in glorified *bodies*. If God has determined that our bodies will be *there*, how dangerous to assume that the physical gathering of our bodies is unimportant when we worship him *here*.

Conclusions

We began by acknowledging that there will be times when a local church will have to decide whether to suspend physical gathering and resort to 'virtual' services. To do this we need to understand the advantages and disadvantages of 'virtual' services. The things we gain are relatively easy to understand—because they are largely physical, visible benefits (less travelling, more comfort, less risk of upsetting people who think we ought not to be gathering, less risk of spreading disease).

But the things we lose are less tangible, less visible. That means we need to be careful not to overlook them. Many of those disadvantages have been outlined above. No doubt the reader will be able to think of others.

Some may say that the Bible does not state *explicitly* that physical gathering is important. That is a very questionable assertion—but even if true, it cannot be denied that the importance of the physical element is strongly *implied*.

Others may argue that 'the ends justify the means'—that 'virtual services' mean that many more people than normal can 'attend' and that they can increase the spread of the gospel. But we need to be wary of this kind of argument. The number of people *participating* in a service of worship is more important than the number of people *listening* to it.

Time will tell whether 'virtual services' are more effective than the preaching of the Word in the context of the physically-gathered church. A sensible starting assumption is that their efficacy will be as limited as any other means which may seem attractive to certain well-meaning Christians in certain circumstances, yet which are not the time-honoured means which God has appointed in his Word. And of course, with the ability to broadcast services from our assemblies (for the benefit of those *unable* to attend) we do not have to choose between assembling and broadcasting. Both can be done at once; provided we take care to keep in our minds the importance of gathering so that we do not think of 'listening in' online as a valid substitute.

It is easy to state these things in theory and looking back. Prioritising physical gathering when it is forbidden by the law—when we run the risk of offending our neighbours, being fined, featuring in the media—is less easy. We do need to count the cost. On the other hand, we should not forget that it is impossible, in the long run, for anyone to lose out by following Christ and his Word; and suffering for righteousness' sake is not to be feared, but welcomed. That said, we do need grace to purify our motives—suffering for *stubborness'* sake is not commended!

Many of us, perhaps, are looking back to the early days of the recent pandemic and how we responded to the restrictions placed on us, and are wondering whether we did the right thing. It is good to look back and acknowledge our failings. But we are also called to look forward. What will the 'new normal' look like for the church? It is notable that at the time of writing, when restrictions on gathering for worship have been lifted, many churches are still choosing 'virtual services'. Will such services become a permanent feature?

We are surely in danger of failing to learn the lessons of the past. Over 50 years ago, Dr D. Martyn Lloyd-Jones recalled preaching at a church where in the morning, two services had to be held because of the number of people who attended—he estimated the total attendance across those two services to be 2,600 people. However, the evening service was broadcast over the radio, and he noted that the congregation was very much smaller—just 400 people. His comments are surely relevant to the situation facing us today as we contemplate what the 'new normal' for the church ought to look like:

> ... if I were the minister of that church I would not broadcast the evening service on the radio ... rather, I would advertise the church in these terms: 'The church which does not broadcast.' Why? Because that method, it seemed to me, would persuade the people to come out for the evening service. As long as they could sit at home and listen to it on the radio, why take the trouble to get your car out of the garage and struggle with the traffic and many other inconveniences? Broadcasting I fear has discouraged people from coming to the House of God and taught them bad habits. But even more serious is the harm it has done to the people's idea of the corporate life of the church. Far too often they think of churches just as places where you sit and listen to a sermon; and now you can get this on the radio or on tapes and so on. So the whole notion of coming together, and sitting together round the Word, and listening to an exposition of it, is seriously damaged. The very facts and statistics

demonstrate that during these last fifty years the life of the church, as such, has deteriorated very seriously.

I suggest, here again, that it is for us to break into all this. The motives which have led men to use these media have of course been obvious. They thought that this was going to do good to their churches, and that people hearing them on the radio would then come and listen in the church. I suggest that it really has not worked out like that; and that you are likely to find in the future that God will revive his work in the church, and that it is those who attend regularly who are the ones who are going to participate most of all in the blessing. That has always been God's way in the past. What is astonishing, once more, is that people do not want to do things in God's time-honoured way. They are content with this detached attitude towards the church. It is a fundamental failure to understand the true doctrine of the Christian church—'the unity of the Spirit in the bond of peace', the gathering together of the people of God. 'Where two or three are gathered together in my name, there am I in the midst.'[24]

---

[24] Lloyd-Jones, D. M. (1998) *Preaching and Preachers*. London: Hodder and Stoughton. p. 251.

~ 5 ~
How should church and state interact during a crisis?

Allan W. MacColl

This chapter explores how the church and the state should relate to one another during a health crisis. The duty of civil government to protect lives during the Covid-19 crisis has brought a level of state intervention to bear upon the activity of the Christian church which has not been witnessed previously in modern Britain. A question which arises, therefore, is whether this degree of intervention has encroached on the church's spiritual freedom. And a further question is whether a time of crisis entitles the state to intervene in the church's own jurisdiction in a way it would not at other times.

The chapter discusses the biblical and theological position on church-state relations and moves on to consider historical examples where the biblical principles were tested in practice. The legacy of the past points the way to how the church should respond to the state's actions during the current crisis and in the future.

1. The scriptural doctrine of church and state

In any area of controversy, the church must search the Scriptures in order to test the spirits and to ascertain as clearly as possible the mind of Christ, the king and head of the church.

The distinction between civil authority and religious authority is made clear from the Old Testament onwards. In 2 Chronicles 26:16-21, we read the account of King Uzziah taking upon himself to enter into the temple to burn incense. He was immediately opposed by the priest who rebuked the king with the words, 'It appertaineth not unto thee, Uzziah, to burn incense unto the Lord, but to the priests the sons of Aaron, that are consecrated to burn incense: go out of the sanctuary, for thou hast trespassed, neither shall it be for thine honour from the Lord God.'

Uzziah immediately fell under God's severe judgment in the form of leprosy, a disease from which he never recovered. This solemn example from Scripture shows that in the Old Testament church, a clear practical distinction existed between the functions of the monarchy and the priesthood, between the Jewish state and the church. This meant that the officers of the state were not to interfere in the administration of the worship of the church, or to take upon themselves the functions of the officers of the church.

The priest's resistance to Uzziah's authority is not by any means the only example in the Old Testament where we find godly people refusing to implement policies and regulations promulgated by civil authority which were detrimental to the life and activity of the church. We have the example of the faithful midwives in Egypt, Shiphrah and Puah, who 'feared God, and did not as the king of Egypt commanded them, but saved the men children alive' (Exodus 1:17). Most dramatically of all there are the examples in the Book of Daniel where both the three young men and afterwards Daniel himself in later life, were remarkably delivered from cruel deaths. They refused to compromise their exclusive adherence to the worship of the Lord though obeying the ungodly decrees issued by the civil authorities. Their faithfulness is commended to all generations and furnishes important lessons to God's people faced with the dilemma of whether to obey or resist laws which run counter to biblical principles. When faced with such a dilemma, the apostles were likewise clear. 'We ought to obey God rather than men' (Acts 5:29).

When it comes to the spiritual jurisdiction of the church, Scripture has much to say.

- Isaiah 9:6-7 speaks of the 'government' being upon the shoulders of the Messiah, the Prince of Peace. Christ reigns spiritually over his church.
- In the New Testament we learn that in the church of Christ there exists the gift of *government* (Romans 12:8; 1 Corinthians 12:28) and there are elders to *bear rule* (Acts 14:23; Philippians 1:1; 1 Timothy 5:17) and *take oversight* of the flock of God (Acts 20:28; Hebrews 13:17).
- These church governors have sacred functions they must perform, such as *ordination* (2 Timothy 2:2; Titus 1:5), *admittance to and exclusion from church fellowship* (2 Thessalonians 3:6) and *determining controversies* (Acts 15:23).
- They must *meet together* in assemblies in order to perform those functions, in the name of Christ, by whose authority they are to meet and deliberate (Acts 15:6).

All these functions are bestowed as gifts from Christ, the king and head of the church (Ephesians 4:11-16). When we further consider that all the blessings which Christ has purchased for his people were obtained at the price of his own precious blood, we must entertain the highest possible regard for the privileges of having church government, church governors and the ordinances of Christian worship and discipline. The freedom of Christ's church in spiritual matters is, ultimately, a freedom purchased in the blood of the everlasting covenant.

The origin, nature, extent and parties who exercise power respectively in church and state are different and are not to be confused.

- *Origin.* The origin of state power lies in the fact that God is the moral governor of the universe. But the source of the spiritual power of the church is the headship of Christ, the mediatorial king of Zion. He is over all things for the sake of his body the church (Ephesians 1:22), therefore nations are obliged to acknowledge his claims (Isaiah 60:12).

- *Nature.* The *coercive* power he gives to magistrates (civil government) over persons and property is of a different nature altogether from the *spiritual* power he vests in the church and exercises through church officers. Civil power is described as 'the power of the sword' in Romans 13. Magistrates act as God's ministers in order to be a terror to the wicked and protectors of the good.

- *Extent.* Civil power extends only to people's *outward activities,* whereas the power of the church takes to do with their *spiritual relations* to God and their fellow men, as far as men can judge of such relations. For example, the state (but not the church) can fine people, confiscate their property, imprison them, and in some situations execute them. On the other hand, the church (but not the state) can preach the gospel, baptise people, include or exclude them from the Lord's Supper, ordain or depose ministers, decide on points of doctrine, etc. When church governors exercise their divinely bestowed authority, they are wielding the 'power of the keys' of the kingdom of heaven as Christ's servants (Matthew 18:18-20). 'Heaven' in this context refers to the church as God's kingdom. What church governors loose and bind in the courts of the visible church on earth, however, is ratified in heaven when they reach authoritative decisions on earth concerning spiritual matters which are consonant with the mind of Christ as revealed in Scripture. Civil governors are to have no jurisdiction here. The Westminster Confession of Faith (1647) teaches that, 'The Lord Jesus Christ, as king and head of his church, hath therein appointed a government in the hands of church officers, distinct from the civil magistrate' (WCF 31:1). The Confession also states that 'the civil magistrate may not assume to himself the administration of the Word and sacraments, or the power of the keys of the kingdom of heaven' (WCF 23:3).

- *Parties.* Again, another difference between church power and civil authority is that the parties who wield these different kinds of power are not the same. Civil rulers and church governors do not have mutual eligibility of office. The ministers of the gospel are not to intermeddle with the work of magistrates in the civil sphere and vice versa.

It should be clear from this outline that civil authority and spiritual authority are fundamentally different in nature. Sometimes people have argued that there can be only one ultimate authority in a nation, and the dispute turns to whether that ultimate authority should be churchly or civil. However, this argument proceeds on the misconception that the nature, scope and exercise of power in both church and state is of the same kind and must inevitably lead to conflict. If instead we bear in mind how different they are, this argument falls to the ground. When both jurisdictions exercise their God-given authority within their own proper spheres according to the principles of Scripture, there ought to be no serious issue of either side over-reaching its own authority to the detriment of the other.

Since the civil authorities during the apostolic era and for the next two centuries did not profess Christianity, there is no reference in the New Testament to the church joining in alliance with the state for the mutual good of the community. The duty of obedience to the 'powers that be' is, however, inculcated by Paul in Romans 13 and this duty was expressed at a time when such abominable tyrants as Nero and Caligula occupied the imperial throne. We are to pray for kings and all in authority that we might live peaceably in this world (1 Timothy 2:2). Ungodly and unbelieving rulers are still entitled to the honour of Christian citizens. But, crucially, the apostle in Romans 13 is referring only to the civil function of the state—to the fact that civil rulers bear the sword since their God-given right and duty is to punish evil. Scripture, however, did not teach that civil rulers are to be obeyed if they command obedience to laws which are contrary to God's own law, or if they attempt to extend their power into the spiritual jurisdiction of the church. The example of the apostles makes this abundantly clear (Acts 4:19-33; 5:29). It is impossible to assert absolute obedience to the civil authorities from Romans 13 or any other statement in Scripture—absolute obedience is due to God alone. Civil rulers are entitled to obedience in civil matters and no more. In a catechism published by the Free Church of Scotland in the period following the 1843 Disruption, the point is forcibly made that if church governors submit to the authority of the state in ecclesiastical matters merely out of a sense of civil obligation, 'they abdicate the function which Christ has conferred upon them, and the civil magistrate comes into the place Christ has assigned to them as the governors of his house.'[1]

What happens, however, when there seems to be an overlap between the civil and spiritual jurisdictions? The church's actions often have civil consequences—for example over a minister's income and dwelling-place—and the church necessarily interacts with the state's laws in many ways, including in the areas of health and safety measures in buildings, charity law or disability access. The classic distinction that theologians made in the past was that the civil magistrate has power *circa sacra* (*about* sacred things) but not a power but not *in sacris* (*in* sacred things). State power concerning religion therefore extends *around* sacred things but not actually *into* the sacred things themselves. The state has no authoritative control over the church's own province—the spiritual affairs of Christ's kingdom. The state should, for example, protect and support the church and call the church to put its house in order if it is manifestly failing in its own duties (this obligation of the state was a view held by the Westminster divines (WCF 23:3)). The state's power of the sword, however, can never be used to take over the church's power of the keys.

If possible, the state and the church should seek to enter into a friendly alliance, mutually supporting each other and working for the good of the community in their separate but co-ordinate spheres of jurisdiction. The principle underlying this alliance has been described as 'a co-ordination of powers and a mutual subordination of persons,' whereby each jurisdiction recognises the supremacy of the other in their respective sphere.[2] This co-

---

[1] Gray, A. (1853) *Catechism on the Principles and Constitution of the Free Church of Scotland*. Edinburgh: Johnstone and Hunter. p. 23.

[2] Cunningham, W. (1991) *Discussions on Church Principles, Popish, Erastian and Presbyterian*. Edmonton, Alberta, Canada: Still Waters Revival Books. p. 153.

ordination and mutual support is implied in the prophecies which refer to the New Testament era. 'Kings shall be thy nursing fathers and their queens thy nursing mothers' (Isaiah 49:23). 'The nation and kingdom that will not serve thee shall perish' (Isaiah 60:12). Promises like these are addressed to the church and indicate that New Testament Christians are to pray for such a mutual supporting between church and state. In Revelation 11:15, it is prophesied that a time will come when 'the kingdoms of this world are become the kingdoms of our Lord and of his Christ.' The principle of 'Establishment' (at least as understood by Scottish presbyterians) is grounded in these promises of Christ to the church, with the corresponding obligations of each nation towards the Christian religion. As the eminent Free Church minister John Kennedy of Dingwall (1819-1884) noted, without the security of state recognition, the civil powers may treat the church fairly and tolerate her activities, but at the same time, they may treat the church on the same basis as another voluntary society, and leave her as vulnerable to state encroachment as any other group in the community.[3] It is for this reason that most conservative Scottish presbyterians have always promoted national recognition of religion by the state as a duty and, if the terms were suitable, have desired to see one national church established with legal protection and support from the civil authorities.

---

[3]See Kennedy, J. (1955) *The Present Cast and Tendency of Religious Thought and Feeling in Scotland.* Inverness: Northern Counties Newspaper. James Begg stated, 'States may enslave churches, and churches may connive at their own bondage; but if the arrangement is otherwise unobjectionable, the best way of securing spiritual freedom, as all our ancestors maintained, is to get the state to recognise the creed and jurisdiction of the church, and to shut out its own courts from interfering with spiritual acts and decisions.' Begg, J. (1874) *Free Church Principles (Memorial with the Opinions of Eminent Counsel in regard to the Constitution of the Free Church of Scotland).* Edinburgh: Johnstone, Hunter and Co. pp. 56-57.

2. Historical background

The Early Church

In the circumstances in which the church found itself in the early years of the New Testament era, relations with the civil authorities assumed a significance that cannot be overstated. The state's actions towards the church proved to be literally a matter of life and death in countless cases. The Scottish Free Church theologian, James Bannerman (1807-1868), writing in the mid nineteenth century, stated that,

> For the first three hundred years of its existence the religion of Christ was in almost perpetual collision with the state, just on the ground that it was essentially a missionary and an exclusive religion, that it would not, and could not, exist in peace alongside of any other faith, that its temples must stand alone, and its deity find no place in the Pantheon. Nor has the essential character of Christianity altered since the days of Nero and Diocletian.[4]

From the end of the Roman Empire

When the Roman Empire became professedly a Christian state, the relationship between the church and the civil power became at the same time much closer and also much more complicated. If we take the entire period from the end of the Roman Empire to the Reformation, it is clear that the struggles between church and monarchy were largely informed by both sides practically aiming at controlling the other. In the Eastern Church, the state assumed supreme authority over the church, and the idea of the church having an independent jurisdiction from the civil power was not recognised. This doctrine is variously known as Byzantinism, or

[4] Bannerman, J. (1974) *The Church of Christ*. Edinburgh: Banner of Truth Trust. Vol. 1, p.142.

Caesaropapism, or (in later years) Erastianism. In the Western Church, however, the situation was to a large extent reversed. The bishops of Rome came to claim a universal jurisdiction over not only the whole Christian church but also over the secular rulers of the world. The claim to complete authority over church and state on the part of the papacy reached its highest practical enunciation during the time of Gregory VII and Paschal II. One practical example of this claim was when Pope Innocent III placed the kingdom of England under an interdict for six years between March 1208 and May 1213, after King John refused to accept the pope's appointee Stephen Langton as Archbishop of Canterbury. The Fourth Lateran Council in 1215 pronounced the atrocious decree that 'heretics' were not only to be hunted down and expelled from Christian lands but that those secular rulers who did not comply in this were to be replaced by other rulers willing to do the pope's bidding.[5]

From that time until 2020, the church in England has been free to worship under the terms of *Magna Carta* (1215) where King John consented for perpetuity 'that the Church of England shall be free, and shall have all her whole rights and liberties inviolable.'[6]

The Reformation

The rise of the modern nation state in the fifteenth and sixteenth centuries coincides with the Renaissance and the Protestant Reformation. The professed alliance between church and state which had characterized the mediaeval period was not challenged at this critical juncture, but it did undergo significant changes. Mediaeval monarchs had always sought to dominate the church for their own ends, mostly by controlling appointments and

[5] See https://www.papalencyclicals.net/councils/ecum12-2.htm#3 [Accessed 24/04/2021].

[6] Carpenter, D. (Ed.) (2015) *Magna Carta*. London: Penguin Classics. p. 69.

benefices and thus tapping lucrative sources of funding. But as modern states became more centralized and powerful in relation both to their own citizens and to the church, so an assertiveness on the part of the civil authorities to control the newly-formed Protestant churches became more evident. Martin Luther (1483-1546) and Philip Melanchthon (1497-1560) both recognised this,[7] though they were far more concessive to state control than John Calvin (1509-1564) and John Knox (d. 1572). All the leading Reformers believed in an alliance between church and state and, in a society where royalty and aristocracy held all the reins of power, they were assiduous in seeking the support of monarchs and nobles in the cause of the Reformed faith.

The great achievement of John Calvin in the field of church polity was his realisation that there was a distinct ecclesiastical government in the church separate from the power of the civil magistrate.[8] Calvin insisted that the church must be free to exercise spiritual discipline and oversight. What made this novel in relation to previous conceptions of ecclesiastical power was the sharpness of the distinction drawn between the two jurisdictions.[9] To this insight we can therefore trace the whole of the subsequent development of presbyterian church government—as well as that of independency and congregationalism—in their view of the

---

[7] Cunningham, W. (1994) *Historical Theology*. Edinburgh: Banner of Truth Trust. Vol. 2, pp. 567-8.

[8] 'When I approve of a civil administration that aims to prevent the true religion which is contained in God's law from being openly and with public sacrilege violated and defiled with impunity, I do not here, any more than before, allow men to make laws according to their own decision concerning religion and the worship of God.' Calvin, J. (1960) *Institutes of the Christian Religion* (Battles Ed.). London: S. C. M. Press. p. 1488.
Institutes 4.20.3

[9] Cunningham, W. (1994) *Historical Theology*. Edinburgh: Banner of Truth Trust. Vol. 2, p. 569.

separate spheres of church and state. More widely, this Calvinist insistence on the freedom of the church to exercise discipline exclusively in spiritual matters was of the utmost importance in the battle against absolutist government and tyranny in the following centuries as it brought home to ordinary people as well as to ruling elites, that there are limits on the power of the civil authorities. Basing his thinking on profound understanding of the Word of God, Calvin rightly saw this as a return to the position and practice of the apostolic church.

England and Scotland became Protestant nations during the Reformation. In both nations the monarch was Protestant and on either side of the border each sought to retain control of the church. In the break with Rome, King Henry VIII (1491-1547) was determined to be head of the church in his realm, and this state of affairs was confirmed in the settlement of the Church of England in the early years of Elizabeth I (1533-1603). In Scotland, King James VI (1566-1625) correctly perceived that presbyterianism was a threat to his claim of unchecked monarchy by divine and absolute right. He thus sought to undermine the church's independent government through the introduction of episcopacy and a gradual conforming to Anglican practices when he succeeded Elizabeth I on the English throne in 1603. In a famous incident in 1596, the great presbyterian leader Andrew Melville (1545-1622) stated unequivocally to King James,

> There are twa kings and twa kingdoms in Scotland; there is Christ Jesus the king of the church, whose subject King James VI is, and of whose kingdom he is not a king, nor a lord, nor a head, but a member.[10]

---

[10] M'Crie, T. (1856) *Life of Andrew Melville*. Edinburgh: William Blackwood and Sons. p. 181.

This captures the essence of the contention of the presbyterians that the jurisdictions of the state and the church were separate, and that the church's spiritual authority was independent from state interference.

Nonconformists and Covenanters

The rise of the Puritan movement in the late sixteenth century in England was mirrored by an increasing resistance by Presbyterians in Scotland to the state's control of the church. This eventually gave rise to the signing of the National Covenant in 1638 and to the famous 1638 General Assembly of the Church of Scotland, which abolished episcopal church government and continued to meet in defiance of the king's commissioner's instructions to dismiss.

Although the ascendency of the Puritans and Covenanters in the 1640s and 50s was short-lived, it did fundamentally affect future church-state relations. While Charles II and James VII and II exercised a tyrannical despotism, they were not able to root out Protestant dissent in England, where more than two thousand Puritan pastors were forced out of the Established Church in 1662 rather than submit to the terms upon which the Anglican Church was to be based. Their view of the spiritual independence of the church led them to reject a settlement that forced them against their conscience to practice what they believed was contrary to Scripture.

In Scotland, 300-400 were similarly ejected from their parishes rather than yield the spiritual freedom of the church to the Stuart claim that the king was supreme in all causes, civil and ecclesiastical. The vicissitudes which affected those Covenanters who opposed the authorities were numerous, especially when some were persuaded to take the indulgences of the government and re-join the Established Church. This had the effect of dividing and weakening the opposition to the royal policy. Some of the more militant Covenanting leaders eventually renounced even their civil allegiance to the Stuart monarchy. Of course, this line of conduct gave the civil authorities a greater pretext for violently crushing all opposition to their regime.

The Covenanters furnish us with a very important example when we are trying to identify the proper extent of the church's independence in relation to the state. In a pastoral address to his congregation written from exile in the Netherlands, one of the most eminent Covenanting ministers, John Livingstone, (1603-1672), emphasised the spiritual independence of the church under Christ's Headship. Livingstone stated that, Christ, 'their only Lawgiver' had invested his church with

> intrinsick power to meet for his worship, and their officers appointed by him, to meet for discipline and ordering the affairs of his house.[11]

Perhaps one of the most succinct treatments was George Gillespie's *One Hundred and Eleven Propositions Concerning the Ministry and Government of the Church.* This document was approved by the General Assembly of the Church of Scotland in 1647.[12] According to Gillespie,

> magistrates shall no less sin in usurping ecclesiastical power, ministering holy things, ordaining ministers, or exercising

---

[11] Quoted in Tweedie, W. K., *Select Biographies*, republished as (2008) *Scottish Puritans.* Edinburgh: Banner of Truth, p. 246. This intrinsic right of convocation and assembly was also asserted by continental divines cited in Gillespie, G. (1846) *Aaron's Rod Blossoming*. Edinburgh: Robert Ogle and Oliver and Boyd. p. 141.

[12] Gillespie, G. (1647) *CXI propositions concerning the ministerie and government of the Church.* Edinburgh: Evan Tyler.

> discipline ecclesiastical, than ministers should sin in rushing into the borders of the magistrate, and in thrusting themselves into his calling. (Proposition 79)

> If it further happen (which God forbid) that the magistrate do so far abuse his authority, that he doth straitly forbid what Christ hath ordained, yet the constant and faithful servants of Christ will resolve and determine with themselves, that any extremities are rather to be undergone than that they should obey such things, and that we ought to obey God rather than men; yea, they will not leave off to perform all the parts of their office, being ready in the meantime to render a reason of their practice to every one that demandeth it, but specially unto the magistrate ... (Proposition 99)

The Ten Years' Conflict

The next major period when church-state relations came to prominence was in the Ten Years' Conflict (1834-1843) which culminated in the Disruption of 1843, when around one third of the ministers left the Established Church of Scotland to form the Free Church. Contrary to biblical principles, the ministers of the Church of Scotland were not only elected by their congregations but were 'presented' by the 'patrons' of each parish, those who possessed property and influence and who were required to materially support the church in each locality.

This practice had led to great conflict and division in the Scottish church during the eighteenth century, especially the Secession of 1733, and it took on even more significance from the late 1830s. The civil authorities—both Whig and Tory administrations—supported the property rights of the patrons, arguing that the right to present ministers to parishes was an inherent property right. This was tested in a number of high-profile court cases, both in the Court of Session (Scotland's highest civil court) and the House of

Lords. Over the period of the Ten Years' Conflict, the church's independence from the state was consistently rejected in principle by the civil courts. The majority of those in the Church of Scotland who were prepared to accept patronage belonged to the Moderate (i.e, non-Evangelical) Party. Their leader in the 1840s, Dr George Cook, expressed the view that, 'When any law is declared by the competent authorities to affect civil right, the church cannot set aside such a law ... So to do would be to declare ourselves superior to the law of the land.' He went on to state that the exercise of civil authority over church court decisions relative to ordination of ministers was necessary in response to excessive claims to spiritual independence by the Evangelicals,

> Such cases would never have occurred but for the false pretensions which church courts have put forward ... The jurisdiction of the civil courts has been invoked to meet claims before unheard of, and when such claims are abandoned all such interference will immediately cease.[13]

In practical terms, therefore, the basic Moderate position was that the church should accept whatever the state chooses to impose on it, in order to continue to receive the support of the civil authorities. The Evangelical party, however, believed that this was fundamentally Erastian as it amounted to conceding that the final jurisdiction over the church's spiritual functions belonged to the civil power. Evangelicals contended that no person should be intruded as minister on a parish where the majority of the congregation were opposed to his settlement. They contended for the principle of 'non-intrusion'—that the rights of the Christian

---

[13] Quoted in Fry, M., 'The Disruption and the Union' In: Brown, S. and Fry, M. (eds) (1993), *Scotland in the Age of the Disruption*, Edinburgh: Edinburgh University Press. p. 34.

people ought not to be overborne by the civil authorities. 'Intrusion' here referred to intruding an unwelcome minister on a congregation. But (as was correctly perceived by the Evangelicals) this form of intrusion represented a wider encroachment or intrusion on the church's rightful jurisdiction. It is the church who has the right to set men apart for the work of the ministry and to settle ministers as pastors in particular congregations. The church's independence in this spiritual matter should not be interfered with by the civil authorities. Otherwise, the church's rights under Christ to govern its own affairs would be fatally compromised.

The opposition to the Evangelical Non-Intrusionists in the Church of Scotland by ministers of the Moderate party was intense and brought the Evangelicals under successive interdicts from the Court of Session. These interdicts were intended to prevent church discipline from being carried out when the civil courts disagreed with the church's decision. They also attempted to hinder the preaching of the gospel by Evangelical ministers in parishes where Moderates had been disciplined for appealing to the civil courts against the decisions of the church courts. A prominent Evangelical, Thomas Guthrie, related his experience of being served with an interdict threatening him with prison for preaching in the parish of Strathbogie in Aberdeenshire:

> In going to preach in Strathbogie ... I was met by an interdict from the Court of Session—an interdict to which as regards civil matters, I gave implicit obedience. On the Lord's Day, when I was preparing for divine service, in came the servant of the law, and handed me an interdict. I told him that he had done his duty, and I would do mine. The interdict forbade me, under penalty of the Calton Jail, to preach in the parish churches of Strathbogie. I said, 'The parish churches are stone and lime, and

> belong to the state; I will not intrude there.' It forbade me to preach in the school-houses. I said, 'The school-houses are stone and lime; I will not intrude there.' It forbade me to preach in the churchyard. I said, 'The dust of the dead is the state's; I will not intrude there.' But when the Lords of Session forbade me to preach my master's blessed gospel and offer salvation to sinners anywhere in that district under the arch of heaven, I put the interdict under my feet, and I preached the gospel.[14]

Guthrie, with the leading Evangelical ministers of Scotland at that time, was prepared to suffer significant civil penalties rather than implicitly obey all the terms of the interdict from the Court of Session. It is exceptionally important to note the crucial distinction he drew between obeying the civil powers in civil things (e.g., to do with the use of buildings), to which he gave implicit obedience, and obeying when the Court of Session interfered with the spiritual right of Christ's ministers to preach the gospel at all. It was at that point that Guthrie and the other Evangelicals could not and did not yield submission. This distinction is also emphasised in the *Claim of Right* of 1842:

> … this government of the church, thus appointed by the Lord Jesus, in the hand of church officers, distinct from the civil magistrate or supreme power of the state, and flowing directly from the head of the church to the office-bearers thereof, to the exclusion of the civil magistrate, comprehends, as the objects of it, the preaching of the Word, administration of the sacraments, correction of manners, the admission of the office-bearers of the church to their offices, their suspension and deprivation

[14] Brown, T. (1893) *Annals of the Disruption.* Edinburgh: MacNiven and Wallace. p. 34.

> therefore, the infliction and removal of church censures, and generally, the whole 'power of the keys' …
>
> … this jurisdiction and government, since it regards only spiritual condition, rights, and privileges, doth not interfere with the jurisdiction of secular tribunals, whose determinations as to all temporalities conferred by the state upon the church, and as to all civil consequences attached by law to the decisions of church courts in matters spiritual, this church hath ever admitted, and doth admit, to be exclusive and ultimate, as she hath ever given and inculcated implicit obedience thereto …[15]

When the Disruption eventually took place in 1843, the issue at stake was the right of the church to exercise her own jurisdiction without interference from the state in the ordination and induction of ministers. For this principle, over 400 ministers were prepared to leave the comfort of their position in the Established Church, with all the financial and social status which this brought with it. The desire to maintain the independence of the church could not have been more clearly emphasised in practical terms.

The twentieth century

Up to the present day, while the Church of England has remained firmly under the control of Parliament, the Nonconformist churches in England have largely enjoyed freedom from state encroachment—certainly in relation to spiritual matters. North of the border, the Church of Scotland was liberated from the shackles of patronage by Act of Parliament in 1874 and since 1921 the state has officially recognised the Church of Scotland's claim to spiritual independence. It is no exaggeration to state that the contending and suffering of Reformers, Puritans, Covenanters and

[15] Hetherington, W. H. (1845) *Authoritative Exposition of the Principles of the Free Church of Scotland*. Edinburgh: John D. Lowe. pp. 27-62.

Evangelicals over the generations have brought us immense privileges in our heritage of religious and civil liberty.

The examples from history, however, from the time of the Roman Empire down to the era of fascism and communism in the twentieth century, show a clear and consistent pattern. All kinds of governments—some heathen, some professedly Christian—have been willing to tolerate the church within their realms provided the church agrees to implement whatever the civil power chooses to impose on it. But when the church refuses to yield, then almost invariably the coercive power of the magistrate begins to be wielded to a lesser or greater extent.

3. When do the state's actions intrude on the church's spiritual freedom?

Ways of identifying state intrusion

The church's spiritual freedom is to be safeguarded at all times, but it becomes a duty to assert it particularly when it is under threat, or is actually curtailed. To help us to ascertain when state action is a threat to spiritual freedom we might pose a series of questions.

Question 1. Who has the power to call (or forbid) public assemblies for worship?

Christ has authorized his church to meet together for worship and government (Matthew 18:20; Hebrews 10:25). In Christ's name therefore his ministers have vested in them an intrinsic and inalienable power to call an assembly to meet and to worship God.[16] This power to convoke an assembly obviously comes into

[16] Cf. the quote from John Livingstone above. John Owen's comments on Hebrews 10:25 include the following: '... those assemblies, those comings together in one place, were the only way whereby the church, as a church,

conflict with the state's lawful power over persons and property only if the state extends its power beyond its legitimate exercise. If, on the one hand, the state forbids us to gather and the church, on the other hand, judges it to be the duty of Christians to continue to hold worship services, who should we obey? Whose authority should have precedence in our thinking and actions?

Of course, we must distinguish between who has power over the *buildings* recognised as places of worship, and who has power over *worship itself*. We accept that the state has some power over the use of buildings. We do not argue that a church should absolutely resist the right of the state to force the closure of public buildings if it believes that this is proportionate and justifiable. But allowing a power to the state over worship itself is a different matter altogether. This distinction is very important to bear in mind. It brings us back to the point that Thomas Guthrie made when he agreed not to preach indoors in Strathbogie but, refusing to be cowed by the threat of imprisonment, continued to preach the gospel in the open air. Control over buildings is not the same as control over gospel ordinances as such. Buildings belong ultimately to the civil power, gospel ordinances entirely to the spiritual power. When the two jurisdictions come into such close contact this distinction must be clearly before our minds.

Question 2. Who makes the ultimate decision?

If the state imposes restrictions on whether and how people travel or meet, locally or nationally, for the public good, the presumption

---

made its profession of subjection unto the authority of Christ in the performance of all those duties of sacred worship whereby God was to be glorified under the gospel. Wherefore a voluntary neglect and relinquishing of those assemblies destroys any church-state, if it be persisted in', Owen, J. (1991) *An Exposition of the Epistle to the Hebrews.* Edinburgh: Banner of Truth Trust. Vol. 6, p. 521.

would be that the church would co-operate and observe these out of respect for the lawful authority of the magistrate and out of concern for the good of others. That presumption in favour of co-operation can only last, however, as long as the state's actions do not interfere with the spiritual freedom of the church. So long as the church agreed that it was proportionate to the dangers confronting us there are, arguably, potential situations where some curtailment of public worship becomes necessary, although only for so long as is absolutely needful. But because the activity to be curtailed is *the worship of God,* it is the church which should be left to make the decision whether it is safe to hold services in such a time of crisis or not—guided by, and responsive to, the advice of the government. Curtailment of Christian worship must be the church's decision and not the state's because Christ has given authoritative control over the church's ordinances only to church officers (ministers and elders) and not to civil rulers. Where the church is free to make the decision, her jurisdiction has not been intruded upon.

But where the church's freedom to decide whether worship is to continue or not is overruled by the civil authorities, and where the state has acted on the assumption that power over assemblies for Christian worship ultimately belongs to the civil authorities, then we can clearly say that there has been an encroachment into the spiritual freedom of the church.

Question 3. When does state intrusion become coercive?

Where the government not only overrules the decisions of the church, but this is then enforced by civil penalties, the encroachment then becomes coercive. We call it coercive because all civil power is based on the power of coercion—'the power of the sword'—and the church's own freedom to wield the power of the keys has been taken from her.

Let us bear in mind that unquestioning adherence to the state's policies or actions can never be an option for a Christian in a sinful world. If a 'stay at home' order impinged on the rights of Christians to meet together over a continued period, the church's cooperation in observing such restrictions ought not to be total and unqualified, since to observe any human laws out of blind obedience is to betray true liberty of conscience (WCF 20:2). Of course, many factors would need to be taken into account in seeking to ascertain whether the regulations were proportionate and just. And whether the state's motives were good or not in imposing the restrictions is not the main issue. In such situations, it is not the state's *intention* that matters so much as the state's *actions*. But ultimately, it must be the case that only the church itself can decide whether to obey the order or not in relation to Christian worship.

Yet if the church obeys the state's injunctions in relation to curtailment of Christian ordinances only out of deference to the civil power, then the church officers are effectively recognising a different supreme power in the church—the state, rather than Christ. Instead of acting as the ministers of Christ, they would be merely acting as the vice-regents of this new supreme power in the church. If the church fails to assert, maintain and defend the spiritual freedom which Christ has given to his church, then the church is guilty of failing her king and head.

The state's actions in the current crisis

We must enquire whether the kind of regulations which we have seen introduced in connection with church services are contrary to the will of Christ for his church? Take Scotland, for example.

Thinking firstly of church buildings. Granting that the state has some power to force the closure of public buildings, was it proportionate and justifiable for the government to close church buildings? During the latest lockdown in early 2021, supermarkets were filled with shoppers and professional sports were encouraged to continue, while a handful of worshippers have been forbidden to gather indoors or outdoors. So, the answer to that particular question in this situation would seem to be that a complete closure of church buildings was disproportionate and unwarrantable.[17] For surely extra mitigations might have helped reduce any further possibility of viral transmission without having to take the draconian and unwarranted step of criminalizing all expression of public or corporate Christian worship. The churches have, on the whole, tamely submitted to this however, and any expressions of dissent from the prevailing conformity have tended to represent a minority position within the various Christian denominations. This surrender to the secular priorities of the state and of wider society is all the more shameful when the decision to close the churches in Scotland at least (in January 2021) was based on political considerations rather than medical ones, involving a determination on the part of the leadership of the Scottish Government not to be seen to give favourable priority to the Christian church over other groups.[18] This shows the civil power regarding the church's spiritual jurisdiction to be no greater than that of any secular organisation or activity, calling it such and regulating it for secular reasons. When the state does this in China (for example) it is regarded as persecution, but when it is done in this country (albeit for more benign reasons) the pressure has been to accept that it is possible to do this kind of evil in order that good may result.

---

[17] Indeed, this was the conclusion of Revd Dr William J U Philip & Ors for Judicial Review of the closure of places of worship in Scotland (2021) CSOH 32.

[18] This was revealed through a freedom of information request. https://www.gov.scot/publications/foi-202000094719/ [Accessed 20/04/2021].

And we must also consider worship itself. We would argue that the restrictions introduced in the lockdown in Scotland from 8th January to 26th March 2021 involve an intrusion of civil power into the jurisdiction of the church in five ways.[19]

1. The civil authorities attempted to take control over the church's right to assemble for public worship and to administer Christ's own ordinances.

2. They made their own declaration as to what constitutes worship (i.e., online livestreaming, broadcasts), which is a matter only for church courts to decide.

3. They specified certain forms of Christian worship which they were willing to permit, such as funeral worship and marriage ceremonies, yet they did not permit ordinary public worship.

4. They criminalised all corporate Christian worship, however small the number assembled may be and irrespective of the safety of the location. Indeed, the police have intervened in a number of situations to ensure that church services with a tiny number of worshippers are completely stopped.

---

19 'From 8 January 2021 it will be a legal requirement for places of worship located within an area having Level 4 restrictions to close for communal worship and individual prayer, until further notice. This means that places of worship are effectively closed for both congregational worship and individual prayer...However, they can remain open for the purpose of broadcasting a service, conducting a funeral, marriage or civil partnership registration, or for a commemorative event for a person who has died.' https://web.archive.org/web/20210117041625/https://www.gov.scot/publications/coronavirus-covid-19-phase-3-guidance-for-the-safe-use-of-places-of-worship/pages/individual-and-congregational-worship/ [Accessed 17/01/2021]

5. They permitted buildings intended for public worship to be used for a variety of secular activities but disallowed their use for the sacred worship of God.

In sum, the government in Scotland (and also the wider UK Government during 2020) assumed complete control over the church's services, acting without hesitation to ban public worship services when they saw fit to do so. The justification of preserving life has prevented the majority of Christian people from protesting to any great degree. But if state control over the spiritual things which belong to the church is wrong at any time, it is necessarily wrong all of the time, even during a public health emergency. The church no longer has exclusive jurisdiction if there are exceptions to the rule. Of course, the civil authorities have not intervened in the church's doctrine and internal government, at least in the sense that they have not reviewed whether specific decisions of church authorities are lawful or unlawful.[20] But this does not address the deeper point that their legislation and advice concerning worship, including the most basic right of the church to assemble for worship, clearly extends into the spiritual and exclusive jurisdiction of the church. By their actions the civil authorities have not respected the proper boundaries between church and state.

The role of the state in times of crisis

Is there any Scriptural evidence that the civil powers are to intervene in the spiritual jurisdiction of the church at certain times of emergency in a way that would be unlawful at other periods? Does war or famine or, in our case, pestilence afford extra powers

---

[20] Arguably, however, they have prohibited church authorities from meeting to make decisions and undermined the Church's doctrine of spiritual independence in practice.

to the state to assume control over the church for the duration of the crisis?

As we noted above, the Westminster Confession of Faith (WCF 23:3) allows the magistrate to intervene *circa sacra* in times when the church is unsettled or disordered. However, it never grants permission to the magistrate to intervene *in sacris*. This distinction stands in even greater relief when the church is in a settled condition and her government and ordinances are administered according to the rules of the Word.

The nearest relevant Scriptural example would probably be when David took the shewbread to give to his men to prevent hunger in 1 Samuel 21:3-6. In this incident it is plain that David consulted with the priest and acted in cooperation with him. Although he requisitioned the bread, he only received it when the priest was satisfied that David was safeguarding the requirements he stipulated. Clearly David did not assume superior power over the whole administration of the worship of the sanctuary when he acted in such an extraordinary manner to preserve life.

Let us remember that the civil obligations of laws passed by civil rulers oblige only in civil matters. Civil authority cannot oblige anyone to obedience in spiritual things. If civil obligations are imposed on divine worship, the Christian is to be prepared to submit to whatever civil consequences may arise, as we see in Hebrews 10:32-34 ('and took joyfully the spoiling of your goods'). But it is always unlawful (in terms of God's laws) to concede to the civil powers an authoritative control over the worship of God, and we cannot acquiesce in such control without sin. We may have to show our respect and subjection to civil government by submitting to the civil consequences of state intrusion (whether fines, imprisonment, etc.) but we must not acquiesce in what they impose that is contrary to the law of God.

But we must again ask, does the government actually have the right to act as they have done? Indeed, does the government have the right to forbid Christian corporate worship at all?

The injunction of the apostle Paul in Hebrews 10:25 is very clear and does not admit of any exceptions. 'Forsake not the assembling of yourselves together, as the manner of some is.' As Principal William Cunningham (1805-1861) pointed out, it seems impossible for a church to be independent of the state unless it has the intrinsic power to assemble to perform its ordinary business as a church of Christ.[21] Cunningham had in mind the rights of church courts to meet to decide ecclesiastical business. But, even more fundamentally than that, it surely must be the case that Christ has given his church a right and imposed a duty to meet together to worship him publicly, for worship is even more fundamental to the church's existence and purpose than church governance. In a public health crisis this duty of meeting together is not in any way lessened for the church, though extra safety mitigations would undoubtedly need to be observed.[22]

The circumstances in which Paul exhorted the Hebrew Christians to continue meeting were such that, through fear of persecution—confiscation of property, imprisonment—many had ceased to attend public assemblies. The apostle instructed them to meet nevertheless, even though such meetings exposed worshippers to dangers to liberty or even life itself. It may be argued that, since

---

[21] Cunningham, W. (1991) *Discussions on Church Principles, Popish, Erastian and Presbyterian*. Edmonton, Alberta, Canada: Still Waters Revival Books. p. 181.

[22] See Chapter 3 of this volume ('Should the church ever suspend public worship?').

contemporary Christian worshippers fully intend to return to public assemblies when it is legally permitted so to do, Hebrews 10:25 does not apply in this case. But that seems to evade the force of the moral duty enforced in the verse. The apostle is telling the Hebrews that whatever troubles may arise they are not to cease to gather together for worship. Since Hebrews 10:25 is relevant to the church of God in all subsequent generations, the practical neglect of its obligations when it is possible to meet for worship in limited numbers must be regarded as a serious issue, to say the least.

The ideal situation would be for the church and the state to cooperate together, each mutually recognising the God-given prerogatives of the other and endeavouring not to usurp supremacy one over the other. In a health crisis, the church would clearly wish to help the state as much as it could and not expose worshippers to undue danger or be the means of spreading contagion in the community. The church should, equally, be able to count on the assistance of the civil powers to ensure that divine worship could be safely conducted and continue—at least in all but the most extreme cases, where even the very attendance of a handful of worshippers in a gathered assembly in the outdoors well-distanced from one another constituted a *severe* danger to life and health. That extreme level of danger has clearly not been the case in any modern pandemic or perhaps in any epidemic in recorded human history. The noble example set by the Puritans who continued to minister to their flocks during the Great Plague of 1665-6 in England[23] stands in great contrast to the contemporary church. Even during a health crisis considerably greater than that of the current situation it should be well-nigh inconceivable for the church to be forced to concede that Christian corporate worship

[23] See Janeway, J. (1847) *Heaven upon Earth: Jesus, the Best Friend in the Worst Times*. London: Thomas Nelson. pp. 23-25.

could be subject to a total ban by the state in every imaginable circumstance. There will nearly always be methods by which Christians can safely assemble to worship in person, provided there is a will to find out the way to perform the duty. Sadly, such willingness seems to be in very short supply in the church at the present time.

4. The church's grasp of spiritual independence

External threats to the church's spiritual independence

The dangers of secularism are increasingly felt in contemporary Britain. The church's witness is ignored or condemned, and the pressure brought to bear on Christians—especially those who work in the public sector—to either conform to the godless and immoral ideology of the age is immense. Those who are prepared to stand out against the promotion of evil and immorality are often brought to suffer reproach and loss in various ways. In relation to the church's whole purpose in general, and her claim to spiritual independence from the state in particular, secularism represents a mortal foe. Godless people in places of authority—when left to their own ways—will not hesitate to use the power of the state to inhibit Christians and the Christian church from challenging the prevailing attitudes and conduct of society. This makes it very difficult for the church to assert biblical principles in a society which refuses to recognise the authority of Scripture. And during a pandemic, when other sectors of society are being forced to restrict their activities, there is evidently little sympathy in government or in wider society for the idea of the church retaining her freedom to assemble for worship.

Another danger lies in the widespread acceptance of religious pluralism. When we outlined the Scriptural position on church-state relations in Section 1 above, we saw that it is the duty of the civil authorities to grant Christianity a privileged place in national life. This view is widely rejected today, not only in the world but also within the church itself. The argument goes that if the state is to have any interaction with religion at all, it should be merely to preserve a level playing field among all religions in a multicultural environment.

In our current situation the practical effect of this kind of thinking is that the Christian church should not be allowed to retain a unique freedom to govern its activities when other religions and sectors in society must submit to unprecedented state intervention. Referring to Christ's statements to Pilate in John 18, James Bannerman rejects such a position.

> … our Lord never claimed toleration for his kingdom and truth upon the footing that it had an equal right, and no more than equal, with falsehood, to be owned and protected by Caesar. Nay, our Lord never claimed toleration for his gospel upon any other ground than that it was *the* truth, and not falsehood, and had a right, which falsehood had not, to be not only tolerated, but also owned and recognised and submitted to by Caesar.[24]

If the state will not give the place to Christ's own church which Christ himself demands in his Word, then it is failing in its duty to the king of nations. It is the church's duty in the face of pluralism simply to state the claims of Christ, the truths of his Word and their application to current issues, whether the state and society will hear or forbear. When the church concedes to pluralistic arguments and relinquishes the authoritative and unique claims of the Word of God and the privileged place that should belong to

[24] Bannerman, J. (1974) *The Church of Christ*. Edinburgh: Banner of Truth Trust. Vol. 1, p.142-3.

the religion of Christ in every nation, it leaves itself exposed to every possible encroachment on its jurisdiction and activities on any possible grounds that the state may choose. Only when the church makes a principled and self-denied stand on the grounds where her king and head 'before Pontius Pilate witnessed a good confession' (1 Timothy 6:13), can the church be expected to possess the blessing of the 'blessed and only potentate, the king of kings and lord of lords,' and also to obtain the position which Christ's church ought to have in the counsels of the nation.

Internal threats to the church's spiritual independence

The unwarranted assumption on the part of civil authorities and the wider public is that the state has final jurisdiction over everything in society, including the church. These threats all tend to produce a situation where government control over the church is accepted. Living in a nation which has become increasingly secularized and where Christian values are marginalised more than ever in public life and in the attitudes of the general population, it is little wonder that this situation would develop (see Chapter 9 of this volume—'How far has our culture impacted the church's response to the pandemic?'). The greater tragedy, however, is when threats to spiritual independence also come from within and are produced by the failure of Christians to grasp the importance of the church's spiritual freedom. Perhaps few today really grasp that our civil liberties and opposition to absolute power actually flow in great measure from the spiritual independence of the church.

The idea that the government has the right to regulate church business seems to be unconsciously accepted in the contemporary church, even in churches that claim descent from the Reformation. For example, there has been very little consistent corporate witness raised against state intrusion into worship over the past year in any

Protestant denomination in Britain. Legal challenges to restrictions on worship both north and south of the border have been raised by groups of church leaders acting on their own initiative. Some of these legal challenges have tended to focus on modernistic human rights arguments rather than appealing to the intrinsic spiritual freedom which Christ has bestowed on his church. Such arguments ultimately can be criticised as amounting to an appeal to Caesar to restore the things that are rightfully in Caesar's gift to concede. Spiritual freedom is, after all, of a different nature from the civil freedoms recognised by the state—even civil freedom to worship. The church's spiritual freedom is bestowed by God, not by the state, and it is a fact which exists whether the state is prepared to concede civil freedom to worship or not. This is all the more tragic given that the presbyterian church in Scotland has its spiritual freedom and constitutional position in relation to the state guaranteed by statute law, even in the Treaty of Union of 1707.[25]

We cannot simply blame the government for its overreach. We must also remember that to concede to the state anything that Christ has reserved to his church is a compromise on the part of the Christian church which is not compatible with God's law. As Cunningham put it:

> When any civil magistrate assumes such jurisdiction or authoritative control in the regulation of the affairs of Christ's church, he is guilty of sin; and when the church submits to the

[25] Revd Dr William J U Philip & Ors for Judicial Review of the closure of places of worship in Scotland (2021) CSOH 32. This case succeeded on the basis of a lack of proportionality and contravention of the European Convention on Human Rights, but not on the basis of historic constitutional legislation protecting the church's spiritual independence (though this was appealed to).

> exercise of such jurisdiction, she too becomes partaker of his sin, and is involved in all the guilt of it.[26]

One of the most troubling aspects of the Covid-19 crisis from the point of view of the church's response to events has been disarray on the part of Christian people as to how to respond to and critically assess the regulations which have been imposed on God's ordinances. This has been evidently true of ministers and office bearers as well as of ordinary Christians. It has often seemed that the prevailing view has been that if the government has required something on health grounds, then we are duty bound to do it whatever the case may be. If, however, there is a failure to grasp the biblical principles which ought to inform our response to the state's actions, then there will consequently and inevitably be a failure to respond appropriately and unitedly. Of course, there may be many reasons for this. One reason may be a lack of appreciation of the scriptural doctrine of the church's relations with the state. Coupled with this may be ignorance and disinterest relative to the historical precedents furnished by the struggles of earlier generations of Christians. There may be a spiritual apathy about an issue that seems somewhat abstract and removed from ordinary practical concerns. But even where we might otherwise expect an intelligent understanding and willingness to contend for biblical principles there seems to be a genuine fear of the consequences—both legal and medical—of challenging the government's regulations, which stifles any willingness to oppose them publicly.

Among the great dangers which are likely to face the church in future may be a combination of these external and internal threats,

---

[26] Cunningham, W. (1994) *Historical Theology*. Edinburgh: Banner of Truth Trust. Vol. 2, p. 586.

with all their sapping effects on the church's faith and morale. And if the current level of disharmony and evident acceptance of state control are anything to go by, the weakening of the church's strength and the diminishing of her place in society can only be greatly hastened by continuing along the trajectory which has been followed over the past year. As leading voices in wider society have already expressed their concern that the lockdown measures represent a potential precedent for curbing a whole range of important liberties—freedom of religion among them—we must be very wary that compliance with laws which are coercive and secular in nature could well bring a yoke of further restrictions on the church of Christ in time to come as a result. Thus, the loss of spiritual independence in the short period of the pandemic poses a significant longer-term danger for the church.[27] But the greatest danger of all is the loss of God's favour and blessing as a just chastisement for a failure to search out and apply the biblical principles which ought always to govern the church's interaction with the state.

Conclusion

How the church should respond to the current levels of state intervention in its activities is a question fraught with difficulties, and each attempted response seems to engender debate and

---

[27] As John Knox put it, 'take from us the liberty of assemblies, and take from us the gospel,' 'if the liberty of the church must depend upon her allowance or disallowance, we shall want not only assemblies, but also the preaching of the gospel.' Knox, J. (1848) *Works of John Knox*. Edinburgh: Wodrow Society. Vol. 2, p. 295-7. For instance, if prayer and preaching the gospel with application to particular sins is seen as 'conversion therapy' now, it is conceivable that the time may come when any kind of activity seeking conversion may be criminalised.

dissension. But there can be little doubt that the church's jurisdiction has been heavily encroached upon during the crisis and that the church has failed to mount an effective and principled challenge to this encroachment.

When the state is not prepared to grant concessions which secure the church's freedom to assemble safely, the Christian is then faced with the dilemma of civil disobedience or compliance—essentially the same dilemma which has confronted previous generations of Christians. The price of disobeying the state in the present may not be as high as that faced by the godly in the past, but it will never be without cost. In contrast, the spiritual cost of conforming to laws which inhibit the blood-bought freedom of Christ's church cannot perhaps be fully measured in this life, but the price will, ultimately, be far higher. The choice between sinning or suffering is a solemn dilemma, but sinning through compromise will bring greater judgment on the individual, on the church and on society in the longer term.

If a similar situation arose in future, would the church repeat the same compliant attitude it has adopted in the past year? The believer is not to seek persecution or to draw attention to their opposition in a way reminiscent of political protesters. Yet the cost of obedience to Christ in secular Britain may well increasingly prove to be a passive, peaceable form of resistance to the restraints imposed by secular authority.

The church's freedom in the spiritual realm must always be upheld. But if this is to take place, the church plainly needs to be more clearly and firmly grounded in the principle of her divinely bestowed spiritual independence. As we have seen, this principle has been very clearly articulated by past generations, who suffered much for their adherence to it. Let us therefore seek by grace to assert, maintain and defend it to the best of our abilities in our own day. While the church should be able to call upon the civil authorities to guide them in their decisions, the church must not allow itself to barter away Christ's rights in his own kingdom for the sake of peaceful compliance with regulations that are contrary to his revealed will. How much better it would be for the welfare of the entire community if, instead of criminalizing corporate worship, the state would help to ensure that the church's most basic activity was being carried out safely! How much better if the rulers of our nation, floundering as they are under divine judgment, recognised the church's freedom to render to God the things that are God's.

~ 6 ~

Exactly how much must the church render to Caesar?

Matthew A. Vogan

> Fear God. Honour the king (1 Peter 2:17).

> The Lord's people are so to honour magistrates as that they forget not the fear of the Lord and the duties comprehended under it, in the first place: without which no duty can be faithfully discharged to any man (Luke 18:2), for this is not only the order of the words here, but of the purpose itself: Fear God. Honour the King. (Alexander Nisbet[1])

> It is true, it is the duty of every Christian to be loyal, yet I think the order of things is as well to be observed as their natures; the order of religion, as well as the nature of it; religion must not be the cock-boat, it must be the ship; God must have what is his, as well as Caesar what is his, and these are the best subjects that are the best Christians. (Archibald Campbell, Marquis of Argyll[2])

In Matthew 22:17-21 Christ's enemies came to him with the purpose of ensnaring him with matters of political controversy. How much should they render to the government to which they were subject? Christ's response was, 'Render therefore unto Caesar

---

[1] Nisbet, A. (1982) *An Exposition of 1 & 2 Peter*. Edinburgh: Banner of Truth Trust. p. 98

[2] Smellie, A. (1975) *Men of the Covenant*. Edinburgh: Banner of Truth Trust. pp. 86-87.

the things which are Caesar's; and unto God the things that are God's.'

The distinction between the things that are God's and the things that are Caesar's needs to be made and understood as clearly as possible. The 'things that are God's' is a particular reference to the concerns of the temple, which had its own coinage in the shekel. Christ shows that he is no enemy to civil government but rather teaches that it should receive what is due to it. Various passages in the apostolic epistles likewise enjoin due honour for those in authority (e.g., Romans 13:1ff; 1 Timothy 2:2; 1 Peter 2:17). Yet such honour is not unqualified. As the Scottish Covenanter David Dickson (c.1583-1662) put it, 'Men should so regard kings and rulers, as they do not mistake God, but respect, honour, and obey him above all.'[3] The claims of Caesar are limited. Not absolutely everything is Caesar's and to be rendered to him as his due. Further, Caesar does not get to decide in principle what is due to him. God limits the role of civil government. In an absolute sense, there is nothing that is not God's, and therefore civil government and its subjects must render glory to God above all as their highest purpose.

This chapter opens with an overview of what Caesar owes to God before exploring various aspects of the question of how much the church owes to Caesar. We need to consider the subject of church and state relations from Scripture to establish how much the church owes to Caesar in principle. Having distinguished civil things and sacred (or spiritual) things we look at how far these areas extend and how much the church owes to Caesar in them

---

[3] Dickson, D. (1981) *Exposition of the Gospel of Matthew*. Edinburgh: Banner of Truth Trust. p. 296.

before drawing the overall conclusion in answer to the question posed.

1. How much must Caesar render to God?

As David Dickson observes, Christ's maxim in Matthew 22:21 does not imply that governments have nothing to do with God and the things that we owe to God. 'It is reason that magistrates be as careful that God have what is due to him in religion and obedience of his commands, as he is careful that their due be given to them.'[4] In practice, however, such carefulness seems to be all too rare.

While governments are primarily concerned with external and temporal matters, they cannot avoid touching on the matters of religion. All governments rule over those who engage in religious activity. This comes into view mostly plainly when religious practices involve murder or similarly obvious and gross transgressions.[5] But more often it enters into the mundane aspects of life. 'There will be still something earthly in the church,' said John Willison (1680–1750), 'as long as she is upon the earth.'[6] Aspects of property, finance, safety, health, and registration of

---

[4] Dickson, D. (1981) *Exposition of the Gospel of Matthew,* (Banner of Truth Trust, Edinburgh) p. 296.

[5] For instance, the Hindu practice of *suttee* or *sati*, the self-immolation of a widow on her husband's funeral pyre which was outlawed by the British empire in 1829. More contemporary examples would be Islamist suicide bombers.

[6] Quoted in M'Crie, T. (the elder), (1807) *Statement of the Difference Between the Profession of the Reformed Church of Scotland...*, Edinburgh: George Caw. p. 147. John Willison of Dundee was a leading evangelical minister in the Church of Scotland in the eighteenth century, well known for many practical writings. The quotation probably comes from Willison, J. (1729) *A Defence of National Churches....* Edinburgh: James M'Euen.

marriages may come within the sphere of civil government amongst various areas of expanding regulation.

It is worth emphasising that civil government as a human institution is bound to fulfil the highest purpose of human beings—to glorify God. This is the most effective way to govern for the good of their citizens. Civil authorities are no more freed from this obligation than those over whom they govern. Individual citizens owe honour to their rulers, but those rulers owe honour to God and his claims. The Bible says to governors as governors, 'Whether, therefore, ye eat or drink, or whatsoever ye do, do all to the glory of God' (1 Corinthians 10:31). Both the light of nature and revelation teach this, 'so that they are without excuse' (Romans 1:20), 'because that when they knew God, they glorified him not as God' (Romans 1:21). This was the great charge against the heathen king of Babylon (Daniel 5:23). The moral law of God has been given for God's glory and the good of humanity, it binds every rational creature at all times and in every situation, including all the dimensions of government. That law is not only holy, but also just and good (Romans 7:12).

While the New Testament does not give express commands or directions to civil government as such, we are able to draw principles from its teaching on the duty of Christians towards government. Government is termed 'the minister (διάκονός, *diakonos*) of God to thee for good' (Romans 13:4). Civil authorities are 'God's ministers' (Romans 13:4) at all times. Paul uses the word *leitourgoi* (λειτουϱγοὶ) here (usually related to priestly service) as language of constant devoted service to God. The idea of ministering is further emphasised as he goes on to say that they are 'attending continually upon this very thing.' It is clear therefore that Paul's language in this passage is prescriptive (setting out how government *ought* to be), not descriptive (setting out what government is or does *in fact*). It does not imply that whatever a government does always serves God and that whatever they do is approved by God. Nor does it follow that we should obey the government no matter what. Indeed, as the Scottish Commissioner to the Westminster Assembly George Gillespie (1613–1648) points out, this passage does not use the language of obedience but rather of subjection (ὑποτασσέσθω, *hupotassesthō*, 'to place under').[7] One may give subjection to authority by suffering the consequences of declining to obey. If there is no third way, we must choose to suffer rather than sin.

The ruler in the state is 'the minister of God ... for good,' 'rulers are not a terror to good works, but to the evil' (Romans 13:3). 'Good' is something clearly defined in Scripture by God. He has 'shown' us what this is and what it is his right to 'require' of us. It includes the justice and mercy of the later Ten Commandments but also the duty of walking humbly with God as our God as required in the first four commandments (Micah 6:8). Nowhere is it suggested in Scripture that the government is limited to the second table of the law in serving God while everyone else is bound by the whole Ten Commandments. The Apostle Paul tells us elsewhere how civil government serves for our spiritual as well as temporal good. By having a regard for the first four commandments it promotes godliness. The purpose of civil government is 'that we may lead a quiet and peaceable life in all godliness and honesty' (1 Timothy 2:2). As John Calvin (1509-1564) points out, this requires positive action in relation to religion and morality that goes beyond merely

---

[7] Gillespie, G. (2013), *A Dispute Against the English Popish Ceremonies*. Dallas, Texas, USA: Naphtali Press. p. 282. 'The apostle urges (Rom. 13), not *obedience* to magistrates for conscience' sake but only *subjection* for conscience' sake' (italics added). Gillespie says of Romans 13, 'There is not in all that chapter one word of obedience to magistrates.'

restraining disorder.[8] Thomas M'Crie observes, 'Rulers are not, in their official capacity, to be indifferent to godliness, any more than to honesty; both are to be countenanced and promoted by them (Ezra 6:8-10).'[9] The Westminster Confession helpfully summarises this point and the historic Reformed view in asserting that governments 'ought to maintain piety, justice and peace according to the wholesome laws of each commonwealth' (WCF 23:2).

Governments cannot indeed avoid involving themselves in matters covered by the first four commandments. Deregulation of the sabbath, for instance, is not a neutral stance. It inevitably impinges on the freedom to worship God. And indeed, the fourth commandment requires those in authority to ensure that it is kept by those for whom they have responsibility (Exodus 20:8-11). The state cannot avoid entering into such areas, and so the question is not whether they will but whether they will do so in a way that upholds rather than counteracts the claims of God's law.

The historic Reformed view considers the state as having a parental role.[10] Experience tells us that parents who deliberately avoid setting boundaries and sanctions for their children inevitably expose them to the sinful tendencies of their hearts. This is why we need law and order maintained. Similarly, parents who raise their children without religious teaching and practice are not giving them a neutral choice but a predetermined one—they are training them in rebellion against God. It is just the same with government. Religion is necessary not only to the welfare but the

---

[8] See Calvin, J. [translated: Smail, T. A.; edited: Torrance, D. W. and Torrance, T. F.] (1964) *The second epistle of Paul the apostle to the Corinthians and the epistles to Timothy, Titus and Philemon.* Edinburgh: The Saint Andrew Press. p. 207.

[9] M'Crie, T. (the elder) (1807) *Statement of the Difference Between the Profession of the Reformed Church of Scotland....* Edinburgh: George Caw. p. 139.

[10] See Heidelberg Catechism, Q104, and Westminster Larger Catechism, Q124.

very existence of civil government and morality. Our nation has discovered by experience that when the gospel and Christian heritage are rejected, you cannot hope to preserve morality. The historic Reformed view understood that Scripture holds out an ideal role for the state of defending and protecting the church and true religion and indeed supporting it. Much of this can be gleaned from prophecy that describes what will happen in New Testament times.[11]

Civil government is not a value-free area. The authorities are not only driven by one ideology or another, they are constantly shaping values within society. Their decisions help or hinder the progress of truth. The question is not whether or not they will be influenced by values, but which values they will pursue. Their decisions will not only be influenced by but will seek to influence ethics, for better or worse. As the American political commentator

---

[11] 'The whole tenor of the declarations, promises, and predictions of the Old Testament, lead to the conclusion that Christianity shall be owned, countenanced, and supported in a national way. God addresses the nations in a collective capacity, reproves them for their idolatry, and calls them to his worship (Isaiah 34:1; 41:1, 21-29). He proposes Christ, as his anointed servant, to them (Isaiah 42:1); declares that he has given him the nations as his inheritance, and that he shall inherit them all (Psalm 2:8; 82:8; Isaiah 52:15; 55:5). Christ addresses himself not only to individuals, but to the whole islands (Isaiah 49:1); nations join themselves to him, own and worship him (Isaiah 2:2; Micah 4:1-2; Zechariah 2:11; 8:20-22); bless themselves, and glory in him (Jeremiah 4:2); all nations and dominions serve him (Daniel 7:14, 27); they consecrate all things in them, and employ them in his service (Isaiah 60:6-12; Zechariah 14:20-21); he owns these nations as his, and blesses them, while he breaks in pieces and wastes others (Psalm 33:12; 145:15; Isaiah 19:25; Psalm 2:9, 12; Isaiah 60:12).' M'Crie, T. (the elder) (1807) *Statement of the Difference Between the Profession of the Reformed Church of Scotland…* . Edinburgh: George Caw. pp. 136-137.

George F. Will (b. 1941) has noted, statecraft is soulcraft.[12] Even a laissez-faire approach to moral values takes a certain position and has an influence.[13] Moral values is an area into which government cannot avoid entering directly or indirectly, the only question is whether they will do so to the glory of God.

2. How much must the church render to Caesar in principle?

There have been four main views about the relationship between church and state. First, the view that the state should control the church, whether partially or fully (Erastian); second, the view that the church should control the state (Roman Catholic); third, the view that there should be a separation of church and state (Voluntary); and fourth, the view that church and state should be in some mutually binding relationship (Establishment Principle). This chapter assumes the latter view.

It is helpful to clarify the contrasts between church and state in terms of authority and jurisdiction. These can be summarised as in the following table.

---

[12] Wills, G. F. (1983) *Statecraft as Soulcraft: What Government Does.* New York: Simon & Schuster.

[13] From the French meaning to leave alone, a policy that advocates minimum interference by government.

	State power	Church power
What kind of power is it?	Coercive, magisterial authority, represented by the 'sword' of punishment and physical force and compulsion	Spiritual, ministerial authority represented by the 'keys' of doctrine, government, order and discipline
How far does it extend?	To people's outward activities and their property	To people's spiritual relations to God and others

Too often the relationship between church and state is characterised by tensions and competition. This ought not and need not be the case if their areas of common concern are considered. There are indeed similarities between church and state that are often overlooked. The better we understand these, the more we are able to resolve tensions and see how there need not be competition but rather mutual help. In particular, both have their authority from God and are answerable to God for their official actions. They are both to serve God and are appointed for the glory of God primarily, and also the good of those over whom they exercise authority. Both are bound to observe the law and commandments of God, and both have certain directions from the Word of God to guide them in their administration. Both have the role of authority and are to be honoured and obeyed according to the fifth commandment. Thus, both are able in principle to help and strengthen each other in their God-given role.

Much current discussion of church-state relations, particularly in North America, appears to depend on the 'sphere sovereignty' view derived from the Dutch Neo-Calvinist thinker and politician

Abraham Kuyper (1837-1920).[14] This idea was further refined and mediated through the Dutch philosopher and jurist Herman Dooyeweerd (1894-1977). On this idea, human life is situated within multiple separate spheres, such as the individual, the family, the church and the state. The sovereignty and jurisdiction of each sphere extends only as far as that sphere extends, and they cannot overreach their bounds.[15] This view is a commendable attempt to restrain and prohibit the accretion and exercise of absolute power in human affairs, and preserve that power for God alone. It is, however, a view that has been developed with an *a priori* commitment to the pluralist principles of social liberalism. Perhaps this is why it makes such a good fit for those with libertarian inclinations.[16]

Additionally, the key question arises, what precisely are the boundaries of these spheres, and who decides? This theory seems to have conflict rather than harmony hard-wired into it. It can even come perilously close to the Roman Catholic view of exempting the church from the rule of law. Instead, these spheres ought not to be seen as mutually exclusive. Experience shows that they legitimately interlace, intersect and overlap in a myriad of ways requiring careful definition. An example would be marriage, where in many jurisdictions, churches assist in registering

---

[14] See O'Roark, D. (2020) 'The Necessity and Vital Importance of Jurisdictionalism (Sphere Sovereignty) to Christian and Societal Liberty: The Biblical Limitations of Civil and Ecclesiastical Power' in Springer, E., Yeager, J. and O'Roark, D. *Coronavirus and the Leadership of the Christian Church: A Sacred Trust Broken.* Willow Street, Pennsylvania: Old Paths. pp. 131-206.

[15] See Wolfe, S. T. (1978) *A Key to Dooyeweerd.* Phillipsburg, New Jersey, USA: Presbyterian & Reformed. A rather opaque book which does not touch on the issues of church and state but aims to summarise Dooyeweerd's philosophy.

[16] Libertarianism is a political philosophy that seeks to maximize individual autonomy and political freedom and is highly sceptical of state power and big government.

marriages on behalf of the state, as this is an area with both spiritual and civil implications and applications. There is a spiritual aspect of solemnizing marriage with vows before God, biblical counsel and having such relations sanctified by the Word and prayer, but there is also the need for legal recognition and registration which may surround the God-ward aspect.

Although the philosopher Dooyeweerd has sought to elaborate the principle of sphere sovereignty with some detail, it is fair to say that many apply the theory at a more simplified level. While he allows the possibility for sphere boundaries 'to touch each other in constant interaction,' he insists that 'one sphere will not encroach on the other.'[17] This theory precludes the biblical ideal of the state giving support to the church within its own jurisdiction. On face value it seems to offer a definitive way to separate what is Caesar's and what is God's, but it leads to conflict by virtue of where it draws the boundaries.

We must seek to draw the boundaries on a biblical basis, however. If, for example, we identify church and state as coordinate jurisdictions which are distinct and independent, then they may have and pursue common objectives with harmony and

---

[17] Dooyeweerd says that the state is bounded by the juridical (i.e., the law and justice aspect of life). He seeks to systematise this by defining different types of 'enkapsis' or 'encapsulation' by which structures and entities interrelate, using analogies from living organisms. His view is that the individual has a correlative two-way relationship with society in the way that an animal does with its environment. But apparently the state has a territorial rather than correlative relationship with other spheres. Presumably the church is within the faith sphere. See van der Vyver, J. D. (2001) 'Sphere Sovereignty of religious institutions: a contemporary Calvinistic theory of Church-State Relations,' in: Robbers, G. (Ed.) (2001) *Church Autonomy: A Comparative Survey.* Frankfurt, Germany: Peter Lang. pp. 645-81.

cooperation.[18] Conflict arises when there is a failure to recognise what is God's and render it to him and when Caesar does not receive his due. We can draw the line between the jurisdictions by taking account of the following three principles—(i) what honour is due to Caesar, (ii) what is due to Caesar in civil things, and (iii) what is due to Caesar in sacred things.

(i) How much honour must the church render to Caesar?

The church must show respect to the government even if they do not receive any respect in return, despite the fact that government is meant to praise those that do well (Ecclesiastes 10:20; Exodus 22:28; 1 Peter 2:18). Part of this honour involves earnestly praying for God's blessing upon their government (1 Timothy 2:1-2). Christians give submission for the sake of the Lord (who has established this order in human society) (1 Peter 2:18).

Honour given to civil government flows from the fear that we owe to God, who has put some of his glory on the civil authorities (1 Peter 3:17; Psalm 82:6). The Lord's people must not, however, honour government in a way that forgets the fear of the Lord, or if what is involved in the fear of the Lord has primacy over their duty to Caesar. They must show Caesar that he too is to exercise his duties in the fear of God (Luke 18:2; 2 Samuel 23:3). Christians must also give obedience as far as they are able unless it requires them to sin (Titus 3:1). The honour and submission they owe may involve patiently enduring their unjust punishment (Acts 23:5). They must show honour by rendering the taxes that are required, so far as this does not oblige them to sin (Romans 13:7). Provided that nothing contrary to God's law is required, the church will be

[18] See footnote 11 above, and Chapter 5 of this volume ('How should the church and state interact during a crisis?')

able to give continual support and respect to government (Ecclesiastes 8:2-3).

(a) The church must render what is lawful according to God's law
We are not to give an absolute or unlimited obedience to civil government. There are times when obedience to civil authorities is not possible because of the prior obedience we owe to God, the higher authority (Daniel 6:10, Daniel 3:18, Acts 4:19-20, Hebrews 11:23). Obedience may only be given in things which are 'lawful,' in the sense of 'consistent with God's law.' If God were to require obedience to government in unlawful things it would counteract both his law and the purpose for which he gave civil government. It is not possible to give blind and implicit obedience to the state in whatever it requires because this would be to place it before God and deny God the things that are his. We must therefore enquire into and examine the lawfulness of what the state requires. We are to walk circumspectly, understanding what the will of the Lord is (Ephesians 5:17).

The church is required to judge and prove all things (1 Corinthians 2:15; 1 Thessalonians 5:21), to discern the things that differ (Philippians 1:10), using the grace of discernment to distinguish good and evil (Hebrews 5:14), in order to hold fast to that which is good. If we give obedience without being persuaded that it is lawful and approved by the Word it is sin (Romans 14:23). To obey and submit the conscience purely on human dictate is to become the servants of men (1 Corinthians 7:23). We must give account of everything to God (Romans 14:13) but if we have not established whether something is good or bad, we cannot be prepared to give account for it.[19]

[19] See Gillespie, G. (2013), *A Dispute Against the English Popish Ceremonies*. Dallas, Texas, USA: Naphtali Press. pp. 285-288.

(b) The church must render that which examination has shown is Caesar's and not God's

Apart from the honour due to civil government, there are civil things in which Caesar has jurisdiction and those things must be rendered to Caesar. Not everything that Caesar may demand is rightfully (according to God's design) Caesar's due. The church must examine all requirements to satisfy itself that it may yield to certain requirements. It must have clarity that what Caesar demands is not in fact God's, because that is not for the church to give. In identifying such areas, it is important that we have clear criteria to make such distinctions. This can be intricate because spiritual things can be closely surrounded by civil dimensions. The following section, therefore, provides criteria to help make this distinction.

(ii) How much must the church render to Caesar in civil things that are around sacred things?

We have established that besides the duty of honour, the church must only render to Caesar that which after due examination is clearly lawful and the things that are Caesar's not God's. Yet this prompts enquiry concerning the things that are Caesar's as they touch on spiritual matters while remaining civil and secular in their nature. How much is owed to the state in this area?

Using the conventional Latin terms, the historic Reformed view made a distinction between the *ius circa sacra* (right or just authority *around* sacred things) and the *ius in sacris* (right or just authority *in* sacred things). According to this view, God permits civil government to exercise authority *around* sacred things, but not *in* sacred things. Civil rulers who sought to invade spiritual things in the Old Testament were punished by God, e.g. Korah (Numbers 16), Saul (1 Samuel 13:9-15), Uzzah (2 Samuel 6:6-8; 1 Chronicles 13:9-10) and Uzziah (2 Chronicles 26:16-22).

As the historic Reformed view made these distinctions it made two further clarifications about the *ius circa sacra*. (a) It is cumulative not privative, i.e., it adds to rather than detracting from the liberties and privileges of the church. Anything the civil authorities do is to help rather than hinder. (b) It must also be objective, i.e., the civil magistrate 'may politically, outwardly exercise his power about spiritual objects or matters, but not spiritually, inwardly, formally act any power in the church.'[20] It is only in such terms that we 'are willing to give to Caesar those things that are Caesar's, *circa sacra*, even about matters of religion.'[21]

What do these distinctions look like in practical terms? This view recognises that the state has a role in preserving peace, order, justice, safety and security. This includes a due authority over persons and property, even when the 'persons' are Christians or church officers, and the 'property' belongs to the church. We understand that if a minister commits a crime he can be brought to justice for it. The state may also require certain safeguards around those who have access to children or vulnerable persons in all kinds of associations including churches.

The type of requirements in civil things that the state imposes will have an indirect or direct impact on the sacred activities of the church. Rationing during war time or some kind of necessary prohibition, for example, might affect the availability of elements for the Lord's Supper and lead to a temporary suspension of that ordinance. A minister who is required to be a chaplain during time

---

[20] Sundry Ministers of Christ within the City of London [edited: Coldwell, C.] (2020) *Jus Divinum Regiminis Ecclesiastici: The Divine Right of Church Government*. Dallas, Texas, USA: Naphtali Press. p.129.

[21] Sundry Ministers of Christ within the City of London [edited: Coldwell, C.] (2020) *Jus Divinum Regiminis Ecclesiastici: The Divine Right of Church Government*. Dallas, Texas, USA: Naphtali Press. p. 131.

of war will be unable to minister to a congregation, yet this does not constitute a direct ban on such a minister preaching in his congregation. Likewise, a minister who is imprisoned for a crime is not directly banned from ministering. If, however, there is a measure of injustice, including being prosecuted for adherence to biblical teaching, this can be brought before the relevant civil courts. The courts do not, however, have jurisdiction over preaching or church discipline.

On a more mundane level, there may be health and safety, or building and fire regulations, for instance, that regulate a church property in the same way as other properties. This may limit the numbers which can attend in relation to the number of fire exits or other considerations. There may be circumstances of national emergency when security requires restrictions that might apply to church buildings as much as to other properties, such as blackout during times of air raid in the Second World War.

If a building is deemed unsafe by the authorities it cannot be used for worship, which has a clear impact. In usual circumstances the reasons for closing the building and the remedies for reopening will be made clear and the process will not be inordinately extended. The government has civil authority to close places of worship for just and lawful reasons (see below for further considerations). As mentioned, the just and lawful reasons are related to the preservation of order, justice, peace, and health and safety.

But if there are injustices, a lack of just and lawful reasons, disproportionate impact, or even outright oppression, redress can be sought by the church through the appropriate channels of civil courts or official review processes. Similarly, the church could seek redress if there was some evidence or suspicion of discrimination or unfavourable treatment compared with other property owners. Civil liberties guaranteed by law can be asserted through the appropriate processes if they are infringed. Usually there will be some precedent or provision that helps determine when regulations are being applied in an unjust way. It is important to note however that all these examples are a matter of civil liberties rather than necessarily an invasion of the exclusive spiritual jurisdiction of the church.[22]

The question of civil resistance would only be raised once all means of lawful redress had been exhausted and there was undeniable intent to persecute the church. If the church must disobey or oppose government for conscience's sake, they must do it with meekness (1 Peter 3:15). Wisdom is required to know the right response and language for the circumstances and nature of the action, whether private lamentation (Amos 5:13), peaceable petition (1 Samuel 25:18), open testimony (Acts 4:8), open rebuke (2 Chronicles 26:18; 1 Samuel 14:45) or resistance (2 Chronicles 26:16-22).

(iii) How much must the church render to Caesar in sacred things?

If Caesar has the right to legislate *around* sacred things, but not *in* sacred things, what in fact are these 'sacred things'? In a word, they are Christ's *ordinances*. Christ as king and head of his church has instituted and appointed certain standing and perpetual ordinances in his church for the purpose of edifying it, and he has given the 'keys' to church office-bearers to administer these ordinances. There are two broad types of sacred ordinances.

[22] This is a legal term: exclusive jurisdiction exists where one court has the power to adjudicate a case to the exclusion of all other courts.

(a) Ordinances relating to the key of order and doctrine. These include public prayer and thanksgiving; singing of psalms; public reading; public preaching; catechising; sacraments.

(b) Ordinances relating to the key of jurisdiction or of discipline. These include ordination of office-bearers; authoritative discerning and judging of doctrine according to the Word of God; admonition and public rebuke of sinners; excommunication; absolution (receiving penitents again); relieving the poor.[23]

Sacred ordinances do not alter across time, location and culture, they are to remain in place until the end of the New Testament age. But in order to implement them in a certain time and place, specific decisions have to be made that may alter according to time and place. Selecting a time and place to gather for worship, and the need for lighting, will take local factors into consideration, for instance. It was not necessary for Scripture to define the countless factors that might arise in specific settings. These are the necessary circumstances of the essential ordinances listed above.

This introduces another historic Reformed distinction—the distinction between the *circumstances* of worship over against the substantial *elements* of worship.

George Gillespie articulated three principles that help to define a 'circumstance'. Circumstances must: (a) 'only be a circumstance of divine worship, and no substantial part of it—no sacred, significant, efficacious ceremony;' (b) 'be such as are not determinable by Scripture;' and (c) be those for which church

---

[23] Sundry Ministers of Christ within the City of London [edited: Coldwell, C.] (2020) *Jus Divinum Regiminis Ecclesiastici: The Divine Right of Church Government*. Dallas, Texas, USA: Naphtali Press. pp. 107-111.

authorities are 'able to give a sufficient reason and warrant' for implementing.[24]

Such limiting principles are necessary so as to maintain these circumstances within biblical parameters and prevent them being abused. We must do all things decently and in order and to edification (1 Corinthians 14:26; 1 Corinthians 14:40). There is no authority in the church except for the purpose of edification (Ephesians 4:12). Circumstances are to be ordered by the light of nature and Christian prudence, following the rules for doing so set down in the Word of God. In applying prudence to such circumstances certain Scriptural rules must be followed. They are the rules for governing all 'indifferent' things (i.e., things that are neither good or bad in themselves and not determinable by divine law or Scripture). There is *the rule of piety*: like the rest of our lives, indifferent things must be to the glory of God and according to his will (1 Corinthians 10:31; Romans 14:7-8; Colossians 3:17). There is *the rule of charity*: we must not use any indifferent thing if it will stumble or harm the edification of someone else (Romans 14:21; Romans 14:19; Romans 15:2; 1 Corinthians 10:23). There is also *the rule of purity*: we must be fully persuaded with adequate reasons in our own mind and conscience that something is permissible (Romans 14:14; Romans 14:5; Romans 14:23).

We have considered how decisions by the government may impact some of the circumstances of sacred things, such as an agreed place for worship, the lighting availability during the hours of darkness, and the availability of the physical elements for the sacraments. We can also consider what the government may decide in a severe public health emergency. For example, the government may

---

[24] Gillespie, G. (2013) *A Dispute Against the English Popish Ceremonies*. Dallas, Texas, USA: Naphtali Press. pp. 260-262.

provide guidance which reduces the risk to public health, and may ask the church, along with other sectors of society, to prepare risk assessments designed to order the circumstances of worship in a way that reduces the risk of infection. This may address the outward aspect of how and where people are seated. The government may ask that churches record the contact details of those worshiping in order that this information can be communicated to the authorities in the event of infection. The government may give guidance about social distancing among worshippers, even if it impacts on the capacity possible for public worship, in a similar way to the capacity possible for fire safety. These are similar to requirements for disabled toilets or ramps, and requirements for designated and marked fire exits. The government may require citizens to use face masks in certain settings, which might include church worship. The responsibility for complying with this lies with the citizen themselves. While there are different views about this point and while it clearly impacts the experience of worship, it still relates to a *circumstance* of worship rather than one of the ordinances itself.[25]

The church should give due weight to the state's guidance on the outward aspects of spiritual things. Yet, in assisting and giving guidance to the church in relation to these matters, civil government cannot instruct, but may only offer advice. As George Gillespie put it, 'the making of laws about things pertaining to

[25] It should be obvious that suspending public worship on the Lord's Day is not a mere circumstance, to be ordered by the light of nature and Christian prudence. Whether the ordinances of worship take place or not goes to the heart of the ordinance itself. It is not a circumstance to do with the context in which the ordinance takes place.

God's worship is an action of spiritual jurisdiction.'[26] Only the church has such spiritual jurisdiction.

The church cannot render anything whatsoever *in* sacred things to Caesar because to do so would be to render the things that are God's to Caesar. Civil government has no *ius in sacris* and the church is in no way a servant of civil authority. The church owes their service and allegiance to Jesus Christ, and to give obedience in sacred things to government would be to give Caesar what is the royal prerogative of Christ. 'The Lord Jesus Christ, as king and head of his church, hath therein appointed a government in the hands of church officers, distinct from the civil magistrate' (WCF 30:1). The government which Christ has appointed in his church is an exclusive jurisdiction in spiritual things and there are no exceptions to it. It is just as invalid for the state to command the church in spiritual things as it would be for any constituted body of ministers and elders to pass a law trying to, for example, suspend public transport within their locality, or confiscate someone's property, or declare war on behalf of the nation.

Civil government cannot exercise church discipline because Christ has not given it the 'keys'. The weapons of civil government are not spiritual but outward, as represented by the 'sword.' This means that the state cannot prescribe to the church whether or how preaching should be undertaken, nor how the sacraments should be administered. Caesar cannot command whether prayer or praise take place, nor how they take place, nor how many times they take place. Only Christ has that authority. These ordinances, and authority concerning them, are not for the church to give

[26] Gillespie, G. (2013) *A Dispute Against the English Popish Ceremonies*. Dallas, Texas, USA: Naphtali Press. p. 304.

away, because it all belongs to Christ. The church only administers these ordinances in his name.

Neither does civil government have any authority whatsoever to forbid or alter any other ordinances Christ has appointed, or to forbid public worship to take place. These are entirely spiritual matters, and it belongs to those whom Christ has appointed to take responsibility for all aspects of the administration of his ordinances and the government of his church. It is therefore not a sufficient or biblical reason to suspend assemblies for public worship that civil government has forbidden it.

Even the closure of *the place of worship* by the authority of the government with lawful reasons cannot be a sufficient reason to suspend *public worship* itself. This is because the state is not a recognised or lawful authority in or over the administration of the affairs of the church of Christ in its worship or government. Even yielding the right of closing a building to government may be technically giving them the ultimate decision on a circumstance of worship (which is therefore *in sacris*) and must be carefully weighed. Ordinarily, assembling decently and in order in the most expedient and convenient way requires a suitable building for the meetings of the Lord's people, but if such buildings cannot be used it does not prevent such meetings taking place. Alternative locations for public worship assemblies (including outdoors) are possible and must be pursued, unless the church officers have come to their own conclusion (warranted by the Word of God) that public worship is not allowable under any circumstances (see Chapter 3 of this volume—'Should the church ever suspend public worship?').

There may be extreme and rare occasions when there may be just and lawful reasons for suspending public worship in any congregation.[27] Those reasons may be various, but they must always be justified from the law of God as that is revealed in Scripture. Only the law of God and adequate scriptural grounds can bind the conscience of those who would otherwise attend public worship to prevent them from this duty. Civil government does not have the jurisdiction to determine these reasons from the moral law. Although those with authority in the church do have this jurisdiction (in a ministerial way), they must make use of the relevant sources of knowledge and information, and may act in cooperation with lawful civil authority, before binding the conscience of any worshipper in any particular congregation and forbidding such a worshipper from attending to what is otherwise their moral duty of assembling for public worship. Ministers and elders are accountable to Christ for such decisions, and for not making any of Christ's little ones to stumble on account of binding their conscience where Christ has not.

3. Objections to denying Caesar the right to suspend or alter Christ's divine ordinances

Given that the jurisdiction of the church in spiritual things is exclusive, there can be no exception to this. Once an exception is made, that principle of complete spiritual independence and exclusive jurisdiction is lost. We ought to be able to leave the matter there, but specific objections are raised that need to be answered.

---

[27] The commandment of the law of God to assemble together for public worship on the Lord's Day does not take precedence over the commandment of the law of God to take all lawful endeavours to preserve our own lives or the lives of others. See Chapter 3 ('Should the church ever suspend public worship?') and Chapter 8 ('Is it ever unloving to go to church?').

'Ordinarily it is wrong to allow Caesar to suspend or alter Christ's ordinances, but this is an exceptional case.'

As we have noted, once an exception is permitted we have abandoned the principle of exclusive jurisdiction in spiritual things. We have allowed the state to share in the government of the church in spiritual things. Scripture never gives any church authority to civil rulers. The church has exclusive jurisdiction in spiritual matters which cannot be qualified, nor can exceptions be made. These are 'the inalienable liberties of a church of Christ, which, alike by their duty and allegiance to their head and king, and by their ordination vows, they [church officers] are bound to maintain, "notwithstanding of whatsoever trouble or persecution may arise."'[28]

'It is only temporary and not a permanent state of affairs.'

The duration does not change the principle. Once an exception is made to the principle of complete spiritual independence and exclusive jurisdiction (even for a short period) it is lost. We may have regular recurring temporary restrictions once the state has been given this authority. Every situation of state control begins with a specific instance or event from which further control is consolidated.

'The Bible commands obedience to rulers, so the church must obey Caesar in this area.'

The Bible commands Christians to honour and be subject to civil government. Christians are also to obey rulers, but not in things which are unlawful as defined by God's law. The relevant verses of Scripture about our duty to civil government cannot be interpreted as commanding churches to give Caesar control over spiritual things. There is no justification for that. We are not

[28] Church of Scotland (1842) *Claim, Declaration and Protest, Anent the Encroachments of the Court of Session.*

absolutely and always to obey civil government, as our conscience can only be bound by the moral law.[29]

'It will be a stumbling block to unbelievers if the church does not obey the government in this matter.'

One cannot choose to sin in order to avoid causing others to stumble.[30] To yield to Caesar the things that are God's is clearly sinning.[31] One might choose to yield the civil liberty of using a building 'lest we offend them' but to give carte blanche to Caesar in spiritual things is not permissible. In fact, to render spiritual things to Caesar is itself intrinsically a stumbling block to ungodly rulers, because it hardens them in the sin of robbing Christ of his crown rights and resisting the claims of Christ's moral law. It will harden them in their intentions to silence the church in declaring things to be sin that are widely celebrated. It is a stumbling block to churches in other nations who look to our nation for an example in spiritual things. It is also a stumbling block to our posterity who will read of compliance rather than a testimony against the invasion of Christ's kingdom. To give away the exclusive jurisdiction of the church in any way harms the edification of others since it makes the ordinances of Christ and the consciences of many subject to merely human authority.

---

[29] The legal opinion in Revd Dr William J U Philip & Ors for Judicial Review of the closure of places of worship in Scotland (2021) CSOH 32 showed in fact that obeying the government in this area required breaking the law, since Lord Braid ruled that it was an illegal breach of human rights.

[30] See Durham, J. (1990) *A Treatise on Scandal.* Dallas, Texas, USA: Naphtali Press. Durham discusses what we should do when a necessary duty such as praying or preaching will cause a stumbling block or scandal, especially to those are obviously hostile to the things of God (pp. 22-23) and also what we should do when a stumbling block will result whatever we do (pp. 28-29).

[31] It is for instance a sin against the second commandment, which requires us to preserve God's ordinances pure and entire.

'The government does have a right (only for reasons of health, order and security) to intervene in spiritual things. It is for good reasons and with good intentions that they have introduced legislation, because they cannot risk some churches not complying with mere guidance.'

Usually governments have reasons of order uppermost in their concerns when they seek to control the church. The early Victorian establishment, for instance, were anxious about popular revolution and saw the claims of the Non-Intrusionists in the Church of Scotland as subversive of social order. Yet these anxieties did not justify interference in what is properly the church's jurisdiction.

As George Gillespie has observed, if any ruler had reasons of order and security for controlling aspects of the worship of God it was Jeroboam. In Jeroboam's time a state of warfare existed between the northern and southern kingdoms, so it was no longer safe for the northern tribes to go to Jerusalem to worship. Surely, as it was putting people's lives at risk, some amendment in worship was therefore sensible, indeed essential. It would also undermine Jeroboam's government if people went to the southern kingdom on a regular basis, so the changes he made to how God was to be worshipped surely only made sense in terms of national security. Yet, plausible as this line of defence might have seemed, none of these reasons were in any sense acceptable to God. Ever after, he was known as 'Jeroboam the son of Nebat, who made Israel to sin.'[32]

---

[32] Gillespie, G. (2013) *A Dispute Against the English Popish Ceremonies.* Dallas, Texas, USA: Naphtali Press. pp. 290-291.

'The state makes its decisions based on specialist technical advice which the church does not have. We have to trust the decision even though we do not have access to the advice.'

It is true that the church cannot hope to develop this specialist advice, yet neither does it need to (since it does not belong within the church's remit). The state simply needs to make available its advice in order for the church to make its own decisions. The specialist argument works vice versa, of course. The state cannot hope to develop or retain its own theological specialist competence, as this is the domain of the church. The state is not equipped to make judgments about the moral dilemmas of whether certain aspects of the moral law must take precedence over others in relation to spiritual matters such as the worship of God. However, the key point is not just a matter of competence, but the fact that the state has not been authorised by Christ to take control in the area of his ordinances.

'This isn't persecution. We are not being stopped from preaching the gospel, or being required to comply with immoral things.'

Even if this is not persecution, it is nevertheless an illegitimate power grab by the government, overstepping its own jurisdiction and intruding into the jurisdiction of Christ's church. It can do so with the best of motives and without any malevolent intention. Yet if the state decides to define what can and cannot come under the definition of preaching (e.g., limiting it to recorded or broadcast messages) as well as how this is delivered and to whom, then the ordinance of the preaching of the gospel is being defined and altered by illegitimate authority. The historic Reformed view is that civil government can no more suspend aspects of the preaching of the gospel than they can depose preachers from the ministry altogether. Ministers are under an obligation to continue preaching and their pastoral work in every circumstance (2

Timothy 4:2; 2 Corinthians 6:4, 8-9; 1 Corinthians 9:16; Acts 5:28-29, 42).

Even in places like China, the preaching of the gospel is not being stopped altogether—the state merely regulates the context in which it is permitted to take place, and overt persecution only takes place when there is resistance to the regulation that the government is imposing for the sake of social order. Few governments have ever proceeded against the gospel as such. They oppose Christians and the church as transgressing social order and being in some way treasonous and seditious because they will obey Christ rather than Caesar. This was the case under pagan Rome, the Stuarts and at the time of the Disruption.

We may not be experiencing outright hostility and ill-treatment because of the church's beliefs. Yet if the church chooses to stand on the principle of its spiritual independence we will begin to face civil penalties. The idea that we have liberty to surrender to the state until the point that they forbid preaching the gospel is fanciful. The more we give to the state the more they are encouraged to take.[33] And when it comes to Christ's ordinances, these are not ours to give in the first place.

---

[33] Revd Dr William J U Philip & Ors for Judicial Review of the closure of places of worship in Scotland (2021) CSOH 32. showed that human rights guaranteed by law such as freedom of worship and freedom of religion were considered by the Scottish Government but intentionally disregarded. Lord Braid's judgment in this case did of course rule that these were human rights breached by the Scottish Government in closing worship. There is also of course some concern about human rights being a casualty of the response to the crisis. Human rights watch groups have been deeply concerned about the way that rights have been undermined and infringed during the pandemic in countries such as France and Slovakia as well as many developing countries and more authoritarian regimes. There has been an increase in widespread

Conclusion

If we can allow the state control over spiritual things to any extent then there is no clear and abiding difference between the things of Caesar and the things of God. It no longer makes sense to render the things that are Caesar's to Caesar and the things that are God's to God because there might be circumstances in which we have to render the things that are God's to Caesar. What we have been seeking to define is well summarised in article 16 of the *Confession of Faith and Religion Of ... Bohemia* (1535).

> They teach also that it is commanded in the Word of God that all should be subject to the higher powers in all things, yet in those things only which are not repugnant to God and his Word. But as touching those things which concern men's souls, faith, and salvation, they teach that men should hearken only to God's Word, etc., his ministers, as Christ himself says, Render to Caesar the things that are Caesar's, and to God those things that are God's.[34]

'Truth to Christ cannot be treason to Caesar.'

Samuel Rutherford (1600-1661)[35]

---

surveillance in many countries, such as Israel and South Korea, all under the pretext of public health.

[34] Quoted in: Sundry Ministers of Christ within the City of London [edited: Coldwell, C.] (2020) *Jus Divinum Regiminis Ecclesiastici: The Divine Right of Church Government*. Dallas, Texas, USA: Naphtali Press. p. 130.

[35] Rutherford, S. (1982) *Lex, Rex, or The Law and the Prince*. Harrisonburg, Virginia, USA: Sprinkle Publications. p. xxi.

~ 7 ~
What does loving our neighbour look like in a pandemic?

Paul Murray

One of the great imperatives of the Christian life is, 'Thou shalt love thy neighbour as thyself' (Matthew 22:39). A question that many Christians have been asking since the outbreak of Covid-19 is, *how do I do that during a pandemic?* If we are to fulfil our God-given duty in our own day, this is a question that needs a biblical answer.

To find that answer, it is essential that we turn to the law of God. Such an approach may come as a surprise to some. However, just as loving Jesus Christ means keeping his commandments (John 14:15), so love to our neighbour is always regulated by law. Law and love are inextricably linked in the Christian life. So, when Jesus was asked what the greatest commandment in the law was, he answered:

> Thou shalt love the Lord thy God with all thy heart, and with all thy soul, and with all thy mind. This is the first and great commandment. And the second is like unto it, Thou shalt love thy neighbour as thyself. On these two commandments hang all the law and the prophets. (Matthew 22:37-40)

Clearly, these two commandments are not distinct from the Ten Commandments; rather, the Ten Commandments as a whole 'hang' on these two commandments. For this reason, the Westminster Shorter Catechism calls love to God and neighbour 'the sum of the Ten Commandments' (Q42). More specifically, the Westminster Larger Catechism describes love to God as 'the sum of the four commandments containing our duty to God' (Q102), and love to neighbour as 'the sum of the six commandments which contain our duty to man' (Q122).

Although we distinguish between the two tables of the law, it is crucial to understand that they are intimately related. The way that we view, and act towards, God will influence the way we view, and act towards, each other. So, William Ames (1576-1633) argues,

> Those who neglect their duty towards men, deny honour to God, contemning him instead. ... Charity towards God, which is contained in religion, produces charity towards men by its own nature.[1]

To rightly love our neighbour in a pandemic, therefore, is to rightly love God in a pandemic. To fulfil such a calling, it is vital that we rightly understand what God's law requires of us. This chapter will, first, set out what our sixth commandment duties are in a pandemic situation. Secondly, it will consider these duties in their broader context and address some of the tensions that arise between competing duties.

1. Keeping the sixth commandment in a pandemic

Introducing the sixth commandment

At a time of heightened danger from an infectious virus, the particular law that will increasingly need to govern our behaviour is that of the sixth commandment, 'Thou shalt not kill.' This is not

[1] Ames, W. (1977) *The Marrow of Theology.* Grand Rapids, Michigan, USA: Baker Books. p. 300.

a law simply prohibiting wilful and malicious murder. As the psalmist shrewdly observed, there is an 'exceeding breadth' to each of the Ten Commandments that goes far beyond the strict letter (Psalm 119:96).

This becomes clearer when we understand the Ten Commandments to be but a summary of the moral law.[2] The fulness of that law is revealed throughout the Scriptures. This is immediately evident in the giving of the civil laws, which are a practical outworking of the Ten Commandments. These laws, which deal with subjects as varied as restitution, hygiene, and textiles, are all applications of the Ten Commandments and they illustrate its exceeding breadth.

To help us discover this breadth, Question 99 of the Westminster Larger Catechism gives eight rules that are to be applied to each commandment. Among other things, these rules remind us that the commandments are to be observed wholly, perpetually, spiritually, meticulously, and publicly. Especially pertinent is the rule that 'where a duty is commanded, the contrary sin is forbidden; and, where a sin is forbidden, the contrary duty is commanded.'

Jesus Christ exemplified this principle of interpretation with regard to the fifth commandment when he said, 'For God commanded, saying, Honour thy father and mother: and, He that curseth father or mother, let him die the death' (Matthew 5:14). Just as honouring father and mother is commanded, so cursing them is forbidden. Likewise, in calling the Ephesian believer to 'steal no more,' the Apostle Paul also calls him to 'labour … that he may have to give to him that needeth' (Ephesians 4:28). A cursory study

---

[2] Question 98 of the Westminster Shorter Catechism says that 'The moral law is summarily comprehended in the Ten Commandments.'

of Scriptural imperatives will quickly reveal the implementation of this principle for each of the Ten Commandments.

The wording of the sixth commandment is terse, with only two words in the Hebrew. The word translated 'kill' in the Authorised Version refers, specifically, to unlawful killing of people. John L. Mackay (1948–2018) explains,

> The verb used refers to the killing of persons; it is never used of animals. It is not the most general word for the taking of human life, and does not include slaughter in war or the judicial imposition of the death penalty. All in all, the rendering 'murder' reflects its range of meaning very well.[3]

As Mackay highlights, there are times when killing is commanded by God. Animals are commanded to be killed for food (Genesis 9:3) and sacrifice (Leviticus 1:1-5), as well as in instances of self-defence (1 Samuel 17:34-36), although cruelty to animals is expressly forbidden (Proverbs 12:10; Exodus 23:5, 11). There are also times when it is lawful to take the life of a person. God has instituted capital punishment for murderers, to be administered by a lawfully constituted civil government (Genesis 9:5-6; Romans 13:3-4). It is also lawful to take a life in the case of a just war (Deuteronomy 20:1-4; Ecclesiastes 3:8; Matthew 24:6-7) and in cases of proportionate self-defence (Exodus 22:2-3). None of these instances of killing are included in the biblical meaning of murder.

What the sixth commandment forbids is the unlawful killing of a person, normally called murder. The seriousness of the sin of taking a person's life does not simply rest on the fact that murder is an attack upon someone's personal autonomy. The gravity of murder goes beyond that to the fact that people are made in the

---

[3] Mackay, J. L. (2001) *Exodus.* Fearn: Christian Focus Publications. p. 352.

image of God. This is the reason given for the institution of capital punishment: 'Whoso sheddeth man's blood, by man shall his blood be shed: for in the image of God made he man' (Genesis 9:6). As Johannes G. Vos (1903–1983) explains,

> Murder affronts God by destroying an image-bearer of God. Thus, the murderer commits sacrilege by failing to regard the image of God in man as something sacred. The real dignity and worth of human life consists in man's bearing the divine image.[4]

The seriousness of murder, therefore, transcends the temporal realm and pierces the eternal. As important as it is to understand the personal consequences of murder for the victim and his or her family, there are also God-ward consequences. Because man is made in the image of God, any unlawful attack upon a human being is an attack upon the God whose image he reflects. As John Murray (1898-1975) writes, 'an assault upon man's life is a virtual assault upon the life of God.'[5] This perspective gives a deeper insight into what it meant for David, after his murder of Uriah the Hittite, to say, 'Against thee, thee only, have I sinned, and done this evil in thy sight' (Psalm 51:4).

Defining the sixth commandment

The cosmic gravity of murder should make us all the more careful to understand the requirements of the sixth commandment. One of the fullest concise explanations of this commandment is that of the Westminster Larger Catechism. Two questions deal with the sixth commandment.

---

[4] Vos, J. G. (2002) *The Westminster Larger Catechism: A Commentary*. Phillipsburg, New Jersey, USA: P&R Publishing. p. 368.

[5] Murray, J. (1957) *Principles of Conduct*. Grand Rapids, Michigan, USA: Eerdmans. p. 111.

> Q. 135. What are the duties required in the sixth commandment?
> A. The duties required in the sixth commandment are all careful studies, and lawful endeavours, to preserve the life of ourselves and others by resisting all thoughts and purposes, subduing all passions, and avoiding all occasions, temptations, and practices, which tend to the unjust taking away the life of any; by just defence thereof against violence, patient bearing of the hand of God, quietness of mind, cheerfulness of spirit; a sober use of meat, drink, physic, sleep, labour, and recreations; by charitable thoughts, love, compassion, meekness, gentleness, kindness; peaceable, mild and courteous speeches and behaviour; forbearance, readiness to be reconciled, patient bearing and forgiving of injuries, and requiting good for evil; comforting and succouring the distressed and protecting and defending the innocent.
>
> Q. 136. What are the sins forbidden in the sixth commandment?
> A. The sins forbidden in the sixth commandment are, all taking away the life of ourselves, or of others, except in case of public justice, lawful war, or necessary defence; the neglecting or withdrawing the lawful and necessary means of preservation of life; sinful anger, hatred, envy, desire of revenge; all excessive passions, distracting cares; immoderate use of meat, drink, labour, and recreations; provoking words, oppression, quarrelling, striking, wounding, and whatsoever else tends to the destruction of the life of any.

These two answers give us a helpful guide to gauge how well we are responding, both personally and corporately, to the current life-threatening pandemic. In summary, it is our duty to do all in our power both to avoid unnecessary loss of life and to promote preservation of life. To come short in this is to come short in love to our neighbour. Speaking of Romans 13:8-9, where the Apostle

Paul calls loving our neighbour the fulfilment and summary of the law, John Murray explains that,

> The sixth commandment, like the others, is one of the concrete ways in which the summary commandment of love is exemplified. 'Love worketh no ill to his neighbour' and must therefore be governed by, and manifest itself in, 'all lawful endeavours' to preserve and promote the life of others as well as our own.[6]

To sin in this domain is, in its essence, to sin the sin of murder. That is not to say that there are not degrees of guilt within the sin of murder. For example, Herman Bavinck (1854-1921) explains that 'the guilt of violation is greater or less to the degree the commandment was violated more or less intentionally.'[7]

As such, somebody who unintentionally passes on Covid-19 to a vulnerable person would not necessarily bear the same guilt as one who intentionally commits homicide. Likewise, someone who is 'angry with his brother without a cause' but does not act upon that anger will not bear the same guilt as someone who acts upon his anger and murders his brother. In such cases, the essence of the sin is the same, but the guilt and penalty vary depending on the particular circumstances and motivations.

Negative love

Loving our neighbour during a pandemic will have both positive and negative elements. By 'negative love' is meant that there are certain things which we ought *not* to do in order to keep the sixth commandment. In short, it is our duty to ensure that we take

---

[6] Murray, J. (1957) *Principles of Conduct.* Grand Rapids, Michigan, USA: Eerdmans. p. 117.

[7] Bavinck, H. (2006) *Reformed Dogmatics.* Grand Rapids, Michigan, USA: Baker Academic. Vol. 3, p. 150.

appropriate care in our actions so that we do not spread a virus that has the potential to kill another person. The sixth commandment forbids such carelessness.

Scripture clearly equates life-endangering recklessness with murder. For example, the children of Israel were told, 'When thou buildest a new house, then thou shalt make a battlement for thy roof, that thou bring not blood upon thine house, if any man fall from thence' (Deuteronomy 22:8). In Ancient Near Eastern culture, the flat roof on a house was commonly used for socialising. Therefore, it was necessary that houses have battlements, or parapets, to reduce the risk of people falling off the roof to their death. Should a fatal accident occur when the parapet was unsafe or missing, the owner of the house would be guilty of murder because he had not taken sufficient care to prevent it happening.

Similar laws and punishments were put in place with regard to dangerous animals (Exodus 21:28-29). In a case where an animal had caused the death of a man or a woman, God commanded that, if that animal had not previously been a threat to human life, the owner would be guiltless. However, if it had shown life-threatening behaviour in the past and the owner refused to put precautions in place, the owner would be guilty of murder and would be put to death.

The sixth commandment principle at play in both instances is that of indirect involvement in someone's death due to negligence. Negligence which leads to death is classed as murder. Bringing this principle up to date, Brian H. Edwards explains,

> The way we build our house, drive our car, walk our dog or sell our produce can be the cause of the death of others; that may

not be our intention, but it can still be the direct result of our actions.[8]

Where death is caused by insufficient attention given to a situation which poses a potential risk to life, the Bible defines such negligence as a form of murder.

This does not mean that, as a society, we must seek to nullify risk altogether. Society at large has generally realised this, even in the pandemic. Although many activities have been significantly reduced since March 2020, many others have been deemed important enough to continue because the risk of transmission is counter-balanced by the importance of the work. Among many other things, supermarkets and hospitals have fallen into this category.

The duty required by the sixth commandment, therefore, is not always the nullifying of risk but, often, the management of risk. In public activities which we consider to be necessary, what the commandment expressly forbids is negligence. We must avoid 'all occasions … and practices which tend to the unjust taking away the life of any' (Westminster Larger Catechism, Q135).

It is on this basis that churches have historically sought to ensure that their buildings are safe and fit for purpose. Similarly, during a pandemic, it is proper that churches make arrangements to allow activities to be conducted in line with reasonable public health guidelines. To refuse to put safety precautions in place where there is a known danger to life would be akin to allowing a dangerous animal to roam the streets.

---

[8] Edwards, B. H. (2002) *The Ten Commandments for Today*. Epsom: Day One Publications. p. 187.

It is also proper that, where applicable, essential activities be suitably reduced in line with risk. Writing during the Wittenberg plague of 1527, Martin Luther (1483-1546) explained his own approach:

> I shall avoid places and persons where my presence is not needed in order not to become contaminated and thus perchance infect and pollute others, and so cause their death as a result of my negligence.[9]

Luther did not lock himself up during the plague. He did, however, take care to avoid places and people where his presence was not needed, so as to guard himself from a breach of the sixth commandment. His attitude is a helpful example of how risk can be lessened, not by the cessation, but by the curtailment of activity.

Self-love

It is notable that the Westminster Larger Catechism does not simply speak of preserving other people's lives, but also our own lives. As it is a gross sin to cause the death of another person made in God's image, so it is a gross sin to cause our own death, as we are made in the same image.

We can be very careful with regards to others while relatively careless with regards to ourselves. We can even do this with an attitude of supposedly holy indifference. However, as Thomas Boston (1676-1732) rightly states concerning our bodies, 'They are not ours, but God's.'[10] They bear his image and, as such, we have no right to endanger them, whether directly or indirectly.

---

[9] Luther, M., as quoted from his book: *Whether One May Flee From a Deadly Plague*, in: *The Banner of Truth Magazine* (2020) **686** (November), p. 26.

[10] Boston, T. (2002) *The Complete Works of Thomas Boston*. Stoke-on-Trent: Tentmaker Publications. Vol. 2, p. 268.

There are numerous ways in which we can be guilty of the sin of self-murder. As Archbishop Ussher (1581-1656) explains, 'We must not think that there are no more ways to kill a man's self, but with a knife.'[11] The Westminster Larger Catechism speaks of practical things such as 'a sober use of meat, drink, physic [medicine], sleep, labour, and recreations' (Q135) as being necessary if we are to love our bodies and nourish and cherish our flesh (Ephesians 5:28-29). The neglect of such things can contribute to an untimely death and is self-murder.

The Westminster Larger Catechism also speaks of the importance of a healthy mental disposition, which includes such things as 'charitable thoughts, love, compassion, meekness, gentleness, kindness; peaceable, mild and courteous speeches and behaviour' (Q135). Again, inattention to such graces can easily lead to mortal danger.

Particularly relevant during a pandemic is the fact that we can be guilty of self-murder by carelessly exposing ourselves to unnecessary danger. We are prohibited from knowingly putting ourselves into a situation of risk without due regard to the possible consequences. Thomas Watson (1620-1686) illustrates this with a biblical example:

> In the law, God would have the leper shut up, to keep others from being infected (Leviticus 13:4). If any should be so presumptuous as to go to a leper, and get the plague of leprosy, he might thank himself for his own death.[12]

---

[11] Ussher, J. (2007) *A Body of Divinity*. Birmingham, Alabama, USA: Solid Ground Christian Books. p. 243.

[12] Watson, T. (1958) *A Body of Divinity*. London: The Banner of Truth Trust. p. 107.

As such, in ordinary circumstances, it is our duty to avoid places where we are liable to endanger our own lives. In extraordinary circumstances (such as a pandemic) where such risks must be taken, it is our duty to minimise the risk as far as is practical.

Medicine and vaccinations

An important aspect of love to both neighbour and self is that we encourage all lawful endeavours to preserve life at scientific, medical, and legislative levels. In our current pandemic, this would include supporting efforts to develop ethical vaccinations and medicines, as well as the implementation of programmes which could help control the spread of the virus.

Just as Elisha told the leprous Naaman to wash in the Jordan (2 Kings 5:10), and as Isaiah told the dying Hezekiah to boil some figs (Isaiah 38:21), so God calls us to make use of the means of recovery that he provides us with, whether medicines, vaccinations or otherwise. We are never to trust in such means without reference to God, but neither should we be so presumptuous as to say we are trusting in God while neglecting the means.

Johannes Vos explains,

> God has mitigated the curse by placing in the world, for mankind to discover, the means by which human suffering can be alleviated and life prolonged. To refuse to make use of these means because we trust in God involves a mistaken notion of what it means to trust in God.[13]

In creating the world, God has filled it with medicines and cures. Part of the cultural mandate of Genesis 1:28-30 is for man to

---

[13] Vos, J. G. (2002) *The Westminster Larger Catechism: A Commentary.* Phillipsburg, New Jersey, USA: P&R Publishing. p. 365.

discover such means of restoring health and to put them to legitimate use.

The appropriate use of such medicines at a personal level also has a strong bearing on our duty to love our neighbour. As Luther explained in the heat of the Wittenberg plague,

> It is ... shameful for a person to pay no heed to his own body and to fail to protect it against the plague the best he is able, and then to infect and poison others who might have remained alive if he had taken care of his body as he should have. He is thus responsible before God for his neighbour's death and is a murderer many times over.[14]

At a time when the risk of transmitting a deadly virus to our neighbour is high, it is imperative that we make use of any legitimate and effective means that will enable us to do our duty safely.

Positive love

Due to their care to 'stay at home and save lives,' many have fulfilled their 'negative' duty to *not* endanger their own lives or the lives of others during the pandemic. However, there is a danger that, in focusing solely on the negative, the 'positive' duty has been neglected. William Ames succinctly states that we love our neighbour in line with this commandment, not just by 'preventing things hurtful' but also by 'supplying things helpful.'[15] Positively, then, we have *a duty to preserve the life of our neighbour*, especially where that is endangered.

---

[14] Luther, M., as quoted from his book: *Whether One May Flee From a Deadly Plague*, in: *The Banner of Truth Magazine* (2020) **686** (November), p. 26.

[15] Ames, W. (1977) *The Marrow of Theology*. Grand Rapids, Michigan, USA: Baker Books. p. 314.

In fulfilment of such a responsibility, Obadiah risked his own life to save the lives of one hundred prophets (1 Kings 18:3-4), the people of Israel defied the king to save Jonathan from execution (1 Samuel 14:44-45), and the saints in the days of Claudius Caesar sent relief to the brethren in Judaea who were preparing for a famine (Acts 11:28-29). These were all outworkings of the sixth commandment obligation to preserve life and they all involved self-sacrifice and self-endangerment.

Such a principle is undoubtedly relevant in our own day. Since March 2020, the vulnerable in society have become increasingly vulnerable. Unemployment has soared, poverty has increased, single mothers have been deserted, the use of food banks has soared, and the elderly have been abandoned.

Archbishop James Ussher wrote that the sixth commandment requires us to 'visit and comfort [our neighbour] in sickness and affliction ... give meat, drink and clothes to the poor and needy ... give relief to the distressed, and succour to the oppressed.'[16] If the vulnerable are within reasonable reach, and if it is in our power, we have a duty to seek to alleviate their needs. Serious questions could be raised as to how seriously the church has taken this positive aspect of the sixth commandment in the current pandemic.

2. Addressing the tensions

There are three particular tensions which complicate loving our neighbour during a pandemic.

---

[16] Ussher, J. (2007) *A Body of Divinity*. Birmingham, Alabama, USA: Solid Ground Christian Books. p. 246.

Positive love vs negative love

The first is the tension between positive and negative love. By getting practically involved in the life of your needy neighbour, there is a risk that you could transmit the virus to them. By not getting practically involved in the life of your needy neighbour, there is a risk that they will be neglected.

In this regard, it is essential that quality of life be included in the decision-making framework. The biblical definition of life, after all, is not the definition of medical handbooks which describe it along the lines of breath in the lungs and a pulse from the heart. Jesus describes life in qualitative rather than quantitative terms when he prays to his Father and says, 'And this is life eternal, that they might know thee the only true God, and Jesus Christ, whom thou hast sent' (John 17:3). Although life is here described in its highest quality, it gives a biblical warrant to view life from a qualitative, as well as a quantitative, perspective. This allows us to prioritise things like enjoyment, happiness, friendship and worship as essential components of life.

Such an understanding of life has not been entirely absent at a legislative level during the pandemic. However, its importance has been largely minimised in the decision-making process, making way for a quantitative view of life which has as its main aim the prevention of death. Such an approach is evidently not without merit, and many have deemed the reduction in the quality of their life a sacrifice which they have been willing to make in the circumstances.

However, there are particular instances in which the isolation enforced to prevent death has been seriously detrimental to the lives of the most vulnerable. Many elderly people in care homes, now deceased, spent the last months of their lives isolated from their families—in some cases, they did not understand why.

Thousands of others have endured life-threatening illnesses and undergone traumatic surgeries and recovery periods without loved ones by their side.

Thousands have died in hospitals—some with Covid-19 and some without—having not seen members of their immediate family for weeks and even months. Mourners, deprived of holding the hands of their loved ones at their death, are also deprived of anything resembling a normal funeral and the comfort and closure that that entails.

For some, lockdown restrictions have been far more detrimental to life than others. Life in a pandemic has been easier for the rich than for the poor, for the healthy than for the sick, for the sound in mind than for the mentally ill, for the happy than for the mourner, for the young than for the old. There has been an alarming increase in anxiety, depression and suicide, and syndromes like dementia appear to have been exacerbated in many. It has left many feeling that life is hopeless and without purpose. It is not without reason, therefore, that, in some cases, the restrictions have been described as cruel and inhumane.

The question as to how such effects could have been overcome is not easily answered. However, such instances are proof that a one-size-fits-all approach, although easier to enforce, does not actually fit all. The evidence shows that, in many cases, the drive to avoid Covid-19 deaths has led to life being treated in a way that is entirely foreign to the sixth commandment principle to preserve life in a way that does not neglect the qualitative. In such cases, it is the duty of the church to strongly counsel the state to take heed to its sixth commandment duties.

Self-love vs love of neighbour

The second tension is between love of neighbour and love of self. Both are required by the sixth commandment, but which takes pre-eminence? The Apostle Paul, who ratifies the principle of godly self-love (Ephesians 5:28-29), also explains that love 'seeketh not her own' (1 Corinthians 13:5). Jonathan Edwards (1703-1758) described Christian love as 'contrary to a selfish spirit.'[17] It is not strictly selfless, but it is comparatively selfless—the opposite of selfish. Edwards goes on to say that this love,

> disposes persons to consider not only their own difficulties, but also the burdens and afflictions of others, and the difficulties of their circumstances, and to esteem the case of those who are in straits and necessities as their own ... He is ready, also, to help them, and take delight in supplying their necessities, and relieving their difficulties.[18]

Christian love is, therefore, always sacrificial. The great example in this regard is, of course, our Lord, who 'loved the church, and gave himself for it' (Ephesians 5:25). It is this sacrificial mind that the Apostle Paul commends to all believers when he writes, 'Look not every man on his own things, but every man also on the things of others' (Philippians 2:4). This counter-cultural tenet is central to true Christian living and is a clear indictment of Christians who selfishly try to skip vaccines queues or use up supermarket home delivery slots in order to protect themselves at the cost of others.

The Apostle Paul not only understood the self-sacrificial nature of love but clearly acted on it. This is how he came to be,

---

[17] Edwards, J. (1969) *Charity and its Fruits.* Edinburgh: The Banner of Truth Trust. p. 159.

[18] Edwards, J. (1969) *Charity and its Fruits.* Edinburgh: The Banner of Truth Trust. p. 168.

> in journeyings often, in perils of waters, in perils of robbers, in perils by mine own countrymen, in perils by the heathen, in perils in the city, in perils in the wilderness, in perils in the sea, in perils among false brethren; In weariness and painfulness, in watchings often, in hunger and thirst, in fastings often, in cold and nakedness. (2 Corinthians 11:26-27)

Clearly, the apostle did not esteem his legitimate self-love higher than his duty to love his neighbour. He was willing to put himself into numerous perilous situations, repeatedly risking his life, in order to fulfil his Christian calling.

The history of the church is filled with examples of Christians who were willing to suffer in order to act on their love to their fellow human beings. They were prepared to endanger their lives and even lose them in their pursuit of furthering the cause of Christ and showing his love to the world.

A striking instance of this can be found in the behaviour of Christians during the Plague of Cyprian in the third century. At the height of this epidemic, 5,000 people were reported to be dying daily in Rome alone.[19] Many of the wealthy pagans fled the population centres for fear of their lives. The church historian Pontius wrote,

> Multitudes lay about the whole city, not bodies, but by this time corpses; and called on the pity of passers-by from the view of a fortune common to both parties. No one looked to aught

[19] Stark, R. (1996) *The Rise of Christianity*. Princeton, New Jersey, USA: Princeton University Press. p. 77.

> beyond his cruel gain ... No one did to another what he wished done to himself.[20]

As the pagans fled the cities, Cyprian, the Bishop of Carthage, preached to Christians about 'the excellence of mercifulness' and urged them to practically serve one another, as well as their pagan neighbours, by tending to the neglected sick and burying the forsaken dead. Pontius records,

> Accordingly ministrations [were] divided among them at once, according to the rank and circumstances of each ... they did good in the profusion of exuberant works to all, and not only to the household of faith.[21]

It was understood, both at the time and since, that such sacrificial acts of love to all contributed favourably towards the growth of Christianity in the third century. Sociologist Rodney Stark explains:

> Christian values of love and charity had, from the beginning, been translated into norms of social service and community solidarity. When disasters struck, the Christians were better able to cope, and this resulted in substantially higher rates of survival. This meant that in the aftermath of each epidemic, Christians made up a larger percentage of the population even without new converts. Moreover, their noticeably better

[20] Pontius, as quoted in: Stephenson, J. (Ed.) (1975) *A New Eusebius*. London: S.P.C.K.. p. 246.

[21] Pontius, as quoted in: Stephenson, J. (Ed.) (1975) *A New Eusebius*. London: S.P.C.K.. p. 246.

> survival rate would have seemed a 'miracle' to Christians and pagans alike, and this ought to have influenced conversion.[22]

It was this same love which motivated godly Christian ministers[23] and doctors[24] to stay with their London congregations during the Great Plague of 1665-1666, even while many other ministers and wealthy nobles were escaping to the relative safety of their country houses. Richard Baxter, who lived through the plague, wrote:

> When Christ shall say, 'Inasmuch as ye did it not to one of these, ye did it not to me,' it will be a poor excuse to say, 'Lord, I was forbidden by the law.' Therefore they resolved to stay with the people, and to go into the forsaken pulpits, though prohibited, and to preach to the poor people before they died; and also to visit the sick, and get what relief they could for the poor, especially those that were shut up.[25]

In 1665, it was illegal for Nonconformist ministers to preach in the pulpits of the Church of England and illegal for doctors to practice medicine without a license. Both non-conforming ministers and non-licensed doctors chose, not just to risk their own lives, but to break the law in order to care for the bodies and souls of the people of London. They defied one authority in order to bow to another authority.

---

22 Stark, R. (1996) *The Rise of Christianity.* Princeton, New Jersey, USA: Princeton University Press. p. 77.

23 Vincent, T. (1997) *God's Terrible Voice in the City.* Morgan, Pennsylvania, USA: Soli Deo Gloria Publications. pp. 49-53.

24 Aitken, J. T., Fuller, H. W. C., and Johnson, D. (Eds.) (1984) *The Influences of Christians in Medicine.* London: Christian Medical Fellowship. p. 70.

25 Keeble, N. H. *et al.* (Eds.) (2020) *Reliquiae Baxterianae: Or, Mr Richard Baxter's narrative of the most memorable passages of his life and times.* Oxford: Oxford University Press. Vol. 2, p. 306.

The contemporary church has a great deal to learn from the way in which Christians of former generations sacrificially loved their neighbours. Surely the same love of neighbour should prompt Christians to take up jobs in care homes, hospitals or supermarkets during a pandemic, and to be sacrificial in the care of those within their reach, regardless of the danger to themselves.

Christians have been willing to risk their own lives, not just because they understood the importance of loving their neighbour, but because they understood that death would be worse for their unconverted neighbours than it was for them. For the Christian, death is the gateway to eternal life whereas, for the non-Christian, it is the gateway to eternal torment. For this reason, Christians have historically viewed their own death with less dread than the death of the unconverted.

This was the view held by Richard Cameron, the Scottish Covenanter, as he prepared himself and his small army to go out to fight at Ayrsmoss in July 1680. Knowing that his army had no chance of winning the battle, and that he himself would almost certainly die, he prayed, 'Lord, spare the green and take the ripe.'[26] In other words, he asked God to spare the lives of those who were not ready to die and to take those who were ready instead. He understood the momentous difference between the deaths of these two groups.

Such is the spirit that should animate Christians in every generation. Yet, there is evidence that this is not always the case. In the Apostle Paul's day, he wrote that 'all seek their own' (Philippians 2:21). What is particularly worrying is that he wrote this about members of the church. The response of many

---

[26] Hewison, J. K. (2019) *The Covenanters.* Edinburgh: The Banner of Truth Trust. Vol. 2, p. 325.

Christians to the pandemic, and their reliance on unbelievers to take risks in order to serve them, indicates that there are many within the church today who 'seek their own.'

It is indisputable that, since March 2020, acts of self-sacrifice have been predominately undertaken, not by members of the church, but by members of other religions or those who belong to no religion. Food banks have often been run, shopping trips undertaken, and prescriptions delivered, not by Christians, but by those who are risking their immortal souls in the process.

At an individual level, Christians have often been quick to receive aid but slow to give it. To an extent, this is necessary in a day where the church is so numerically weak. However, questions need to be asked of the attitude of Christians who have been sluggish in their response to serve their neighbours, especially Christians who are young and able-bodied. Is it right that the unconverted should be the ones who risk their lives to serve them? This is surely a contradiction of the biblical pattern and a telling indicator of the spiritual condition of the church.

Having an understanding of the eternal risks involved, therefore, Christians ought to be at the forefront of hazard-filled endeavours to love their neighbours. Like Epaphroditus, even when threatened with death, they are not to regard their lives (Philippians 2:28), knowing that their lives are 'hid with Christ in God' (Colossians 3:3). 'Greater love hath no man than this, that a man lay down his life for his friends' (John 15:13).

Body vs soul

The third tension concerns loving our neighbour's body and loving his soul. In all our attempts to preserve bodily life, we must not neglect our duty to preserve the life of the soul. One of the most solemn features of the pandemic has been the almost complete absence of reference in the public domain to the souls of those who have died. The days when disasters would be summarised by the number of 'souls lost' have been replaced by a modern reference simply to 'deaths.' As the church becomes increasingly accustomed to hearing of death in this strictly physical sense, there is a real danger that it imbibes the materialistic worldview which neglects spiritual realities.

To love our neighbour biblically is to love our neighbour's soul, as well as their body. That this dimension of spiritual love is included it in the sixth commandment is evident from the clear Scriptural evidence which speaks of harming another person's soul as murder (Ezekiel 33:7-9), and harming our own soul as suicide (Proverbs 8:35-36; John 3:17-19).

On this basis Thomas Watson spoke of injuring another's soul as 'the greatest murder of all, because there is more of God's image in the soul than in the body.'[27] Similarly, Thomas Boston asked,

> When God says, *Thou shalt not kill,* doth he only take care for the body? No; doubtless of the soul too. He looks not to the cabinet only, overlooking the jewel. The soul is the man, at least the best and most precious part of him.[28]

If the soul, therefore, bears the clearest imprint of God's image—if it is the jewel in the cabinet—it is incumbent upon us to ensure, not just that we care about our neighbour's souls, but that we prioritise them.

---

[27] Watson, T. (1958) *A Body of Divinity*. London: The Banner of Truth Trust. p. 106.

[28] Boston, T. (2002) *The Complete Works of Thomas Boston*. Stoke-on-Trent: Tentmaker Publications. Vol. 2, p. 262.

Framing this duty positively, William Perkins (1558-1602) wrote, 'as concerning [our neighbour's] soul, we must endeavour by all means to win it to the faith.'[29] The Puritans, and those of a like mind, understood evangelism to be not merely a duty enjoined by the Great Commission and other New Testament passages but a matter of obedience flowing from the moral law.

Such a duty to souls is certainly complicated in a pandemic. However, it remains a duty, and not one that the church is at liberty to put on hold for a year. Indeed, if anything, it is a duty that becomes all the more pressing with the prospective imminence of death.

Such a situation clearly brings to light the tension between loving our neighbour's body and loving their soul. In most cases, one would hope to fulfil both duties without jeopardising the other. However, if an occasion should arise where there had to be a choice made between loving the body or loving the soul, it would be our duty to love that part of our neighbour which will not die—the soul. So, the English Puritan John Milward (1619-1683) wrote,

> Our love to our selves is, or should be orderly: we must first, and chiefly, love our souls, and then our bodies. The soul is of far greater worth than the body ... In like manner we ought to love our neighbour; we must desire and endeavour that it may be well with him in every respect, both as to his body and outward estate, but chiefly that his soul may prosper ... To give a man bread when he is hungry, or clothing when he is naked,

---

[29] Nicols, T. (Ed.) (1654) *An Abridgement Of The Whole Body Of Divinity, Extracted From The Learned Works Of That Ever-famous, And Reverend Divine Mr. William Perkins*. London: Printed By W B. For Will. Hope, At The Blue Anchor, On The North-side Of The Royal Exchange. p. 89.

> is something; but to convert a soul to God, is a greater kindness by much.[30]

The current situation also highlights the tension between self-love and loving the soul of our neighbour. Just as our duty is to love our neighbour's soul more than their own body, so it is our duty to love their soul more than our body. The way that countless Christians throughout history have acted in life-threatening circumstances pays tribute to this. A couple of examples will suffice.

In August of 1832, there was a cholera outbreak in Inverness. Rev Robert Findlater (c1753-1832), the minister in what is now the East Church, Inverness, had been away from his congregation at the time, preaching in Breadalbane, Perthshire. Having heard the news, he returned to Inverness as quickly as he could. Though, as his biographer explains, 'several families fled to the country … he deemed it his duty to remain at his post, publicly and privately exhorting his people to improve the visitation.'[31] As such, on his return, he preached twice on the Lord's Day on suitable texts and attended a prayer meeting on Tuesday evening. On Wednesday morning, he took ill with cholera and he died on Friday.

To some, this may seem like a tragic waste of life. However, Findlater wittingly risked his life out of love for those under his spiritual care and, in doing so, he played a part in what was to

---

[30] Milward, J. 'How ought we to love our Neighbour as our selves?' In: Case, T and Annesley, S (Eds.) (1674) *A Supplement to the Morning-Exercise at Cripplegate.* London: Thomas Cockerill. p. 52.

[31] Findlater, W. (1840) *Memoir of the Rev Robert Findlater.* Glasgow: William Collins. p. 308.

become a revival of religion, not just in the Highlands, but over much of Scotland.[32] During his short illness, he showed no regret.

It is notable that, at such times, churches were not closed. On the contrary, the government appointed a day of prayer on March 21st, 1832 and, as Tom Lennie records, 'The day was observed with remarkable reverence and solemnity all across the land.'[33] The leadership of both church and state well understood that, if the outbreak was a judgment from God, it was more dangerous to close churches than it was to keep them open. As such, in some places during the outbreak, churches were thronged and prayer meetings were held almost every week night. To some, this may seem idiotically reckless. However, it really demonstrates a calculated balancing of the physical dangers with the spiritual dangers, and a deliberate prioritising of spiritual health over temporal concerns.

During the same cholera outbreak, a young Gustavus Aird (1813-1898), later the minister of Creich Free Church for over half a century, became a zealous evangelist for the cause of Christ, and risked his own life in the process. His biographer writes concerning the time,

> The fear of God fell upon the community, and the religious life was quickened. The young student shared in the general revival, and found vent for his enthusiasm in many ways. In particular, he made a point of visiting all the non-church-going people in his neighbourhood. He visited some before church-time on sabbath morning, and led them out along with him. He

---

[32] See Lennie, T. (2015) *Land of Many Revivals*. Fearn: Christian Focus Publications. pp. 263-277.

[33] Lennie, T. (2015) *Land of Many Revivals*. Fearn: Christian Focus Publications. p. 263.

> left the house early and knocked at several doors by the way, saying: 'I see you are getting ready,' or 'Are you not ready yet?'[34]

The stories of Robert Findlater and Gustavus Aird are encouraging reminders that godly zeal and self-sacrifice have often reaped their spiritual harvest in the past. But these stories are also challenging to a modern church that must confess that such a spirit has largely been absent in the current crisis.

At such a time when many are fearing that which can 'kill the body,' it is incumbent upon the church to continue to fervently call men and women to be reconciled to 'him which is able to destroy both body and soul in hell' (Matthew 10:28) through the gospel of Jesus Christ. At a time of increased awareness of death and fear of what it holds, this is an opportunity for the church to zealously call men and women to prepare to meet their God and to remember that 'he that winneth souls is wise' (Proverbs 11:30).

The danger of absolutes

The Christian religion is, in many ways, a religion of absolutes. The lines between righteousness and unrighteousness are normally clearly drawn. However, that does not negate the fact that tension can arise between our different responsibilities. For example, it is not always clear where the balance should be struck between preserving our own lives and preserving the lives of others. Likewise, the equilibrium between caring for the soul of our neighbour and yet not carelessly endangering our neighbour's life is not always easy to define.

In approaching these questions, the church needs to pray to be 'filled with the knowledge of [Christ's] will in all wisdom and

---

[34] Macrae, A. (no date) *The Life of Gustavus Aird.* Stirling: Aneas Mackay. p. 30.

spiritual understanding; that [she] might walk worthy of the Lord' (Colossians 1:9-10). Only the wisdom of God can enable us to both understand and traverse the grey areas. When there are so many grey areas, the church needs to be careful when applying absolute applications from the sixth commandment principle. There will be absolutes which need to be communicated, but they should be carefully thought through and wisely applied. A few examples serve to illustrate the need for such an approach.

If the leadership of a church say that public worship will be temporarily postponed on the basis that the social interaction required would breach the sixth commandment, what counsel would that leadership give to a schoolteacher whose council requires her to teach in school or an electrician whose employer asks him to go out to site? In working, are they breaching the sixth commandment and, therefore, being unfaithful to God and unloving to their neighbour? If not, does that mean that the teaching of children or the wiring of a new building is more essential than public worship?

Should a minister visit an unconverted adherent in his church who is very ill? Going to see that person carries the risk of unwittingly transmitting the virus to him. However, the minister feels a great burden for the eternal soul of this man and knows that a face-to-face meeting will give him more opportunity to exhort him and pray with him. What should he do? Should he prioritise the body or the soul?

There can also be tension between different commandments. For example, a woman is told that her mother is being discharged from hospital with Covid-19 and that a care home will not admit her because she is carrying the virus. The woman feels that it is her duty to take her mother into the home in fulfilment of the fifth commandment. However, her husband has a lung condition and, should he contract the virus, it could be fatal. Which commandment should she keep?

Each of these instances shows the danger of hastily absolutizing applications of the sixth commandment. In these case studies, and in many others, the Christian conscience will have an important part to play because, sometimes, decisions will have to be made when there is no definitively black or white territory. However, when there is a measure of uncertainty as to what is right in any given situation, two principles must define Christian decision-making. The first is that decisions must always be based on the Word of God, and not pragmatic factors. The second is that, although both body and soul should be cared for where possible, should there have to be a choice between them, the soul must be given priority.

Conclusion

As Christians we are called to love our neighbour's body and soul, not just in a pandemic, but at all times. During a pandemic, however, particularly relevant is the sixth commandment's call not to endanger but, rather, to preserve the spiritual as well as the temporal life of our neighbour. As a church, we should not baulk at the complications that such a situation has brought into our experience but, rather, rejoice at the new and meaningful ways in which we can do our duty before both God and our neighbours.

If we take our current responsibility with the utmost seriousness, and approach it with the highest diligence, we will still find that we come short of loving our neighbour as we ought to. Nobody will be found to have perfectly observed the sixth commandment during the pandemic. We will all incur guilt. However, in understanding our sin in this area, we would do well to heed Thomas Boston's pastoral counsel as he concluded his own chapter on the sixth commandment:

> Now, sirs, examine yourselves in this matter; and who will not be brought in blood-guilty, guilty of their own and their neighbour's blood, the blood of their souls and bodies! God's law is spiritual and sees the guilt of blood where we plead 'Not guilty.' Let us be humbled and convinced, and apply to the blood of Christ, that we may be washed from it.[35]

[35] Boston, T. (2002) *The Complete Works of Thomas Boston.* Stoke-on-Trent: Tentmaker Publications. Vol. 2, p. 276.

~ 8 ~
Is it ever unloving to go to church?

Jonathan D. Moore

1. 'To the law and to the testimony' (Isaiah 8:20)

One of the most common arguments raised in defence of the churches which, for the past year, have chosen to go along with the widespread cancellation of the public worship of God, is the notion that it would be 'unloving' for the churches of Christ to gather together for worship when there might be a risk of thereby spreading the virus named SARS-CoV-2. Given the undeniable centrality and importance of love in the life and witness of the Christian church (1 John 3:23; John 13:35), that argument, coupled with the mainstream narrative concerning the Covid-19 pandemic, ends all discussion for many, and goes a long way to explain why many congregations immediately closed down their services without so much as a whimper of protest, and indeed why many churches did so even prior to the civil authorities requiring it. Conversely, church leaders and members who have conscientiously gathered for public worship against prevailing 'advice', or even legislation, have been dismissed and denounced—often unlovingly—as being 'unloving.' This brief essay recognises the serious and emotive nature of this charge and seeks to calm emotions on all sides by bringing to the question a greater measure of objectivity and a broader perspective than has often been the case.

Love is the fulfilling of the law

Before any of us can know with an absolute certainty whether it is ever unloving to go to church,[1] we have to be clear on what it is to be unloving. We can all recall times when we believed others had been 'unloving' to us and we were very quick to tell them so. But if we are honest, it was often simply an emotional response that undergirded such a charge. It was because we felt insulted, hurt, threatened, or some such other emotion. But the fact is, feeling insulted, hurt, or threatened can just as easily be because somebody has acted towards us in a loving way. For example, they may have told us the truth about ourselves, pointed out our sin, or exposed our hypocritical irrationality. The Pharisees and many others in Jesus' day felt insulted, hurt, and threatened by our Lord's actions precisely for those very reasons, but he was, of course, totally blameless and love incarnate.

The fact is, the only way to know whether a person's actions towards us are truly loving or not is to evaluate them, not in terms of our own emotional response or in terms of our culture's ever-changing fashions and philosophies—still less the latest meme we came across on social media—but in the cool light of God's Word and specifically the believer's infallible rule of conduct, God's law. After all, 'he that loveth another hath fulfilled the law' because 'love is the fulfilling of the law' (Romans 13:8, 10). How can we know that we truly love others? Answer: 'when we love God, and keep his commandments' (1 John 5:2).

---

[1] By this phrase we do not mean to deny or overlook the fact that the church of Christ is fundamentally a people and not a set of buildings. We simply follow, for the purposes of this essay, the popular shorthand for attending the stated services of the public worship of God in which are observed Christ's appointed ordinances of the New Covenant.

The first table of the law

The moral law of God is 'summarily comprehended in the Ten Commandments' (Westminster Larger Catechism, Q98; Westminster Shorter Catechism, Q41). These were written by God himself and given to Moses in the form of two 'tables of stone' (Exodus 31:15-16). The first table of this Decalogue comprised the initial four commandments which summarise 'our duty towards God,' and the second table comprised the remaining six commandments which summarise 'our duty to man' (WCF 19:2). The first table was further summarised by our Lord as 'the first and great commandment,' which is to love God, and the second table as 'the second like unto it,' which is love to our neighbour as ourself (Matthew 22:36-40). More specifically, the first table requires us to worship and glorify God (first commandment), in the way he has appointed (second commandment), reverently (third commandment), and at the set times he has appointed (fourth commandment). So clearly, it is imperative that we 'go to church' and particularly on the Lord's Day.

The second table of the law

But it is in the second table of the Decalogue and in the sixth commandment in particular ('Thou shalt not kill,' Exodus 20:13) that we find a possible ground for concluding that 'going to church' may sometimes in fact be unloving. The sixth commandment forbids 'the taking away of our own life, or the life of our neighbour unjustly, or whatsoever tendeth thereunto' (Westminster Shorter Catechism, Q69). Conversely, it requires of us 'all lawful endeavours to preserve our own life, and the life of others' (Westminster Shorter Catechism, Q68). Although 'the law of the LORD is perfect' (Psalm 19:7), how to apply it in a fallen world is not always immediately clear. Tensions and apparent contradictions can appear to exist between the various precepts, and even between the ten commandments themselves. Our concern here is whether the requirements of the first table can be overruled, modified, or temporarily suspended in order to fulfil our moral duty in the second table to make 'all lawful endeavours to preserve our own life, and the life of others.' Should my public worship of God ever be suspended in order to help preserve the life of my neighbour? Should the first table of the law ever come in at second place behind the second table of the law? Does the greatest commandment ever give way to the second greatest?

Balancing the two tables of the law

The first table is first for a very good reason: it takes priority over the second table. This stands to reason. God is God and man is man. God is the infinitely glorious creator and sovereign Lord. Man is a creature and a sinful one at that. God is to be worshipped and served. Man is to perform that worship and service. How could it be otherwise? And yet if a fire were to break out in a church building right in the middle of the Lord's Supper there is not a congregation on earth that would resign itself to the flames due to the priority of the worship of God over the temporal needs of sinful man. Yet the congregation that is making a beeline for the fire exit has not suddenly fallen into pragmatism, but can still be applying both tables of the law of God in a principled, internally coherent, and God-glorifying manner. But how exactly does that work in terms of ethical reasoning?

In keeping with a long tradition of Christian ethics, the Reformed Orthodox theologian Francis Turretin (1623-1687) makes a distinction between those aspects of the first and second tables which are 'moral' and those which are 'ceremonial.' The worship of God involves many external or 'ceremonial' acts, but these are not to be treated as more necessary than upholding the moral requirements of the second table. As Turretin puts it, 'the ceremonial of the first table yields to the moral of the second.'[2] As well as others who make the same point,[3] Turretin appeals to Hosea 6:6, 'I desired mercy, and not sacrifice.'[4] This rhetorical statement is not, of course, an absolute negative, but a recognition that, firstly, among other things, the offering up of worship to God is made void if devoid of love, and, secondly as a corollary, that if in any situation there must of necessity be a binary choice between loving our neighbour and engaging in the externals of public worship, then God would always require love to our neighbour 'first' (Matthew 5:23-24).

It is this applicatory principle that lies behind the more familiar concept of the normal requirements of the fourth commandment (the sabbath of the first table) being legitimately interrupted by 'the duties of necessity and mercy' (in acknowledgement of the second table) (WCF 21:8). It is this same principle at work when our Lord recognises that even rescuing a suffering animal, never mind a neighbour, may be a sufficient justification for a departure from normal observance of the first table of the law (Luke 14:5). It therefore follows that Scripture clearly teaches that certain circumstances or 'ceremonials' of the first table (the worship of

---

[2] Turretin, F. [translated: Giger, G. M.; edited: Dennison, J. T.] (1992-1997) *Institutes of Elenctic Theology*. Phillipsburg, New Jersey, USA: Presbyterian and Reformed. Vol. 2, pp. 35-36 (Section XI.6.vi).

[3] E.g., the Scottish Covenanter, James Durham (1622-1658), *The Law unsealed: Or, a practical Exposition of the Ten Commandments*. Glasgow: Robert Sanders. (1676) p. 5; and the English Puritans John Ball (1585-1640), *A short Treatise: Containing all the principall Grounds of Christian Religion*. London: William Welby. (1617) p. 182; *The Power of Godlines both doctrinally and practically handled*. London: Abraham Miller. (1657) pp. 8-9; and Thomas Manton (c.1620-1677), *One hundred and ninety Sermons on the hundred and nineteenth Psalm* London: T. P.. (1681) p. 814 (Sermon 132).

[4] See also the similar teaching of Proverbs 21:3; Isaiah 11:1; Amos 5:21-24; Micah 6:6-8 and our Lord's application of the text in Matthew 12:1-8.

God) may and must be modified if that is the only way a breach of the moral requirements of the sixth commandment can be avoided.

But exactly how and at what point? Where can we draw a line between the necessity of worshipping God in the manner and at the times he has appointed, and the duty of preserving human life? In the extreme case of the fire mentioned above, the answer is clear, and nobody is left syllogising in the pews. But what about less clear-cut situations? What if it is five church members who claim they can smell a gas leak? Does that merit the immediate termination of the worship service? How about two church members? And what if there are reports that there is a new coronavirus at large?

Applying the two tables of the law: biblical quarantine

Thankfully the Lord has not left his people in the dark in this matter of obedience to the two tables of the law. The Ten Commandments are a summary of a much larger body of biblical law. The whole of God's law must be taken into account if we are to know how to keep the Ten Commandments in different contexts and callings, and to apply them to different scenarios. Despite our natural, fallen desire to limit, marginalise, and explain away God's law in order to carve out for ourselves more areas of autonomy and pretended liberty, the fact remains that God's commandments are 'exceeding broad' and touch every area and aspect of our lives (Psalm 119:96).

Concerning the topic in hand, in his infinite wisdom and knowing the end from the beginning, God has been pleased to place in his law specific instruction on the containment and removal of infectious diseases from society in a way that upholds both tables of the law. We find in 'the leprosy laws' of Leviticus 13 and 14 that there is in fact even such a thing as biblical quarantine, that is to say, the enforced isolation of a person infected with a very serious disease which, upon close inspection by the appointed authorities, appears to be one that might spread.

It is important in our context to note that the community as a whole had a responsibility to identify and present such people who appeared to have 'the plague of leprosy' (13:2). It was not left to someone to volunteer themselves as and when, or if, they deemed it convenient or appropriate. And that is quite understandable in light of the fact that the ensuing detailed inspection (13:9-44) could then result in the person being immediately 'shut up' or isolated for up to fourteen days (13:4-5). Even if his skin complaint proved harmless, he was now taking a significant social and financial hit for the sake of the health of the whole community. The best outcome he could hope for at this point was to be released on the fourteenth day with his skin problem declared to be non-contagious (13:6). The worst outcome must have been the nightmare he was dreading for each one of those fourteen days of solitary confinement: to be formally pronounced 'unclean' (13:8) and to attain the judicial status of 'leper' within the community. His temporary quarantine then became a permanent state of isolation from the healthy members of the community: 'All the days wherein the plague shall be in him he shall be defiled; he is unclean: he shall dwell alone; without the camp shall his habitation be' (13:46).[5] This state of isolation might in some instances even last for the rest of his life, even if it were the very king himself (2 Chronicles 26:21).

This isolation meant permanent separation from his family and, presumably, from his earlier calling in society in most cases. But far worse from a spiritual point of view, this isolation by definition also involved exclusion from the gathered worship of the people

[5] He did not need to be 'alone' in the absolute sense since social interaction between lepers themselves was permitted (e.g., 2 Kings 7:3; Luke 17:12).

of God. Here at least, it would clearly have been unlawful, and therefore sinful and unloving, for this leper 'to go to church' as it were, not simply because he was ceremonially unclean but because he was contagious with a serious disease. Furthermore, this non-attendance at public worship was to be actively supported and enforced by the governing authorities. Therefore, the concept of it being 'unloving to go to church' is not something alien to God's law but a scenario which it not only anticipates but actively brings about through its own precepts in certain exceptional situations. The leper could not claim he was being 'persecuted' by this quarantine or inability to worship God in the usual manner. He had to submit to God's providence and acknowledge God's gracious provision for the health and cleanliness of his entire people as they waited for the Messiah to come. In this way the priority and sanctity of God's house and worship was upheld for the whole community, at the same time as the importance of the physical health and well-being of the community.

Applying God's law to modern epidemics: The principles

But the obvious question at this point (at least for the God-fearer) is how this law applies today. We know that, when they were first given, the statutes of Leviticus 13 for diagnosing and containing infectious diseases made Israel stand out from the pagan nations as exceedingly 'wise and understanding' (Deuteronomy 4:6). There were no sniggers about 'primitive' Hebrew medicine back then. In fact, scholars and historians of medicine have since recognised that these statutes were actually 'cutting-edge' healthcare at the time and far superior to the approaches of the surrounding pagan nations and remained so for many centuries thereafter. But the international response would hardly be the same now if Leviticus 13 were to be adopted wholesale by health care practitioners today as 'best practice' in the prevention of infectious skin diseases and epidemics. But notwithstanding the huge advances of modern medicine, we know by deduction that Leviticus 13 is still to this day 'profitable for doctrine, for reproof, for correction, for instruction in righteousness' (2 Timothy 3:16),[6] and we know that we should 'delight in [it] after the inward man' (Romans 7:22). But how does that work in practice, given that Leviticus 13 is linked to the law of sacrifice of the Old Covenant?

The abrogation of the ceremonial law

At this point we must take into account the following considerations. Leviticus 13 is inseparable from Leviticus 14 and it is there that the ceremonial nature of God's law of leprosy is brought to the fore. In the overall context of ceremonial uncleanness, Leviticus 13 shows that the LORD cared for the physical health of his people and the need to be 'healed.' But Leviticus 14 points to his care for the spiritual health of his people, and their need to be 'cleansed' in addition to being 'healed' (14:3-4). It reveals his willingness and readiness to receive the cleansed back into the fellowship of his presence. This cleansing was to be accomplished by God's appointed priest shedding the blood of lambs as part of a larger ceremony (14:12-14, 19-20, 25). In biblical theology sickness and sin are related via the Fall. In biblical law infectious skin diseases are similarly linked to a lack of wholeness, to uncleanness and judicial defilement. They remove the ability to dwell with a holy God in his holy house. Nothing less than the shedding and sprinkling of blood can therefore cleanse from this corruption—and, by analogy, from the sin that plagues our heart (1 Kings 8:38)—and bring us into his holy presence. This is why Leviticus 13 and 14, now fulfilled in Christ's finished work of redemption, are indeed seen by the Christian church as part of the ceremonial law which was 'abrogated, under the new testament.'[7]

---

[6] 'Righteousness' (δικαιοσύνη, *dikaiosynē*) means, in this context, 'right conduct'.

[7] WCF 19:3 appeals to Colossians 2:14, 16-17; Daniel 9:27; Ephesians 2:15-16.

To reintroduce today, for example, the animal sacrifices of Leviticus in any context would be a perversion of the gospel.[8]

The abiding moral duties of the ceremonial law

But it would be a mistake, albeit a relatively common one, to assume that the 'law of leprosy' is therefore irrelevant for Christian ethics and is now only of use for the very occasional preaching of a gospel sermon. Yes, we no longer observe the ceremonial law today as if we were still under the Old Covenant. But in no point and at no stage in human history can any part of God's holy law be seen as immoral or unjust. In other words, there are what the Westminster Confession calls 'divers instructions of moral duties' in the ceremonial laws, even though in the New Covenant these laws are 'now abrogated' (WCF 19:3).[9] Some leading Reformed theologians have called this a 'moral equity' in the ceremonial laws.[10] Whatever we may wish to call it, this important principle

---

[8] This basic point is without controversy amongst orthodox Christians, but it is worth noticing in addition here, that even that aspect of the biblical law of leprosy which provided Israel with a practical defence against infectious diseases contains internal evidence that it was only designed for literal observance under the Old Covenant. The requirement for resurgent 'black hair' to appear before being able to pronounce a patient 'clean' (13:37) was meaningful for a Semitic people, but, if taken literally, would hardly provide much encouragement today for a convalescing blond Anglo-Saxon. In other words, it was clearly not intended to be implemented literally when the New Covenant was to take the true religion to all nations (cf. Matthew 28:18-20).

[9] By way of example, the Westminster Assembly cites here the ceremonial laws concerning leaven and the Apostle's appeal to them in 1 Corinthians 5:7. The implication is that Paul is not simply indulging in a 'spiritual metaphor' but directly bringing out from this ceremonial law a latent moral duty.

[10] For example, the father of English Puritanism William Perkins (1558-1602) states that 'the equitie of those lawes ceremonial ... do still bind us' (William Perkins (1616-1618) *The Workes.* London: John Legatt & Cantrell Legge. Vol. 3, (i) p. 17 [on Heb. 11:4]). The Westminster Divine Edward Leigh (1603-1671) recognises that, 'These were ceremonial Laws, but there is a moral equity of

of an abiding moral kernel in Old Covenant statutes is evident in the Apostolic appeal to Deuteronomy 25:4 in 1 Corinthians 9:8-12 and 1 Timothy 5:17-18. We should recognise, therefore, that there are abiding moral principles in the ceremonial law of Leviticus 13, and, as it happens, they are of particular relevance to the current preoccupation with Covid-19.

Applying God's law to modern epidemics: The details

Now that we have seen how there are abiding moral duties in God's ceremonial law, how should we apply his law of infectious diseases to today's situation, 'not in the oldness of the letter' but 'in newness of spirit' (Romans 7:6)? We readily acknowledge that when we move in this way from 'the letter' to 'the spirit' of the law (2 Corinthians 3:6), things become less clearly defined and more fluid. But this is actually part of the genius of biblical law and Christian ethics, not a defect. Energised by the Holy Spirit, it is what actually enables the church to apply God's law fittingly and appropriately to all nations and cultures until the Second Coming of the Son of God, the Law Giver.[11] But the Lord never promised that obedience would be easy or straightforward. This life is a continual battle against the all-pervasive effects of sin and the dark forces of lawlessness at work in the world, and, sadly, in the church too. But the Lord did give us his Word, his law, and his Holy Spirit. So what do they say?

The need for quarantine

Potentially fatal contagious diseases are a fact of life in a fallen world under the curse. God has made ultimate provision for that fact in the redemption of body and soul in Christ. But meanwhile in biblical ethics it is therefore sometimes legitimate for governing

---

them which is perpetual' (*A Systeme or Body of Divinity*. London: A. M. for William Lee. (1662) Section 8.4, p. 857).

[11] Compare Matthew 28:18-20 with Acts 7:38.

authorities to implement a policy of quarantine as a means of containing serious dangers to public health through the enforced (non-voluntary) isolation of highly contagious people. The resulting inconvenience to some members of society is therefore not *inherently* unjust or some immoral violation of 'human rights.' It is not *of necessity* a 'medical tyranny' which must be strenuously resisted in defence of civil liberties. In our highly individualistic and selfish society, such messages about rights and liberties have their own special attraction, but God's law clearly requires that we be willing to undergo considerable personal inconvenience, and even genuine suffering, for the good of the wider society in which we live.

The seven-day periods in Leviticus 13-14 undoubtedly have a ceremonial aspect, pointing, like circumcision, to the resurrection of Christ on the eighth day[12] and the resulting new beginning and healing that flows from Christ's atonement (Isaiah 53:5; 1 Peter 2:24). Yet it also contains the moral duty of recognising that the needs of public health cannot be met by policies tailor-made to suit every single individual. No doubt some quarantined Israelites began to meet the requisite change in skin condition well before the seventh or fourteenth day, but nevertheless they still had to wait patiently and submit to the law that was there for the good of all. Things cannot always go the way we would prefer and so we must patiently cooperate, where possible, with agreed policies and procedures, despite the inevitable inconveniences.

We must also recognise that the occurrence of deadly contagious diseases in this fallen world calls us to humility in the face of the damage to creation brought about by our own disobedience both in Adam and in our own lives. Part of this humility must also

---

12 That is, the first day of the new week, or the day after the seventh day (hence the 'eighth day') of the previous week.

involve taking contagious diseases seriously in submission to God's providence. This will manifest itself, among other things, in an appropriate and proportionate concern for cleanliness and sanitation, both for ourselves and others, and a willingness to behave responsibly for the good of society at large. There is no place for bravado or an uncaring disdain for the health or vulnerabilities of other members of society. To return to our title, there are sometimes occasions, therefore, when a person should not attend public worship: times when he believes himself to be sick with a contagious disease. And in certain contexts of extreme danger, such a principle can even be legitimately enforced by the governing authorities (through a biblical quarantine policy). This much is surely not only warranted but required by the moral duties latent in Leviticus 13 and the chapter's application of the sixth commandment to public health. In certain extreme cases, therefore, it is indeed 'unloving to go to church.' The ceremonial requirements of the first table of the law must always yield to the moral duties of the second table. True love to our neighbour and to society as a whole is always the keeping of God's law.

The limits of quarantine

Yet not all quarantine policies are biblical ones. If they ride roughshod over the clear limitations of biblical quarantine they become immoral and even dangerous to the communities they purport to be helping. Taken to an extreme, as we see today, they can even end up causing far more suffering and death than the targeted disease ever could, by destroying the religious, social, and economic fabric of society which undergirds its long-term overall health and prosperity. It is vital that we recognise the following characteristics of a biblical and proportionate quarantine policy.

Firstly, the targeted contagious disease must be known to be deadly or devastating in its impact in order to justify the considerable social and economic impact that quarantine can have on the person concerned and their immediate family and connections. Whatever the precise identity of 'leprosy' in Bible times,[13] it was certainly more serious than a coronavirus which the vast majority of people can readily fight off without medical intervention. In biblical times a leper of any age was as good as dead,[14] not just someone who had temporarily lost their sense of taste or smell or needed a couple of days in bed. Even before banishment, biblical 'leprosy' was always inherently devastating, and could often be intensely painful and terminal.

Secondly, the person quarantined must be visibly and self-evidently sick with the targeted contagious disease (symptomatic), or the medical authorities must at least have objective reasons for believing the person's sickness is probably due to that disease. Diagnostic tests designed to play a subordinate and confirmatory role in the presence of known symptoms are not to be used on their own where no symptoms are present. There is no justification whatsoever in biblical law for quarantining perfectly healthy or asymptomatic people. To do so would be to lose all sense of proportion and to make the eradication of a disease more important than life itself. It would be akin to banning all drivers from the roads just to be sure that all dangerous drivers have been successfully banned. Yes, that would largely achieve its narrow goal and technically save some human lives, but only by making the overall situation much worse and destroying many, many

---

13 There is no consensus among modern scholars as to the precise identity of the various diseases in Leviticus 13, and there most probably never will be. But the moral principles in the chapter do not depend on identifying any of its diseases with Hansen's disease (modern leprosy) or any other disease known to modern science. Indeed, in God's providence this lack of clarity simply directs our focus to the abiding moral and spiritual lessons.

14 Cf. Numbers 12:12 ('as one dead'); Josephus, *Antiquities of the Jews*, 3.11.

more human lives in other ways through the destruction of the livelihoods of countless safe drivers and of the society that depends on them. Boasting in the mainstream media about how many lives have recently been saved from road accidents would not make up for this monumental blunder.

Thirdly, the fact that a person is quarantined does not mean they are not attended to and visited by an appointed representative of the church. The priest in Leviticus 13-14 continues to engage with the sick person, to answer their questions and concerns, to explain the word of God to them, and, in short, to minister to them in their affliction. They are sectioned off, yes, but not abandoned by the representatives of Christ. The priest is there to restore them as soon as possible. Clearly the priest might conceivably have caught a disease himself while engaging in these official duties, especially as he had to inspect the skin so closely as to be able to discern the colour of hairs in the infected region. But that was his occupational hazard. It came with the job, even as it comes with the job of (at least) elders today to visit the sick and not make their own health considerations a sufficient ground for disobeying the Lord's command (James 5:14-15; Matthew 25:31-46; 1 John 3:16). If it is said that this in effect nullifies the quarantine, we reply that it does not nullify a biblical quarantine because a biblical quarantine keeps a sense of proportion and deals with the diseased person holistically. It does not force them to die alone and ban all visits from relatives and pastors. Jesus himself embodied the spirit of this law when, without breaking it, he made himself accessible to banished lepers and ministered to them.

Fourthly, every effort must be made to confirm a recovery as soon as reasonably and administratively possible and return the person to the community. The importance of the health of society at large does not mean that the needs of the individual and their dependents have no value at all and that at the whim of a health official or politician they can be sacrificed 'for the greater good' by means of indefinite or excessively long periods of enforced isolation or 'lockdown'. That may pass for a legitimate approach in China or North Korea, but it is not biblical. Public health and the liberties of the individual must be held in balance with a due (i.e., biblical) sense of proportion. Until 2020, the principle of proportionality had played a central part in decision-making in modern healthcare.

Fifthly, and most importantly for our essay title, the public worship of God is to continue even if there is a widespread outbreak of a known[15] contagious disease in society. And it is precisely because of the protection afforded by an accompanying biblical quarantine policy that such a practice is reasonable and responsible. The sick are isolated, the vulnerable are protected, and the healthy continue to worship God—just like in Leviticus 13. The idea that the tabernacle or temple worship was suddenly to be cancelled due to a sharp increase in a disease, no matter how contagious, is alien to the law of God and completely incompatible with the priorities and sense of proportion in a biblically shaped worldview.[16] In fact, it was precisely in order to keep the public worship of God running that lepers were banished from it. The leper's freedoms and preferences were subordinated to the far higher priority of the public worship of God. Effectively quarantining the whole of society so that even the public worship of God must be 'locked down' does not square with biblical law but only with a society that believes the public of worship of God is a trivial, marginal, and largely irrelevant sideshow—a 'non-

[15] If it is not known, then the requirements above for an accurate diagnosis cannot yet be implemented for a biblical quarantine.

[16] Equally incongruous would have been a 'Zero Leprosy' public policy as a precondition for returning to normal tabernacle worship!

essential service.' Such a society has lost its moral compass (adherence to God's law) and the fear of God. In contrast, 'the spirit' of the law is that when a pandemic strikes there should ordinarily be an *increase* in public worship, rather than a decrease, as the church responds to the voice of God in providence by especially calling upon the name of the Lord for mercy, forgiveness, and healing in Christ, and as she seeks to minister to those in need and in distress. Only when a quarantine policy and general approach honour these five principles can it hope to be a biblical and therefore a truly lawful and therefore a truly loving response.

The verdict

In light of the above analysis, and weighed in the balances of God's law and justice—as the actions of all civil magistrates are (cf. Daniel 5:27)—the response of the civil authorities of our day to the Covid-19 pandemic must be found wanting in the vast majority of cases. Although civil magistrates, politicians, and other shapers of public policy are joyfully to acknowledge, with trembling, their moral obligation to uphold God's law (Psalm 2:10-12; Romans 13:3-4), time and time again we find that the restrictions they have recently placed upon the churches of Christ, as well as society at large, are contrary to God's law and have no basis in God's revelation of moral equity. In terms of our assigned question, they have acted lawlessly because acting against God's supreme law. When the 'remedy' of the recent policies of civil authorities proves to be much worse than the disease, it will be therefore largely because the wisdom and equity of God's law has been disregarded in the civil sphere.

But there are no grounds here for the churches to be smug at the failure of the politicians. It is important to remind ourselves that God's law applies to the church with an even greater urgency since judgment begins with the house of God rather than the world (1 Peter 4:7). It applies particularly to church leaders since they will be judged more strictly than everyone else (James 3:1). It follows that churches ought to be taking a lead in principled obedience to God's law and that Christian leaders should be vocal on how exactly a biblical balance is to be maintained between the first table of the law and the sixth commandment. The church should be teaching and witnessing to the state and society at large on the moral requirements of God's law, rather than setting it aside in order to do whatever the state or social pressure demand of her. It is always better 'to obey God rather than men' (Acts 5:29). Yet instead we have seen the churches join hands with the state in forbidding healthy Christians to 'go to church' and justify this complicity with error by redefining love in a way that conflicts with God's law, the true rule of love.

It is this objective, divinely revealed rule of love in all its breadth that ought to be at the foundation of Christian unity in responding to the many vexed issues raised by the occurrence of pandemics in the modern world. The balance and proportionality of God's perfect law should rein in excessive actions and reactions on all sides, and nip in the bud both anarchic and totalitarian tendencies. Agreement on the application of God's law in every detail may not be possible, but a common commitment to honouring the moral principles of God's law concerning infectious diseases should not only result in a general consensus, but also provide a solid basis for exercising judgments of charity towards those Christians and churches who finally end up differing from us in their conscientious application of it to a particular geography, community, or congregation. The only fundamental alternative to God's law is every man doing what is right in his own eyes—a sure recipe for godless and deadly practices from the surrounding culture to move in and fill the moral vacuum (Judges 17:6; 21:25).

2. 'According to the glorious gospel' (1 Timothy 1:11)

Given the prejudices and presuppositions of a large part of the modern Western church, the establishment of our case from the law of God has taken much longer than we need to spend here on the establishment of our case from the gospel of God. The disproportion in length of this second section is therefore not to be mistaken as indicative of the ideal emphasis. A particular emphasis is often demanded by the defects of the hour, even as the apostle's first letter to the Corinthians might well have included even greater coverage of more central doctrines had the Corinthian Christians not been embroiled in some disputes and malpractices in other areas.

A confirmed case of inverted priorities

The reason we do not cease to 'go to church' during a respiratory virus season and cancel services so as not to be seen to be 'unloving' to the small minority of people who could be at serious risk were they to become infected, is not simply because of our reading of the 'moral duties' contained in the doctrine of biblical quarantine in Leviticus 13. No, the gospel itself cries out that we view the public worship of God and the role of the church in society as completely different from the way in which godless civil governments and secular society view it. True love to our neighbour is to tell him by words *and deeds* that we really believe that God's gospel and worship are of supreme importance both for us and for him.

In the past year, the authorities formally pronounced the public worship service of the Christian church as a 'non-essential service'—less essential in fact than off-licenses which have yet to be shut down 'because of Covid'. It has even gone so far as to pronounce fundamental elements of Christian worship as too risky, and many churches have yielded unthinkingly to their 'advice' that God's praise must no longer be sung publicly at all, never mind loudly (cf. Psalm 98:4). We are told by the state that the sacraments or ordinances of baptism and the Lord's Supper are redundant at this time and that their administration is under the state's jurisdiction and within the state's remit to cancel.

But we must not put all the blame on the civil authorities. Church authorities for the most part have encouraged this situation with their lame, immediate, unthinking, and uncritical compliance with such questionable, unbiblical, and even illegal encroachments.[17] In fact, many churches voluntarily closed down or curtailed their public worship and ministries well in advance of any formal directive to do so. Some still continue to outcompete one another in an apparent quest to create the 'safest' worship space ever known to man—or at least to the two-dozen people—maximum—who are allowed entry. In many cases the churches' identity crisis and the accompanying low view of the importance and centrality of the ordinances of Christ's appointed worship have been exposed on a national and international scale.

But this did not happen overnight. Many churches voluntarily transforming themselves into registered charities did not help their mindset in the run-up to the Covid-19 pandemic. In effect many such churches had for decades already been saying to the state, 'In return for some tax rebates, please treat the church of Christ just like any other human organisation, and we promise to submit to all your rules, just as if we were a soup kitchen or a charity of voluntary dog groomers.' In 2020 the authorities took such

---

[17] Restrictions imposed upon churches by the Scottish Parliament have been declared unlawful in the Court of Session (*Opinion of Lord Braid In the cause Reverend Dr William J U Philip and others*, 24th March 2021, https://www.scotcourts.gov.uk/docs/default-source/cos-general-docs/pdf-docs-for-opinions/2021csoh032.pdf?sfvrsn=0, [Accessed 16/04/2021]).

churches at their word and shut them down more or less for the best part of one year—although strangely it allowed charities for dog grooming to continue operating despite the theoretical risk of groomer-owner transmission of the virus. Indeed, for a time in the UK, shops, pubs, and restaurants were allowed to open their doors on the Lord's Day, but not the churches of Christ. Pets could be professionally groomed and beer swilled, but converts could not be officially washed (i.e. baptised—Acts 22:16) nor the wine of the Lord's Supper tasted.

The church and gospel of Christ as central

So if the church of Christ is not just yet one more charity hoping to do a little good at the edges of a broken society, what is she? If she is not just another self-help group requesting from the civil magistrate permission to be able to catch up with shops, pubs, and restaurants in opening her doors on the Lord's Day, what exactly is she?

Well, the Bible is quite clear, and its message is glorious. The church of Christ on earth is the dawn of God's new creation. She is the body of the risen Saviour of the world who has committed to her trust the good news of eternal salvation, the forgiveness of sins, peace with God, and everlasting blessedness in the age to come. She has been entrusted with this good news and the means of grace, and her urgent call goes out to all creation to partake of this full and free salvation. So central is the church of Christ to the salvation of this world and therefore the good of society as a whole that outside of her 'there is no ordinary possibility of salvation' (WCF 25:2). This cannot be said of a gym, health spa, or even of a para-church organisation.

Only the true church of Christ is the salt and light of the earth, preserving and illuminating a rotting and darkened society (Matthew 5:13-14). Only in her are leaves found for 'the healing of the nations' (Revelation 22:2). Had the church of Christ in Sodom exceeded just nine in number, the whole city would have been spared and the day of judgment delayed for their sake (Genesis 18:32). While there are still people to be saved in this world through the preaching of the gospel, the church of Christ is preserved, and the Second Coming and the Final Judgment are delayed (Romans 9:29; 2 Peter 3:9).

In the light of this wonderful reality it should come as no great surprise that God's command in the New Covenant is still that all his people (save for those who in his providence are temporarily sick with infectious diseases) gather together if at all possible in order to 'continu[e] steadfastly in the apostles' doctrine and fellowship, and in breaking of bread, and in prayers,' 'not forsaking the assembling of [them]selves together, as the manner of some is' (Acts 2:42; Hebrews 10:25).

In times of national crisis when many are dying horrific and lonely deaths due to a deadly virus, the church of Christ, in keeping with her historic practice in previous plagues and pandemics, should therefore be demonstrating her love for the lost, the dying, the bereaved, the lonely, the frightened, and the confused, not by mimicking a secular order of priorities, closing down church life, and retreating into her own cosy houses and online meetings, but by being even more actively engaged in publicly preaching the gospel, visiting the sick, pastoring the bereaved and downcast, and showing a despairing world how we have been delivered from the 'fear of death' through Jesus Christ who 'giveth life unto the world' (Hebrews 2:14-15; John 6:33). We have an infinitely more glorious message than this world's offer of pseudo-salvation through lockdowns, big government, and 'big pharma'!

Conclusion: Appearing to love versus actually loving

In our superficial day, when anti-intellectualism, anti-confessionalism, and antinomianism are rampant in the churches, the charge of being 'unloving' will no doubt continue to carry much weight and be enough to intimidate many church leaders and members into submitting to the novel concept of shutting down the public worship of God whenever the advent of a new coronavirus variant is announced. But at this point there is a call to self-examination for every one of us. Do I want to go along with an antinomian, culturally determined, false conception of 'love' or to love 'in deed and in truth' (1 John 3:18)? Do I want the world to think I am a nice Christian more than I want God to see that I am an obedient Christian? Is it my desire and the desire of my congregation simply to *appear* to be loving in the eyes of other Christians and the world, or is it my desire and the desire of my congregation *actually* to be loving? To be more concerned with appearances than reality seems to lie behind much modern evangelism and 'church growth strategies', but it is also the essence of hypocrisy. When we are in our right mind as Christians there is, of course, no doubt about the right answers here. But has Covid-19 found us out of our right mind, with a wrong order of priorities, and in the grip of a far bigger threat than any seasonal respiratory virus?

It used to be a matter of common sense in the modern West that the sick should be isolated, the vulnerable protected, and the rest of society left to get on with their lives. But as the mainstream narrative now commends the locking down of the rest of society, including those who simply want to go to church, it has been necessary for us to demonstrate how both the law and gospel of God come down on the side of now-not-so-common sense.

When we consider the central and glorious role which the church of Christ and her worship and service of God have in the salvation of this world, and do so in the light of the Ten Commandments and Leviticus 13, we see that there is perfect harmony between God's law and God's gospel. The unnecessary cancelling of public worship for healthy church attenders is a breach of God's holy law and revealed will, and also a practical denial of the centrality of the gospel and kingdom of our Lord Jesus Christ. To suspend the worship and saving ministry of the church unnecessarily in the face of any disease is therefore not loving at all.

In a world overridden with the rampant plague of sinful unbelief and man-centred secularism, the church must continue to bear loving witness to the coming of Christ's kingdom and the supreme need everyone has of salvation in Christ through his church. May God grant to his people the grace, clear-sightedness, and courage to be *truly* loving to a sin-sick world at this time of national and international chaos and confusion.

~ 9 ~
How far has our culture impacted the church's response to the pandemic?

Matthew A. Vogan and Catherine E. Hyde

Instinctively, Christian believers neither need nor want to be conformed to this world, but rather, as Paul exhorts us, we should be transformed by the renewing of our mind (Romans 12:1-2). 'The world' which Paul refers to is the whole scene of human history, which is not only passing away, but also antagonistic to God. Its principles are shaped by this. Christians, however, are 'transformed' as we are by grace changed increasingly into the likeness of Christ, so that we increasingly come to have more Christ-like thoughts and preferences and desires and attitudes. To the renewed mind, God is the great reality, and eternal things have the priority. This is evident as we exercise the grace of discernment to identify and pursue the 'good, and acceptable, and perfect, will of God' (Romans 12:2).

The trouble is that in a time of crisis, under the pressure of the circumstances, we can react in a way that is not fully consistent with our renewed thought patterns. We can instead find ourselves responding according to the unspoken assumptions of the unrenewed world around us—assumptions and instincts which perhaps we thought we were largely free of.

A time of crisis and trial can therefore have the spiritual benefit that it shows us what is in our heart (Judges 3:4; 2 Chronicles

32:31). Israel often had this humbling experience (Deuteronomy 8:16; Deuteronomy 8:2). When everything has been turned upside down, we should take the opportunity to reflect on whether we have responded with integrity, as those who are being transformed into the likeness of Christ, or whether the crisis has exposed any underlying problems in our hearts.

This is a particularly pressing question for the church in relation to the pandemic of 2020. In the twenty-first century the church finds itself in strange secularist territory and struggles to know how to respond and adapt. The religious, political, and ideological environment we inhabit is so markedly different from what even very recent generations could even have imagined. The challenges of our time bring real and constant dilemmas for the consistent Christian and the faithful church. These have only been magnified by the crisis.

Like many, including the government, the church was caught off guard and unprepared for the pandemic of 2020. There was an understandable sense of fear and alarm arising from the lack of knowledge of the disease and its effects. We were dependent on other sources of information. The church felt compelled to close its doors, disperse its congregations, and concede to civil government. As recently as the year 2019, the likelihood of most of these actions would have seemed non-existent. Christians across all sorts of denominations placed such a high value on open doors, face-to-face gatherings for worship and fellowship, and the right of the church to make its own decisions about worship independently of the government, that these would have seemed unassailable principles of the Christian church. So how can we understand what led us to make these our responses in this time of trial?

This chapter will explore some aspects of our cultural context which may help to explain the church's response to this crisis. Clearly we cannot avoid inhabiting an environment pervaded by principles that reject God. Yet as Francis Schaeffer (1912-1984) observed, pluralistic secularism 'in the long run is a more deadly poison than outright persecution.'[1] It works slowly but surely and pervasively. The constant onslaught of secularism means that we are inclined to concede smaller skirmishes to save our ammunition for the bigger battles. But while we are defending the main points of entry, have we let the enemy sneak in by a secret means? God's grace means that in our heart of hearts, as believers we are not ultimately conformed to the secularism and materialism of this world. Yet do we not have to confess that, under pressure, when beset by sudden and unexpected adversity, some lingering remnants of our old worldly ways of thinking and acting have been exposed? It can be shocking to realise the degree to which we have not been able to insulate and isolate ourselves from the contagion of such thinking. Uncomfortable as this exposure is to our natural sensibilities, it can have a beneficial outcome, if with the Lord's help we repent and believe afresh.

1. Our view of God

Relegating God to the sidelines

The most basic and ultimate reality is that *God is*. There is one God, and the one who *is*, is triune—Father, Son, and Holy Spirit. These three persons are one God, the same in substance, equal in power and glory (WCF 2).

[1] See https://www.inspiringquotes.us/author/8503-francis-schaeffer [Accessed 01/05/2021].

Yet this is something which our contemporary culture fundamentally rejects. Although many people believe in a god of some kind, it is a step too far for the carnal mind to accept what the one living and true God makes known about himself. More crucially, it is too much to accept that everything must be centred around God. Instead, if God is acknowledged at all, it is with the pagan assumption that we must harness him to serve our needs. We have a man-centred view of God and of everything else.

So, instead of grounding our understanding of ourselves and our context in an acknowledgement of the one true God, our culture prefers to package up our world into areas where we will concede that God has some involvement, and areas from which we can comfortably exclude God. This secularism is instinctive to our fallen hearts (human pride has always said 'No' to having God in our thoughts (Psalm 10:4)), but it is strikingly, pervasively characteristic of the cultural context we inhabit. We treat religion (the acknowledgement of God in belief and worship) as merely a compartment of our lives, something that is optional and voluntary, just one of many personal interests that people can choose to have or not as they please.

Christians in our day do of course push back against this, insisting that Christianity has a place in the public square and defending the validity of the Christian voice and Christian praxis even within a non-Christian majority. We do not believe that Christians should have to conceal or deny their convictions. We resist the idea that Christian values are antithetical to public service even though they may conflict with an equalities agenda.

But when it came to a public health crisis, we responded in general as if human expertise and human regulations were the final word, and as if human concerns and physical wellbeing were supremely important. We conceded that it was in everyone's best interests to suspend gatherings for God's worship, even though those 'best' interests were only physical and temporal, not spiritual or God-ward. The only relevant matrix was apparently the 'four harms' caused by Covid-19: the direct health impact of the virus, impacts on other health areas, impacts on society and impacts on the economy. These are profound issues, but spiritual harm did not register in public policy, except as a tiny aspect of society. This approach influenced the definition of essential and non-essential activities. Christopher McKnight Nichols, associate professor of history at Oregon State University, observed that such definitions were influenced by cultural values. He said that 'the process of designating "essential services" is as much about culture as any legal-political reality about what is necessary to keep society functioning.'[2]

We listened carefully to the messages coming from central government and public health experts and took on board their regulations and guidance as if everything depended on our compliance, even though 'everything' here was only the numerical reduction in the spread of a temporal disease to locally manageable levels. The recourse we made to basic theological and ecclesiological principles was more or less an afterthought. Along with those who did not really know God at all, we responded without God first of all, and did not take much time to consider whether, either in reference to our own principles or in the eyes of a watching world, our message and response was really any different from theirs.

---

[2] Quoted, Selsky, A. 'What's essential? In France: pastry, wine. In US: golf, guns.' Associate Press March 28, 2020.
https://apnews.com/article/f81fafc80efc9488ca706505b6789806
[Accessed 17/04/2021].

We accepted, additionally, that worship is non-essential. This is an essentially secular view, where religion is a private matter at the margins of life and society. We accepted it when ministers were not classified as key workers, although delivery drivers were. We did not classify pastoral care as essential, rather as just an add-on that we could more or less do without. We were reluctant to call attention to the fact that worship is a transcendent and metaphysical (indeed, a heavenly) reality that stands apart from all kinds of other activities.

Again, this coincides with the essentially secular assumption that there is no belief which is axiomatic for everyone, but everyone's beliefs are contested and contestable. Our preference was to avoid making metaphysical claims which compete with anyone else. We did not feel confident about claiming special treatment for the church in relation to Covid restrictions. Such exceptionalism would harm our reputation, we fretted—it would make us seem too egocentric and inconsiderate of others. Faced with the assertion that other people find their ultimate meaning and fulfilment in the gym or the garden centre, we were unable to counter-assert that there is a higher priority to worshipping God. Surely this reveals that in the church, despite our opposition to outright secularism, we subconsciously feel vulnerable to pressures from other belief systems and none. And this does not simply signal some level of capitulation to secularism, but it also worryingly testifies to the fragility of our own beliefs. Somehow, we are sufficiently haunted by the alternatives out there that the thought of standing above them seems too much to ask.

Resisting God's providential involvement

Of course, the Triune God does more than exist. He is involved moment by moment in upholding, directing, disposing, and governing all creatures, actions and things, from the greatest to the least, by his most wise and holy providence (WCF 5:1).

Yet part of our culture's endeavour to push God to the fringes of our lives includes overlooking God's providential control of all things. We prefer, by and large, to disregard how little control we have over our own circumstances (who our parents are, when we were born, the community we grew up in, the opportunities available to us, the influences we are exposed to). Instead, we do our best to maintain the illusion that we are in control of our own destiny. Whatever happens, as twenty-first century Westerners we never dream of seeing it as coming from a personal God who is continuously involved in every detail. Such (we think) were the assumptions of a superstitious, pre-scientific age, before we developed the naturalistic understanding to which we have progressed. We will think of what happens instead as the things that life (impersonal, and not divine) throws at us. And, whatever happens, we will stubbornly insist, 'I am the master of my fate: I am the captain of my soul.'[3]

In the pandemic, naturally we acknowledged that no individual can tackle a public health crisis single-handedly. Nevertheless, we had great faith in ourselves collectively to be able to beat the virus and save lives. Nations acted as though matters of life and death were entirely in their hands. Our governments passed legislation to permit DIY abortions during lockdown, and classified travelling for the purpose of assisted dying as a reasonable excuse for leaving home. So we acted as if we had the right to facilitate people losing their lives in *these* ways, while straining every muscle to avoid people losing their lives in *other* ways—to coronavirus,

[3] From *Invictus* by William Ernest Henley (1849–1903).

specifically—according to our own ungodly preferences and priorities.

This thinking also seeped into the church. We decided that we would follow the measures that experts and the authorities set out (without particularly checking how far these measures supported rather than undermined vital practices, especially forms of worship). We decided that we would prioritise survival rates (without weighing this in the balance against concerns for other aspects of health and wellbeing, including spiritual priorities). We took it for granted that our measures would be effective (without necessarily remembering that the power to make means effective rather than futile belongs to God).

In addition, in the church many were willing to attribute the health crisis to natural causes.[4] We did not see it as something that God had arranged and ordered in the minutest detail. Prominent evangelicals were anxious to absolve God of all responsibility, or argued that it was arrogant to think that we could discern a divine purpose in sending it. Even those who felt that God was in some way speaking loudly against the nation's rebellion against him did not seem stirred up to intercede for the nation. Instead, it seems we needed just to pray for a vaccine and ride out the storm as best we

---

[4] This extends a trend which has been noted in relation to the cholera outbreaks of the nineteenth century. According to Lennie, 'by all accounts, the religious community of the time saw the 1832 cholera outbreak as a direct result of the will of providence,' but later outbreaks in the 1840s and 1850s were met with a 'much more muted religious response' (Lennie, T. (2015) *Land of Many Revivals.* Fearn: Christian Focus Publications. p. 267). Disease was interpreted in medical and scientific terms *instead of* rather than *alongside* an awareness of providence, and responses were made in terms of better housing and sanitation *instead of* rather than *alongside* days of prayer and humiliation (Morris, R. J. (1976) *Cholera 1832: The Social Response to an Epidemic.* London: Croom Helm. p. 202).

could. Christ tells us that the message of such unusual providential occurrences is always a call to everyone to repent (Luke 13:1-5). Yet few wanted to ask the unsettling, uncomfortable question as to what we were being called to repent of as individuals and churches.

Recalibrating the Christian hope

The one living and true God does more than arrange things in providence. He also brings sinners from spiritual death to spiritual life. Those who believe in the Son will 'not perish, but have eternal life' (John 3:16). The Christian hope refers to more than earthly and temporal blessings. It aspires higher than natural life and looks beyond the grave, to eternity and eternal life—to 'being made perfectly blessed in the full enjoying of God to all eternity' (Westminster Shorter Catechism, Q38). Those who live by grace on this earth have the expectation of glory in the world to come. 'For the Lord God is a sun and shield: the Lord will give grace and glory ...' (Psalm 84:11).

Yet as God is pushed increasingly to the periphery of our lives in the West, the things that are seen and temporal take on an increasing significance for us. Life is comfortable and well provided for. There is much to enjoy here for many years. We lose the sense that there is something beyond this life. This can be the case even for Christians, as R. C. Sproul (1939-2017) has pointed out.

> It's not so much that the contemporary Christian has consciously embraced worldliness, it's more that we have been so influenced by a manner of viewing the world that anything beyond this world seems obscured by eclipse. Gone is a vital sense of Providence. The world is seen as operating according to its internal mechanistic laws. The hand of Providence is not so much regarded as being invisible; it has been erased

> altogether. Gone is the blessed hope of heaven. Though interest abounds in the return of Jesus, the contemplation of heaven itself has been banished from our thinking. Our thinking is earth-bound, trapped within the confines of the terrestrial.[5]

Perhaps this is why busy activity features more largely than spirituality and deep communion with God in the Christian life today. What is unseen and eternal becomes very vague, misty, unreal, and low priority in our lives. Instead what seems very real and important to us is the here-and-now. We expect to live life to the full *before* we die, instead of afterwards. Then, as a believing spirit wanes, so does joy and peace in believing. As unbelief escalates, so does hopelessness and fear.

Fear is not always irrational or sinful. Indeed, fear is often the genuinely most appropriate and natural response to the threats we face. But those whose horizons are filled with God—his glory, his awesome majesty, his compassion—can put natural fears in perspective. When the people of Jerusalem were afraid of an impending Assyrian invasion, God told Isaiah not to share their fear but, instead, 'Sanctify the Lord of hosts himself; and let him be your fear, and let him be your dread' (Isaiah 8:11-13). When Jesus sent out his disciples, on an onerous mission and at risk of real persecution, he told them, 'Fear not them which kill the body, but are not able to kill the soul: but rather fear him which is able to destroy both soul and body in hell' (Matthew 10:28).

The pandemic has shown that in the church we are often as vulnerable to fear as those who are without God and without hope in the world. Clearly the cruelty and bloodshed of the Assyrian army, and the threat of being taken to law, physical harassment

---

[5] Sproul, R. C. (1991) 'Foreword' in Burroughs, J. *A Treatise of Earthly-Mindedness.* Ligonier, Pennsylvania, USA: Soli Deo Gloria. p. i.

and psychological pressures, are truly fearsome. The same can be said of the fear of catching a new and poorly understood disease, the fear of unwittingly spreading disease to others, and the fear of social stigma and public shaming for stepping out of line. Yet God is more to be feared, and with God on our side, these fears need not be paralysing and all-consuming.

2. Our view of earthly things

The less trust we place in God, the more trust we put in other things—things which, by definition, are idols. Some of the most prominent idols of our contemporary culture are science and medicine, technology, health and safety, and consumer goods.

It is of course not unique to our generation that periods of economic prosperity and affluence can coincide with lessening commitment to the Lord (Deuteronomy 32:15). This was essentially the situation of the people of Israel at the time of the prophet Hosea. The Lord had saved them and installed them in a most comfortable position, and they had flourished under the Lord's generous provision. But perversely they turned his goodness towards them into reasons why they no longer needed him. According to the lavish, extensive pastures the Lord gave them, they became full, and the Lord's accusation was, 'They were filled, and their heart was exalted; therefore have they forgotten me' (Hosea 13:6).

So, as we reflect on the pandemic, another metric for self-examination might be the extent to which we have put our trust in sources other than God himself—even things which on one level we are thankful to acknowledge as signs of his goodness towards us.

Science and medicine

As our Father in heaven, God protects us and provides for us. What he provides for us is not necessarily an easy life of material comfort and physical health, but certainly he provides for us in ultimate things, in spiritual ways.

However, advances in science and medicine have created conditions for the majority of people in the West where an easy life of material comfort and physical health is simply taken for granted. We have credited ourselves with eradicating so many diseases, and finding treatments and interventions for so many other illnesses, that it seems obvious to transfer our confidence away from God's providential care and put a large part of our faith in science and medicine instead.

As Christians, even when we acknowledge God's fatherly care and provision, we still act as though we deserve protection from disease and untimely death, and we still take substantial comfort from knowing that if we get ill, the NHS will be there for us. Indeed, secular commentators (even before this crisis) have referred to the NHS as our national religion.

In the pandemic, therefore, believers shared at least some of the fear of the wider population in the face of a new disease. The safety net offered by science and medicine suddenly appeared much less secure than we had assumed. The triumph of science and medicine was suddenly exposed as much more incomplete than we liked to think. The threat that the NHS could be overwhelmed prompted us to affirm that NHS workers are heroes, and confronted us with the realisation that without a functioning NHS, things would be a lot more uncertain and scary for us. We might have to endure more bodily discomfort and physical unpleasantness than we are used to. And, to the extent that we had slacked off in our confidence in God's fatherly care, we were perhaps more concerned than we should have been when these secondary supports started to look precarious.

Technology

Our culture is steeped in the view that technology is always a good thing. Part of the secularism of our context has been faith in human progress, only momentarily shaken by the coronavirus crisis. We are surrounded with successful innovations, from the domestic (fridges, vacuum cleaners) to the digital (laptops and smartphones). It is therefore easy to believe that technological innovations have no (or only a few manageable) downsides, and that adopting new technologies is by definition progress.

Undoubtedly lockdowns, imposed with a view to slowing the spread of coronavirus, would have been much less feasible without digital technology. Large numbers of people were able to stay at home only because of the possibility of remote working, online shopping, online doctor consultations, and online schooling. Likewise, Christians were facilitated in complying with the 'stay at home' order by the availability of digital technology. Thanks to audio and video streaming, preachers could continue to share messages with congregations, and indeed broadcast to larger numbers, including numbers of people who would not normally come to church to hear a sermon. Members of congregations could continue to feel connected to their pastor, and each other, thanks to video conferencing.

Yet because technological solutions were so readily available, we did not think too carefully about what we lose by switching to digital. At the societal level, a picture is developing of significant damage to family relationships, workplace relationships, businesses, health, and education—none of which can be repaired by online solutions. The gap between the digital 'haves' and 'have-nots' has been both exposed and exacerbated as people in poverty (both financial and digital) have been forced to choose between paying for essential household necessities or for more data to access essential services.

Among believers, unease about excessive screen time and warnings about social media consumption were largely forgotten in the rush to connect online. Older people in the churches, who had not perhaps previously made very much use of digital technology, suddenly embraced it. Compared with younger people, older people seemed perhaps more susceptible to regarding virtual and real-life alternatives as much of a muchness (possibly because of the novelty, and how it compensated for some loneliness they might have otherwise felt, and possibly because of the convenience it offered).[6]

The usefulness and ubiquity of digital technology also fosters the idea that we can control nature. The Westminster divines wrote in the seventeenth century of Christian worship including 'circumstances common to human actions and societies' which are to be 'ordered by the light of nature and Christian prudence' (WCF 1:6). Yet in the twenty-first century it seems that through technology we can dispense with circumstances such as physically gathering in the same space, and what we regard as common sense is filtered now through the illusion of the apparently limitless possibilities of the virtual rather than what is real.

Health and safety

It is a mercy that our working and living environments are much more safe and much healthier than they have been historically, or compared with the developing world. It is right and proper to

[6] See also Chapter 4 in this volume, 'How important is it for believers to gather together physically to worship God?'

avoid ill-health and hazards to our own and other people's welfare.

However, we sometimes come close to acting as though health and safety concerns are an end in themselves. In the pandemic, we accepted the assumption that we were in such a risky situation that we had to take unprecedented steps to avoid danger. The risks were, however, framed mainly in earthly terms, from the perspective that the worst thing that can happen to us would be something like either suffering physical ill-health, or spreading disease to others, or contributing to overwhelming the NHS.

As Christians, we appear to have given mere survival a higher priority than spiritual wellbeing. We preferred to close churches for worship, in order to stop the spread of the virus, rather than to preach with greater urgency, in order to bring more souls out of hopelessness and spiritual death into spiritual life with a good hope for eternity.

This approach would make sense if our main goal was only reducing death rates and preserving physical life—if we only needed more time to try and achieve our best life now. But life is more than food, and the body is more than clothing (Luke 12:23). We do not save our life just by preserving it. Survival is not our greatest need, nor our highest ambition.

Instead, we largely overlooked the spiritual risks in our health-related risk assessments. We did not sufficiently consider the risk of letting unbelievers go to eternity without hearing the gospel, or the risk of declining in holiness or spiritual comfort when we cannot access many of the ordinary means of grace. We did not think about whether our duties to one another would become very difficult (if not impossible) without each other.[7]

To a large degree our culture has embraced the trend of seeking to eliminate rather than manage risk. This is in spite of how unrealistic it is to think that risks to our bodily health and safety can ever be reduced to zero, given the uncertain environments we belong to and the prevalence of disease and disability. We seemed largely to forget that a lost eternity is not merely a risk but a certainty for those outside Christ, yet that this certainty can be eliminated when we are united to Christ.

Commodities

Our culture is to a large extent preoccupied with the acquisition of consumer goods. Our society and economy depend on encouraging as many people as possible to keep acquiring goods and services in ever-increasing amounts, on the assumption that the more we consume, the better off we will be. This plays on our natural desire to have more (in terms of things, products, goods) than what would just meet our basic needs for food, clothing and shelter. When we buy things in response to advertising (aspiring to a desirable lifestyle or social status), because we are dissatisfied with the adequately functioning items we already have, and especially if it is simply for the pleasure of purchasing, and without

[7] These might include speaking with each other (Malachi 3:16), demonstrating love for one another (John 13:34-35; 1 Thessalonians 4:9), striving together for the gospel (Philippians 1:27), by love serving one another (Galatians 5:13), bearing one another's burdens (Galatians 6:2), submitting ourselves one to another (Ephesians 5:21; 1 Peter 5:5), teaching and admonishing one another (Colossians 3:16), comforting one another with God's words (1 Thessalonians 4:18), encouraging and edifying one another (1 Thessalonians 5:11), exhorting one another (Hebrews 3:13), provoking one another to love and good works, not forsaking the assembling of ourselves together, but exhorting one another (Hebrews 10:24-26).

a plan or a budget, we are betraying ourselves as followers of consumerism.

The gospel and spiritual things have easily been misrepresented in this context. The impression can be given that Christ is something that will make an already comfortable life go that bit better, or something that will deal with some of our needs and regrets. The gospel becomes subconsciously marketed as a commodity. The impression is that it is not essential to life but something extra that improves it.

For long enough now, we have expected our churches to try to market themselves to us as providing *things* which will enhance our lives. The atmosphere in worship services (perhaps especially in terms of what and how we sing, although also including people's social, communal interactions) has been regarded as more important to making worshippers feel comfortable and satisfied than to honouring the God we ostensibly worship. The concept of a worship service has been reimagined so that it is less about us serving God and more about serving ourselves and others. The idea of shopping around to find a church that suits us is regarded as perfectly acceptable. When we feel we stop getting what we want out of a church, we feel entitled to move on to have our perceived needs met elsewhere. The concept of worship as something we do for God (in response to God, out of obedience to God, for the purpose of glorifying God) is fading from our consciousness. We tend to place much more focus on what *we get* out of worship than on how in our acts of worship we *serve God.* We have acted less as worshippers and more as consumers, with worship itself as the commodity we consume.

The pandemic has exposed this with particular reference to preaching. Preaching is clearly an act of worship from the point of view of the preacher: speaking God's words from God's Word to God's people, honouring God's authority and God's truth and God's redemptive purposes and God's call and obligation to the preacher to be God's ambassador. It is also an act of worship from the point of view of the hearers. Hearers assemble out of obedience to God's call, to glorify God by obediently hearing God's Word preached by God's ambassador, and obediently responding with repentance towards God and faith in God.

But to the extent that we have reframed preaching as something that is there primarily to meet our needs (even our spiritual needs, and even our spiritual needs as defined in Scripture), to that extent we have commodified the sermon. It is recast as something therapeutic for us rather than honouring to God. So, during lockdown (and sometimes also after lockdown), we have assumed that in order to continue consuming this lifestyle-enhancing product, all we need is a workaround to keep individually accessing this kind of message. Since a remote or virtual facility will give us this, we are content with streamed worship. A streamed message will do practically as well as an in-person message to satisfy our wish to hear something from the Bible and something to do with salvation, and give us spiritual benefits we would like to experience in the form of raised affections and devotional warmth.

Staying at home instead of assembling for in-person worship thus lets us present ourselves within our communities as responsible citizens who make sacrifices analogous to other people's sacrifices when they forgo visits to shops and restaurants. It lets us present the God we follow in terms that fit the expectations and wishes of our neighbours—someone who understands when we have to treat his requests as temporarily unrealistic, and who prefers us to keep ourselves healthy than risk anything for the good of our souls. And we can continue to think of ourselves as loving neighbours because we are doing our bit to stop the spread of the virus, even though it costs us in terms of how lovingly we are acting towards our worship-worthy Saviour.

3. Our view of ourselves

Although our culture provides us with a number of idols which we serve to a greater or lesser extent, these are themselves all subservient to the greatest idol of all—self. As believers, we have genuinely abandoned ourselves to the Saviour. When grace renews us, the deepest desire of our hearts and the most basic inclinations of our wills is to lose ourselves in Christ. Every believer can ultimately say with Paul, 'I am crucified with Christ: nevertheless I live; yet not I, but Christ liveth in me: and the life which I now live in the flesh I live by the faith of the Son of God, who loved me, and gave himself for me' (Galatians 2:20). Nevertheless, even as believers whose truest identity is in Christ, we can still betray ourselves when our 'I' asserts itself in less Christ-like and less God-honouring ways.

Individual autonomy and expressive individualism

Our culture prominently exalts individual autonomy. We regard it as highly important for individuals to be able to express their inner, authentic selves in a way that feels to them to be true to themselves. We value people's freedom to follow their hearts, wherever that takes them, and we acknowledge that everyone is entitled to be celebrated for who they really are in themselves.

Such individualism does however sit uncomfortably with the identity of a believer as one of a community. Of course, Scripture insists on the need for personal dealings with a personal Saviour, and presents redemption as something purposed, purchased, and applied for specific individuals. Believers have come to realise by grace that following their hearts will lead to disaster and destruction. 'There is a way that seemeth right unto a man, but the end thereof are the ways of death' (Proverbs 16:25). Instead of seeking for people to 'accept me for who I am,' the believer wants to be accepted by God for who Christ is, and for what Christ has done. 'We have turned every one to his own way; and the Lord hath laid on him the iniquity of us all' (Isaiah 53:6).

Those who are individually saved are not saved into isolation. We are members of a body, sheep in a flock, branches of a vine, stones which make up a building. We are each other's brothers and sisters, adopted into a family with a loving heavenly Father, an Elder Brother, and a Comforter. Rather than introducing constraints and restraints which we should resist because they stifle our individuality and render us inauthentic, the relationships and responsibilities which are conveyed by these ways of conceptualising the believer's identity are precious and life-enhancing.

Somehow, however, we have become used to thinking of the church as only there to serve and affirm *me*. We tend to see corporate worship as an individual exercise—I go to hear a message for *me,* which describes *my* case and meets *my* needs. If I 'didn't get anything out of it,' I can legitimately conclude that it was of no value. While we need to take the Word to heart personally, that is different from listening or believing individualistically, or self-centredly, or exclusively for ourselves. Although our pastors are called to preach to the whole flock, so that we would all be edified together and grow together, we do not always view ourselves as embedded in a congregation as we listen. Perhaps we scarcely think about our role of praying for the preacher while listening or encouraging him by our attention. Nor do we always fully recognise our shared attendance at corporate worship, including our shared listening to the preached Word, as itself an integral (in fact, foundational) part of Christian fellowship. Fellowship is seen as something we do outside the service.

In the pandemic this shift in thinking—towards individualism and away from corporate religion—has contributed to the ease with which many of us switched to connecting remotely to online broadcasts. As long as we are able to hear the message as individuals, we have not felt it acutely painful to go without the contact with our pastors alongside our fellow members of the congregation and co-communicants.

Emotivism

We live in a post-truth culture. Objective facts are less influential in shaping opinion than appeals to emotion. In this context, information serves only to reinforce what we feel, rather than reflect reality. Because our philosophers and opinion-shapers prefer not to explain morality in a transcendent way, there is a tendency to say that moral statements merely express emotions or attitudes.

This influence is most noticeably seen on social media, where things that provoke a strong emotional reaction are more widely shared. However, whether or not we use social media we cannot avoid this influence. Traditional media is of course influenced the same way, as are our friends, relations and acquaintances. In the debates over coronavirus-related restrictions, masks and much more, the polarised opinion has been largely driven by fear (of the virus or the opinion of others) on the one hand and outrage (at the loss of freedom and those restricting it) on the other.

For Christians, there is a danger that we become subtly influenced by this post-truth, emotivist outlook so that our message and convictions are more influenced by how they make us feel, or by the response of other people. The danger is then that at decisive points we respond with emotion first, and then reach for the information that justifies or backs up our gut reaction, turning a blind eye to what supports the opposite case.

During the crisis it has seemed as though we have engaged with issues less on the basis of principle and more on the basis of how it makes us feel. All sorts of scriptural, theological, ethical and ecclesiological principles have been conspicuous by their absence from the church's discussion in the coronavirus crisis. Instead, we have often seemed to respond out of fear, with strenuous disapproval directed towards those who see things differently from us, and with less forbearance and understanding than we should have.

4. The way forward

Acknowledgement

As we emerge from this time of crisis, we can only recognise that in many ways, life will not be the same again. We should take the opportunity to reflect on what it has shown us about ourselves spiritually. To the extent that we have been exposed as being complacent and lacking in spiritual preparation, we must resolve not to remain like this any longer. This is not about pointing the finger at a godless society. Believers will always be situated in a context where there are pressures and ideologies and received wisdom which are hostile to God and to grace. The question for us in the church is how far we have resisted this hostility and retained our integrity before the Lord.

As we take stock and identify where we have been less Christian and more worldly in our responses, we should accept the fact that *this* culture, with all its own characteristic ways of expressing its hostility to God, is the culture which *we are part of*. Nehemiah had a clearer conscience and did more obvious kingdom work than most of us will ever have or do. Yet when he reflected on his people's history and current practice of turning away from the gracious and merciful God, he did not blame *them*. He confessed, '*We* have done wickedly' (Nehemiah 9:33). In much the same position, Ezra prayed, 'O my God, I am ashamed and blush to lift up my face to thee, my God: for *our* iniquities are increased over our head' (Ezra 9:6). Similarly, when Daniel, a man greatly beloved, set out to make confession, he included himself with the people. '*We* have sinned, and have committed iniquity, and have done wickedly, and have rebelled, even by departing from thy precepts and from thy judgments' (Daniel 9:5).

It may be unsurprising that we have conformed to this assertive and demanding culture, considering how many other institutions, social norms, and individuals have struggled to stand out against its pressures. Yet as the Lord's people, we have stronger motivations, better incentives and more effective (divine) resources to be, by the Spirit, not conformed to this world, but transformed increasingly into the likeness of Christ.

Penitence

The uncomfortable part of repentance is identifying our sins, accepting that they are sinful, and admitting that because God is so good and gracious, we have no one to blame but ourselves. All the supplies of grace and courage we will ever need in order to be rightly counter-cultural are stored up in Christ for us. We have no real excuse for compromising and worldliness. But we must not simply reach a true sense of our sin. We must also turn to God and apprehend his mercy in Christ. The deep legalism and hardness of our hearts often makes us afraid of acknowledging our sin because we suspect that this will make God less likely to help us. But God sees our sin whether we confess it or not, and if we cover our sin we will not prosper. Self-destroyed and self-condemned, we can only turn to God. After all, 'there is more pity to be found at the hands of an offended God than in all the world beside.'[8] The very God we have sinned against is the one who has mercy on sinners. He is the one who graciously invites us to acknowledge him as sovereign and to forsake the other things we have secretly trusted in. He commends himself as king and head of his church and people, their only lawgiver. 'I will be thy king: where is any other that may save thee in all thy cities? and thy judges of whom thou saidst, Give me a king and princes?' (Hosea 13:10)

Faith

When Hosea challenged Israel for drifting away from their allegiance to the Lord, he pointed out that they had destroyed themselves. This sinfulness of this perverse self-destruction is aggravated because God himself was their helper. But that same fact is the very thing for faith to take hold of—the fact that God is their helper. 'O Israel, thou hast destroyed thyself! But in me is thy help' (Hosea 13:9).

This does not negate the fact that God can be angry with his own people and can even act very fiercely against them (Hosea 13:7-8). But even in this, he is not their enemy, he is their helper. He disdains the puny, worthless things they turned to for help when they turned their backs on him (Hosea 13:10). But with equal intensity and in equally vivid terms, he trounces and despises their real worst enemies—death and the power of the grave (Hosea 13:14). Christ's obedience and sin-atoning death and new resurrection life are the triumphant realities that our faith has to

[8] Dickson, D. (2020) *Sermons on Jeremiah's Lamentations.* Dallas, Texas, USA: Naphtali Press. p. 79.

lay hold of. 'O death, where is thy sting? O grave, where is thy victory? … Thanks be to God, which giveth us the victory through our Lord Jesus Christ' (1 Corinthians 15:55-57).

As believers, we have a hope beyond this life. Disease and social pressures and legal penalties are fearful in their own way, but on our side is the Lord Jesus Christ, the great Jehovah, 'death of deaths, and hell's destruction.' 'I beseech you therefore, brethren, by the mercies of God, that ye present your bodies a living sacrifice, holy, acceptable unto God, which is your reasonable service. And be not conformed to this world: but be ye transformed by the renewing of your mind …' (Romans 12:1-2).

~ 10 ~
How can we move on from this crisis?

This book has been written out of profound loving concern for the church and a desire to learn from the experience of the Covid-19 crisis. We need to look forward, but how will we move out of this period of testing?

The future need not be bleak. No one has a deeper love and concern for the church than Christ himself. He continues to make rich promises to us, and by faith we may be sure that the Lord will yet bless us if we turn to him.

One passage of Scripture which offers a highly desirable vision of blessing following a time of trial is Psalm 133.[1] This short psalm vividly displays a faithful, hopeful longing for the blessings of unity after bitter disunity, and community after tragic scattering. To conclude this collection of essays, we would like to use Psalm 133 to give content and direction to our hopes for the future of the church.

1. Blessing is prefaced by self-examination

As we start, we must ask what the Lord requires of us as we set these desirable blessings before us. What is the appropriate path out of these trials in seeking the blessing of God? While this book

[1] For the background to Psalm 133, see Robertson, O. P. (2015) *The Flow of the Psalms: Discovering their Structure and Theology*. Phillipsburg, New Jersey, USA: Presbyterian and Reformed Publishing Company. pp. 211-212.

strives to consider the issues involved in a calm and reasoned way, this should be more than an intellectual exercise. This review should prompt us to much reflection—to 'consider our ways,' as Haggai puts it (1:7-8). It should drive us to our knees in our deep concern for the church's worship and witness. We need to intercede for it and seek divine help to turn from the ways in which we have turned aside from clear duty.

Self-examination for the church need not be a doleful thing. When the goal of it is to bring us back to the Lord, it has the promise of blessing attached.

This book has raised the question of whether the church failed the Covid test. That is something we must answer at all levels: individual Christians, office bearers, congregations, and denominations. If we are making excuses, or looking for scapegoats, rather than saying, 'Is it I?', we are not responding appropriately to the chastisement the Lord has sent.

We need to ask ourselves, did we make mistakes? Now that we have more time and space to reflect on the past year, we must bring our decisions and actions to the touchstone of the Word of God and to the witness of the church in history. How do we measure up? Were the decisions we made based on hasty pragmatism? Were they wrong in the light of Scripture? Did we fail the test? Did we fail to stand in our duties in a trying day? Did we fail to look to the Lord for help, turning to science and medicine rather than sanctifying the Lord God in our hearts (Isaiah 8:11-14)? Did we fail our brothers and sisters and undermine the witness of the church by our unloving attitudes and behaviour?

A commendable willingness to reflect and confess has already been publicly demonstrated by the Archbishop of Canterbury.

As he admitted,

> I got quite a few things wrong at the beginning and I learnt quite quickly. I didn't push hard enough to keep churches available for at least individual prayer in the first lockdown. We also said clergy couldn't go in, and personally I feel I made a mistake with that. I can make all kinds of excuses. I still think I was too risk-averse.[2]

2. Blessing may follow chastisement

> The Lord commanded the blessing. (Psalm 133:3)

Psalm 133 shows us the church experiencing the blessings of fruitfulness through an abundant dew as well as the extensive holy consecration and renewal that comes from the anointing oil of the Holy Spirit. Those blessings are greatly to be desired: they are beneficial, beautifying and delightful. Psalm 133 directs the church to seek the blessing of unity from God alone. He is the only one who can command it.

We can all agree that these blessings are the great needs of the church. The Lord is sovereign and may or may not choose to bless us, but we can be sure that he will not bless our disobedience. Rather he will chastise it.

The pruning of chastisement is painful, but if we are rightly exercised by it, it can produce a harvest of 'the peaceable fruit of righteousness' (Hebrews 12:11). If we fail to respond to it we can only expect further chastisement. We cannot earn God's favour,

---

[2] Mance, H. (2021) 'Justin Welby: We have a case of national PTSD.' *The Financial Times*. Online: https://www.ft.com/content/8e831398-8a44-4d8c-b1bc-1642278e5ebb [Accessed 08/04/2021].

yet equally we cannot expect any of the blessings we long for if we are negligent about our responsibilities. The love, unity, pursuit of peace and coming together emphasised in this psalm are part of our calling as one body.

3. Longing for the blessing of Christ's presence

> It is like the precious ointment upon the head, that ran down upon the beard, even Aaron's beard: that went down to the skirts of his garments. (Psalm 133:2)

The blessings of Psalm 133 come from the abundant anointing of the Holy Spirit. They flow from Christ as the head, who has been anointed with this 'oil of joy' (Psalm 45:7) for the benefit of his church and people. How much we need 'the oil of joy for mourning, the garment of praise for the spirit of heaviness' (Isaiah 61:3)! This comes from the Redeemer's anointing with the Holy Spirit without measure (Isaiah 61:1).

The good ointments of Christ, and their fragrance, are his graces received out of his fulness (Song 1:3; Psalm 45:2). It is from the head that 'all the body by joints and bands having nourishment ministered, and knit together, increaseth with the increase of God' (Colossians 2:19). This is experienced through the ordinary means of grace—especially the Word, sacraments, and prayer—means which are simultaneously ordinary and heavenly. The church as a body gathers to Christ and in his name. There, in the gathered church, his name is as ointment poured forth (Song 1:3) and there the beauty of the Lord is seen in a unique way (Psalm 27:4). His presence is promised where even two or three are gathered together in his name (Matthew 18:20). The Lord Jesus loves to walk amid the seven golden candlesticks of his church. The Lord will meet with us in all places where he records his name (Exodus 20:24).

It is instructive that Christ gives the promise of his presence in the context of restoring unity amongst the brethren within the church—that is the context of the Matthew 18 passage. When the brethren are kept apart, self-seeking, contention and pride have the opportunity to establish a root of bitterness. When the brethren gather, then Christ is in the midst and there is to be united prayer and use of the authority he has delegated (Matthew 18:19-20).

We need to value Christ's presence in the public means of grace. How much have we missed it? We have surely underestimated the importance of this principle of Christ's presence in our approach to worship over the past year. His precious presence is easily sinned away (Song 2:7). If someone asks, 'Where is thy beloved gone?' would it really be accurate for us to reply that our beloved has gone down into his garden to eat and to gather lilies—that he is right here with us and we and he are enjoying each other's company—or would we have to confess that Christ has withdrawn himself and turned aside (Song 5:6)?

Christ is seeking real and true communion with his beloved people. We see this in his knocks at the door of the church of Laodicea (Revelation 3:20). The imagery of him standing at the door suggests they feel that they can get on very well without his manifest presence indoors with them. Some are so satisfied with themselves that there seems no sense of need of having Christ nearby and among us. It is possible to rest satisfied with something less than communion with Christ among his people. Are we keeping him out? He knocks both by his providence and also by his ordinances. It is a louder knock when he combines the two, adding knocks in providence because we have not been listening to the knock in the ordinances. He is doubling his knocks when his ordinances are removed in his providence.

Let us therefore prize Christ's presence in the physical gatherings of his people, even if only two or three are there for whatever reason. Here is where the Lord commands his blessing in a unique way. In the midst of God's judgements, his mercies know no bounds. We should seek to recalculate the value of God's gifts to us, particularly gifts like the public means of grace (especially the sacraments), the liberty to worship, union and communion with our brethren, people we can worship with and a place where we can gather to worship. These are immense gifts to the church from a gracious God. If we have treated them lightly in the past, and have not valued them while we enjoyed them, we should be thankful to have them restored to us, and rejoice when we have again been allowed to partake of them.

4. Longing for the blessing of dwelling together

> Behold, how good and how pleasant it is for brethren to *dwell together* in unity! (Psalm 133:1)

Recovering a desire for the intangible presence of God in the midst of his gathered church will lead us to place more value on the goodness and pleasantness of brethren dwelling together in unity. The terms brought together in Psalm 133:1 make it seem almost impossible to emphasise it more: *brethren, dwelling together, in unity*. Rather than seeing religion as an insular, individualistic thing—all about me, and my blessing—we should widen our horizons to include growing together (Ephesians 2:21), bearing one another's burdens (Galatians 6:2), and appreciating the church as a glorious body with Christ as our glorious head (Colossians 1:18).

Worship is not primarily for social ends, or for mental health benefits, or for keeping up a tradition, or something performed to be seen of men. It is for the glory of God. Whilst isolated from one another, many expressed the longing to be back together again in person with one another. The situation was not natural. Gathering for worship is a spiritual and not a merely social imperative. We need each other and must recognise the importance of the body and edifying one another. This book refers to the many 'one another' duties we owe to each other and which are scarcely possible if we are not gathered together in person. We must 'dwell together' as the household of God. If our individualistic mindset has been painfully exposed by the chastisement of isolation and scattering, let us forsake it and not the assembling of ourselves together. Let us value as never before this blessed duty so that we may 'consider one another to provoke unto love and to good works' (Hebrews 10:24).

5. Longing for the blessing of brotherhood

> Behold, how good and how pleasant it is for *brethren* to dwell together in unity! (Psalm 133:1)

Brotherly love is a gift from heaven flowing from the love of Christ to his people through the ministry of the Comforter. The fragrance of brotherly love rejoices the heart and is attractive to those who observe it. Indeed, it is what identifies Christ's disciples to a watching world (John 13:35). We need love and the right spirit towards one another as brothers and sisters in the adopted family of God the Father. This edifies the church for its good and makes it attractive. We must seek peace and pursue it (1 Peter 3:11). The blessed responsibility of striving for unity requires us to put on love and deny ourselves (Colossians 3:14).

Thomas Boston (1676-1732) preached about how the church's beauty is 'marred with division.' 'There is no danger from enemies without, like that from divisions within,' he said.[3] It is not only sad but dangerous that responses to Covid-19 have become a source of such contention and division in the church. When Covid-19 itself has reminded us how short and uncertain our lives are, can we afford to live at variance with our brethren? Should we not rather take the opportunity to learn to love one another (Galatians 6:1-2)? If we think a brother has been 'overtaken in a fault,' by all means we ought to seek to 'restore him' to the right way (Galatians 6:1). But this must be done 'in the spirit of meekness' and tenderly—as tenderly as if we were resetting a broken bone, according to the metaphor in the original. We must remember that we too are ready to be tempted to other faults even in our pursuit of principle. Are the divisions in the church one of the reasons God has sent his judgements in the first place?[4]

It is much easier to begin acting in a contentious spirit than it is to stop, and much easier for a dismissive attitude to the brethren and the unity of the church to take root than it is to root it out. Yet lovelessness and disunity in the church are not only damaging to believers, but also transparent to the world, and a huge factor in giving unbelievers an excuse to reject religion. Letting ourselves be carried away with an undue sense of the importance of our

---

[3] Boston, T. (edited: Miller, S.) (2002) *The Complete Works of the Late Rev. Thomas Boston, Ettrick*. Stoke on Trent: Tentmaker Publications. Vol. 7, p. 611.

[4] Thomas Vincent (1634-1678) gave this as the reason for the Great Plague of 1665. See Vincent, T (1997) *God's Terrible Voice in the City*. Morgan, Pennsylvania, USA: Soli Deo Gloria Publications. pp. 110-111.

cause and our own need to be right can often have harmful ripple effects far beyond the consequences of the issue itself. Rather than becoming partisan, we should be willing both to accept sympathetically other people's acknowledgements of where they slipped up, and also to acknowledge with frankness when we ourselves have got things wrong.

Let us strive after the fervent love that we ought to have for one another, rather than strive with one another (2 Timothy 2:24). 'Let there be no strife, I pray thee, between me and thee ... for we be brethren' (Genesis 13:8).

6. Longing for the blessing of standing fast in unity

> Behold, how good and how pleasant it is for brethren to dwell together *in unity*! (Psalm 133:1)

Coming together in unity means standing fast together for the same things. It means unity of mind and principle as well as unity of affection. We are to love the truth and peace (Zechariah 8:19). 'Now I beseech you, brethren, by the name of our Lord Jesus Christ, that ye all speak the same thing, and that there be no divisions among you; but that ye be perfectly joined together in the same mind and in the same judgment' (1 Corinthians 1:10). Truth and a gracious love for the truth helps to unite. God has promised to give us one heart and one way and we should seek to have it (Jeremiah 32:39, Ezekiel 11:19).

We must stand together for the liberties we have been given in Christ and not surrender truths for which others have suffered. When it comes to the sole headship of Christ we must hold fast the head (Colossians 2:19), and not allow any human authority (intentionally or otherwise) to usurp his prerogatives. He has given spiritual responsibilities and authority to the church alone and we cannot allow civil government to have these without disobedience to Christ.

We must also stand together in our duty, not stand back from it. A knowledge of the past would have informed us that the imposition of lockdown on churches was infringing church privileges for which our forefathers had made great sacrifices—personal, financial, their homes, their family and even their lives. If we had remembered this, would we perhaps have been less willing to give up these freedoms so hurriedly? We also appeared to have lost sight of the cloud of witnesses who laboured tirelessly in times of plague and distress in the past, ministering both to material and spiritual needs. Yet in 2020 the church seemed to lose all sense of purpose. Instead of stepping up to the mark, the church stepped down.

Paul's words seem very apposite to the church of our generation, 'For when for the time ye ought to be teachers, ye have need that one teach you again which be the first principles of the oracles of God; and are become such as have need of milk, and not of strong meat' (Hebrews 5:12-14). We were unprepared for a crisis of this nature and magnitude because we had become so unskilful, both in our awareness of our past and our grasp of timeless doctrines. In many respects our knowledge of church history and our understanding of doctrine (especially that of the church and its worship, and the relationship between the church and the state) have been so rusty that we have had no foundation on which to build our response to the difficulties raised by the pandemic. Yet we will not experience the blessing of standing fast together without a shared recovery of where we have come from and what we stand for. We must recover our history, and teach it to our children, so that the church in the time to come may stand strong in these principles.

7. Longing for the blessing of holy consecration

> Like the precious ointment upon the head ... that went down to the skirts of his garments. (Psalm 133:2)

Here is the spiritual vitality and renewal we seek. The anointing oil of Christ as high priest flows down to his people to consecrate them for holy service. This is true of all his people, and of those whom he has commissioned for the ministry. In many ways we have all missed opportunities—formal and informal—to serve the Lord.

Considering God's mercies, his chastening love, and our failures and sins in time of trial, we each should seek to rededicate ourselves to his service. This rededication is needed at all levels within the church: as congregations, as ministers and office bearers, and as individual Christians.

Ministers have failed to heed the advice of Richard Baxter (1615-1691), 'to preach as a dying man to dying men.'[5] Instead we have failed at our post, being more afraid of dying, than of having the blood of dead men upon our hands. We have failed to minister to the sick and the dying. We have failed to preach the gospel according to the appointed Scriptural pattern at a time when it was most needed. As Baxter says concerning the Nonconformist ministers who stayed in London to minister to those caught up in the Great Plague of 1665,

---

[5] Baxter, R. (1821) *The Poetical Fragments of Richard Baxter*. London: Pickering. p. 35.

> When Christ shall say, 'Inasmuch as ye did it not to one of these, ye did it not to me,' it will be a poor excuse to say, 'Lord I was forbidden by the Law.' Therefore they resolved to stay with the people, and to go into the forsaken pulpits, though prohibited, and to preach to the poor people before they died; and also to visit the sick, and get what relief they could for the poor, especially those that were shut up.[6]

Who is on the Lord's side? As ministers we need to seek a fresh sense of the weight of the call, the burden of responsibility, the honour of duty, the reality of eternity, and the solemnity of having to give an answer to Almighty God for our failures in the ministry. 'Them that honour me I will honour, and they that despise me shall be lightly esteemed' (1 Samuel 2:30).

As a church, we need to be stirred up by the question, 'Watchman, what of the night? Watchman, what of the night?'—'The watchman said, The morning cometh, and also the night: if ye will enquire, enquire ye: return, come' (Isaiah 21:11-12). May we work with renewed vigour while it is day, for 'the night cometh, when no man can work' (John 9:4).

Yet God's mercy remains great towards his church in the midst of chastisement. 'As many as I love, I rebuke and chasten' (Revelation 3:19). The love of Christ to his church persists despite our failures. The glory of the Lord as seen in the witness and worship of the church has been sadly dimmed. Yet the Redeemer loves his church with an unfailing love, and so he chastens us rather than cut us off. May a realisation of that love, magnified by a sense of our utter unworthiness, have a constraining influence

[6] Keeble, N. H. *et al.* (Eds.) (2020) *Reliquiae Baxterianae: Or, Mr Richard Baxter's narrative of the most memorable passages of his life and times.* Oxford: Oxford University Press. Vol. 2, p. 306.

upon us, drawing us to love and serve him more. 'For the love of Christ constraineth us' (2 Corinthians 5:14).

The Lord's people have the greatest comfort on which to rest, to live, and to serve—the fact that we are not our own, we are brought with a price (1 Corinthians 6:19-20). This fact should make us 'heartily willing and ready from now on to live for him' (Heidelberg Catechism, Q1).

8. Longing for the blessing of vitality and fruitfulness

> As the dew of Hermon, and as the dew that descended upon the mountains of Zion. (Psalm 133:3)

This speaks of a copious, abundant dew that will revive all that grows and cause corresponding fruitfulness. The picture has an echo of the beauty of Hosea 14, where the backsliding church returns to the Lord in humble confession and is met with precious promises of blessing and fruitfulness. Then the Lord 'will be as the dew to Israel' (Hosea 14:5), guaranteeing beauty, strength and fruitfulness. Our great longing is that the remnant of the Lord would take root downward and bear fruit upward (Isaiah 37:31). As the cooling, refreshing dew generates fruitfulness and vitality, so it must be in spiritual terms. The Lord's blessing is associated with our unity of purpose, principle and affection. When these things are manifest a greater fruitfulness is to be hoped for.

Such a condition contrasts with the prevailing lethargy of our times. Perhaps our greatest sin as churches is the state of, and satisfaction with, lukewarmness. There is outward profession and activity, yet a lack of power, warmth and spiritual vigour. Many duties can be done without zeal to God, but this is not acceptable to Christ, though it may be enough for us and others. We can perhaps learn from the church of Laodicea (Revelation 3:14-22). There was nothing to rebuke them for in terms of deviation in doctrine, worship, practice, or reputation, but they were also the only church that had nothing to recommend them. We must become more dissatisfied with the mere form of religion, more uncomfortable with a religion which ticks the boxes for duty but has no implications for our material comfort and leaves no impact on our relationships with each other and the world. The church of Laodicea were very self-satisfied in their condition, and in their pride and complacency they were blind to their true danger. The danger is that we become harder and grow worse in this condition. Few conditions can be more dangerous. We should take the advice given to Laodicea, 'Be zealous therefore, and repent' (Revelation 3:19). Even to such a church, Christ makes the precious promise of a crown. Yet he also emphasises that we are to be overcomers, and overcoming is something that cannot be done lukewarmly and half-heartedly. There must be wrestling and suffering in overcoming, just as Christ himself had to experience before he was enthroned (Revelation 3:21).

9. Longing for the blessing of eternal life

> For there the Lord commanded the blessing, even life for evermore. (Psalm 133:3)

Life for evermore is *the* blessing—the blessing of blessings. It includes all other spiritual blessings. How much our world needs it! We must value it highly in the church. We need an eternal perspective, not one dominated by secularism. We have been entrusted with a unique message of hope, that there is life more abundant in Christ (John 10:10). The church has the privilege of giving witness to this, in season and out of season. The everlasting gospel is a sweet savour of life (2 Corinthians 2:14-15)—a fragrance and a pleasing aroma that the church must exude as much as possible.

In the days to come, we need to show the world that we trust in God—not just to keep us safe, but as a sovereign God who has the right to govern us, and in whose hands our times are cast, and a gracious God who is working all things for the good of his people and his honour and glory. During the pandemic the world might well have asked, 'Where is now their God?' (Psalm 115:2).

Confessing that we got it wrong before the world would not be weakness. Instead it would start to dispel the fog we have unthinkingly created around what should have been a clear display of God's glory. Removing the spot from God's glory would be the first step to a closer and more God-glorifying walk in the future.

Conclusion

Although we have arguably made a worse initial response to the coronavirus crisis than our forebears did to analogous crises, is it possible that we could take the opportunity now to make a better longer-term response? Can we find the humility to accept that in the heat of the moment we failed—yet find the zeal in the coming days to seek that the Lord would give grace and re-establish the church in unity and restored community?

True repentance means not only acknowledging what we have done wrong but forsaking it and turning towards what is right with a renewed vigour. When the Puritan preacher James Janeway (1636-1674) reflected on the response of the people of

London to the Great Plague of 1665 and the Great Fire of 1666, he feared that the voice of the Lord had not been heard.[7]

Yet Janeway gives us a hint as to how our beliefs and behaviours should be shaped in the aftermath of some tumultuous months and years in the sub-title he gave his book: *Jesus Christ, the best friend in the worst of times.*

In order to move on, let us seek the Lord's help to trust more wholeheartedly in Jesus, not fearing what man or nature may appear to throw at us. Let us remember that King Jesus reigns over every circumstance in the world, the church and our lives, for the good of his people and his honour and his glory. What he does with us must surely be the best thing for us, because he ultimately has his people's best interests at heart. If faith can hold onto that, then we will know what Janeway called 'heaven on earth'—perfect peace (Isaiah 26:3)—despite what horrors may be going on around us.

> 'For I am persuaded, that neither death, nor life, nor angels, nor principalities, nor powers, nor things present, nor things to come, nor height, nor depth, nor any other creature, shall be able to separate us from the love of God, which is in Christ Jesus our Lord' (Romans 8:35-39)

---

[7] Janeway, J. (1847) *Heaven upon Earth: Jesus, the Best Friend in the Worst Times*. London: Thomas Nelson. pp. 26, 28.

Also available from Ettrick Press

A Call to the Church in the Pandemic
by David Campbell

Messages from Captivity:
Sermons from Ezekiel
by Allan W. MacColl

The Adoption of Sons:
A Practical and Experimental Treatise
by Thomas Houston

Walking in the Light:
Notes of prayer meeting addresses
by Hugh M. Cartwright

For more new releases, visit: www.ettrickpress.co.uk